*A*dventure Guide to
Georgia

Blair Howard

HUNTER
PUBLISHING

HUNTER PUBLISHING, INC.
130 Campus Drive
Edison, NJ 08818-7816
Tel (908) 225 1900; Fax (908) 417 0482
E-mail: hunterpub@emi.net
Web site: www.hunterpublishing.com

1220 Nicholson Road
Newmarket, Ontario L3Y 7V1, CANADA
Tel (800) 399 6858; Fax (800) 363 2665

ISBN 1-55650-782-8

© 1997 Hunter Publishing

Maps by Lissa K. Dailey & Kim André

PHOTO CREDITS
Cover photo: Fox, *Index Stock Photography*
Photos on the following pages were generously offered by the
Georgia Department of Industry, Trade & Tourism:
72, 81, 105, 117, 140, 168, 173, 215, 242, 245, 251, 253, 263, 272
Photos on pages 103 and 108 © Kevin C. Rose
All other photos by the author.

About The Author

Blair Howard was bitten by the travel bug more than 30 years ago when, during a stint in the Royal Air Force, he spent a year in paradise on a tiny island in the middle of the Indian Ocean. From there, his travels have taken him to the Far East, North Africa, across most of Europe, to the islands of the West Indies, the Bahamas, Bermuda and to almost every state in the Union.

With camera in hand, he wandered from one location to another, finally settling in a small rural town in Tennessee. But there's no cure for wanderlust. So, taking advantage of his new-found home, he set out once again, this time to write about the lands that surrounded him closer to home.

Today, after many miles on the road – and some 260 magazine articles and nine books – he's still at it, visiting and revisiting his favorite spots.

Other titles by Blair Howard for Hunter Publishing:

Adventure Guide to the GREAT SMOKY MOUNTAINS
(1-55650-720-8/$13.95/340pp)
Adventure Guide to the BAHAMAS
(1-55650-705-4/$12.95/176pp)
Adventure Guide to BERMUDA
(1-55650-706-2/$12.95/176pp)
Adventure Guide to the GEORGIA & CAROLINA COASTS
(1-55650-747-x/$13.95/280pp)
Adventure Guide to TENNESSEE
(1-55650-743-7/$13.95/320pp)
BATTLEFIELDS OF THE CIVIL WAR Volume I
(1-55650-603-1/$11.95/310pp)
BATTLEFIELDS OF THE CIVIL WAR Volume II
(1-55650-685-6/$12.95/288pp)

We'd Love to Hear From You!

Hunter Publishing makes every effort to ensure that its travel guides are the most current sources of information available to travelers. If you have information that you feel should be included in the next edition of this guide, please write Blair Howard, c/o Hunter Publishing, Inc., 130 Campus Drive, Edison, NJ 08818. Feel free to include price updates, your personal experiences while traveling, and ways in which you feel this book could be improved.

Contents

Maps

Introduction

The Nature Of Adventure

Adventure, for most people, means an excursion into the great outdoors: hiking, fishing and boating. And certainly the major portion of this book is devoted to that type of experience. But here in Georgia, adventure can mean much more than outdoor recreation. This is an area rich in history and culture, and the location of some of the most delightful, intriguing and exciting towns and cities in the nation. With many interesting places to see and historic sites to visit, adventure can also mean sightseeing; Atlanta is an adventure all its own.

But adventure means different things to different people. While to some it means hiking over snow-covered trails in Alaska, mountain climbing in Nepal, or a safari through the far-off jungles of the Amazon, to many it means a spin of the roulette wheel, shopping in a suburban mall, or a gourmet dinner in a fine restaurant. Most of the above, and more, can be enjoyed within the bounds of Georgia. The peaks are not as high as they are in the Himalayas, the snows not as deep as they are in Nome, but the jungles of the Chattahoochee National Forest, the swamps of the Okefenokee, and the great wildlife refuges can be just as dense and mysterious as those in Central America.

Here in Georgia adventure can mean driving the backcountry roads in search of some exciting new experience. It can mean shopping: antique stores, gift shops and craft fairs abound throughout the state, not to mention some of the finest shopping malls. And, for the gourmet adventurer, it can also mean great new experiences in fine dining and opulent hotels. And gambling? Yes, you can do that, too.

So, while this book is a guide to the outdoor adventures, it's also a guide for those of you who would rather spend your time in relative comfort, within the bounds of civilization, close to the shops, stores, restaurants and fun-time attractions that have made places like Atlanta, Savannah and Augusta famous.

How To Use This Book

With so many adventures to choose from, and so many attractions to see and experience, deciding which will be the most enjoyable for you and yours might be a problem. You could settle down and read the whole book from cover to cover and mark the most appealing spots; you could use it to plan your trip; or you could carry it along with you.

Georgia's rural areas can be a bit mundane, but much of its countryside, especially in the north and east, is very beautiful, often wild and dramatic. Some of the adventures listed in the index as "scenic drives" are designed for the pure pleasure of driving, with just enough attractions and stops along the way to keep things lively; maybe you'd like to take time out for a picnic. So, let the top down, the wind blow through your hair, leave all the anxieties of the busy world far behind and enjoy!

To make things as simple as possible, we have taken the following approach to the order of this book. First, each type of adventure is briefly covered on pages 25-42. There, you will find out what's available and where. Second, each geographical region is described in some depth. This is followed by practical information under the headings that follow.

GETTING AROUND

The driving directions for each trip assume that you're approaching a given destination via an interstate or major highway.

Route maps scattered throughout the book show you approximately where the sites are, and which main roads provide the most direct route to them. In many cases, however, you'll still need a good, up-to-date road map. The Official Georgia Road Map is available at any in-bound welcome center. It is quite good and will provide adequate main road information, along with the locations of some of the more popular sites, parks and attractions. If you want to really get off the beaten path, you'll need something more detailed.

The majority of destinations in this book are best reached by car; with a few notable exceptions, they do not lend themselves to public transportation. If you've arrived at your base destination without wheels, you can rent a car at the airport or at any of the downtown rental company offices; if not, you'll have to limit yourself to those trips that can be done easily by metrobus, cab, or on foot. There are plenty of excursions organized by local companies, and, in some cases, you can get where you want to go via Amtrak or Greyhound. Schedules are often inconvenient, though.

Some of the trips to outlying areas, especially the beaches, can be done by bicycle. Rentals are available almost everywhere; ask at your hotel.

ACCOMMODATIONS

For each base city or area you'll find several hotel listings. These are not recommendations, merely hotels where we have had good experiences. Rates are indicated by multiple $ signs.

$ indicates a daily in-season rate of $50 to $75
$$ means $76 to $100
$$$ designates a rate over $100

Hotel Reservation Terms

When it comes to making reservations, hotel people talk a different language than the rest of us, and some of the terms they use might have different meanings from what you would expect. The following might help make things a little clearer.

Oceanview means exactly what it implies, a view of the ocean, not a room on the oceanfront. Your room might be at the top of a hill and the ocean a tiny blue spot several miles away in the distance. If being near the water is important is important to you, ask when making your reservation.

Oceanfront means the room or property faces directly onto the ocean and is located on the ocean side of the street.

An *efficiency* is minimally equipped to prepare and serve meals, The minimum includes, but is not limited to, a stove, refrigerator, sink, and appropriate cooking and serving utensils.

American Plan means with meals.

European Plan means without meals.

CAMPING

Here you'll find listed campgrounds large and small, those run by state and national park services, and even by commercial operations. These are not the only campgrounds to be found in Georgia, just the ones we know and can recommend.

FOOD & DRINK

Always the high spot of any vacation, dining must be an important consideration when choosing a destination or day out. Several choice restaurants where the atmosphere is inviting, the service always good, and the food even better, are listed for each base city and destination. Many are the long-time favorites of experienced travelers. Some are not quite so well known and offer a culinary experience that's decidedly different. Seafood and Low Country cooking are the ultimate experience in coastal Georgia, and you'll find many of the restaurants listed here offer interesting and tasty variations on the theme. Many more throughout the state feature regional specialties not generally found elsewhere. The approximate price range is shown as:

$ – inexpensive
$$ – reasonable
$$$ – luxurious and expensive

Fast food outlets are, of course, scattered around almost everywhere and don't take up much of your sightseeing time. An even better alternative is to picnic. Georgia must be the picnic capital of the world; there are picnic areas everywhere, some beside the ocean and others in places where you'd least expect them. They offer the opportunity to take time out and enjoy a quiet lunch in the sunshine. Aaaah.

WHEN YOU ARE THERE

Weather

This can range from almost temperate in the north to subtropical in the south. Rainfall can sometimes be a problem – expect afternoon showers in coastal areas – but on the whole, Georgia is very much a sunshine state. You'll find the local climate described for you in the *When You Are There* section.

Opening Times & Fees

When planning a day out or a tour, be sure to note the opening times of the various sites – these can often be a bit erratic, especially on weekends. Anything unusual that you should know before starting out, such as "don't make this trip on a Monday," is summarized in the *When You Are There* section.

Entrance fees listed in the text are, naturally, subject to change – and they rarely go down. On the whole, though, considering the cost of maintaining the sites, admissions are quite reasonable.

Facilities available at each site are listed, along with the address and phone number. These often include restaurants or cafeterias, cafés, information counters, gift shops, tours, shows, picnic facilities, and so on. Useful telephone numbers and relevant area codes are given at the end of each listing.

Handicapped travelers: Access varies with each individual's needs and abilities, so no firm statement can be made about any site. It's always best to phone ahead.

Group Travel

If you're planning a group outing, always call ahead. Most sites require advance reservations and offer special discounts for groups, often at a substantial saving over the regular admission fee. Some sites will open specially or remain open beyond their scheduled hours to accommodate groups.

Suggested Tours

Two different methods of organizing days out are used in this book, depending upon local circumstances. Some are based on structured itineraries, such as walking tours and scenic drives that follow a suggested route, while others just describe the local attractions for you to choose from.

Major attractions are described, some in extensive detail, some in only one or more paragraphs, beginning with practical information for a visit.

About Georgia

The largest state east of the Mississippi River, Georgia plays a major role in the economy of the southeastern United States. Atlanta, the state capital and largest city, is the commercial, transportation, and financial center of the entire region. Thousands of national concerns have their corporate headquarters in Atlanta, and one of the city's downtown intersections is known locally as the Wall Street of the South. Although many think of Georgia as a rural state – small towns and agriculture – the urban manufacturing centers are more truly representative of the modern state.

Georgia is the only state named for an English king. King George II granted the original charter for the "land lying between the Savannah and Altamaha Rivers" in 1732. Over the years it has had such nicknames as the Buzzard State, Cracker State, Goober State and Peach State.

Geography

Georgia has an area of more than 59,000 square miles, nearly as large as all New England. Of that, more than 854 are covered with water. It ranks 21st in the nation in size. This is a state of contrasts, of mountains, lakes, rivers and ocean. From Rabun Gap to Tybee Light, it slopes from almost a mile high down to sea level. Brasstown Bald Mountain, near Rabun Gap in the northeastern corner of the state, is the highest point. Located in the Blue Ridge Mountains, it rises to a height of 4,784 feet. The original 18th-century Tybee Lighthouse, which was one of the first public structures in the state, still guides vessels into the port of Savannah.

Georgia extends over five natural regions: the low Coastal Plain; the central Piedmont Plateau; and, in the extreme north, the Blue Ridge, the Valley and Ridge, and the Cumberland Plateau regions of the Appalachian Highlands.

THE COASTAL PLAIN

It was here, along its Atlantic coast, that Georgia was first settled in 1733. The new colony was established as a haven for England's poor and as a buffer between the Northern colonies and Spanish Florida. The waterpower of Georgia's rivers first attracted industry. Following the rivers, the early Georgians spread inland. They crossed the Coastal Plain and the rolling uplands, venturing as far as the Blue Ridge Mountains in the north.

Georgia's Coastal Plain occupies about 60% of the land area of the state. It lies south of a line running from Augusta through Milledgeville and Macon to Columbus. This dividing line between the Coastal Plain and the Piedmont Plateau to the north is called the fall line. It is marked by a belt of hills, where the hard rocks of the plateau meet the softer rocks of the plain. Rivers and streams flow rapidly over the fall line on their swift descent to the plain.

The Coastal Plain is divided into two sections along a watershed between the Ocmulgee and the Flint rivers. East from the Ocmulgee is the Sea Island region, which drains into the Atlantic Ocean. From the Flint River west is the East Gulf Coastal Plain, which slopes southward to the Gulf of Mexico.

The East Gulf Coastal region is largely a flat limestone plain, deeply cut by narrow valleys. The Flint and Chattahoochee rivers flow south and join on the Florida border to form the Apalachicola River.

The Sea Island section of the Coastal Plain is so named because a chain of islands parallels the coastline. They are the exposed tops of a submerged ridge. The so-called valley between the islands and the mainland is part of the Intracoastal Waterway.

Salt marshes and freshwater swamps border the coastal mainland, broken by the mouths of the Savannah, Ogeechee, Altamaha, Satilla, and St. Mary's rivers. In the extreme southeast, extending into Florida, is the great wetland wilderness called the Okefenokee Swamp.

Inland from the coast, the land rises in a series of terraces to an upland district of rolling hills with rounded summits 50 to 100 feet high. Here are sandy areas known as pine barrens, where longleaf pine grows in abundance.

THE PIEDMONT PLATEAU

The Piedmont Plateau lies to the north of the Coastal Plain and occupies about 30% of the state's total area. This is Georgia's most densely populated section. Here, among the rolling uplands that slope northward from the fall line toward the mountains, most of the state's important cities are located. Altitudes range from 500 to nearly 2,000 feet. Four great rivers, the Chattahoochee, Flint,

Ocmulgee and Oconee, cut deep, narrow valleys through the woodlands and forest. To the north, a series of isolated hills rise sharply against the skyline, great masses of rock that resisted erosion while the surrounding land was worn down. These include Stone Mountain, near Atlanta, and Kennesaw Mountain, near Marietta. In the northeast section of the Piedmont lies the Dahlonega Plateau, a deeply eroded region of steep, forested hills and narrow valleys where the peaks rise some 1,800 feet above sea level near the Blue Ridge Mountains. Here, through a deep gorge, the Tallulah River falls 360 feet over a distance of four miles.

THE BLUE RIDGE

The Blue Ridge is to the north. These mountains, together with the Valley and Ridge and the Cumberland Plateau regions, are all a part of the Appalachian Highlands. The mountains here rise an average of 3,000 feet above sea level; the peak of Brasstown Bald Mountain, the highest point in the state, is 4,784 feet high.

THE VALLEY & RIDGE

The Valley and Ridge sits to the west of the Blue Ridge. This is a region of folded mountains where the old rocks, resistant to erosion, stand out as long, narrow ridges. It's a heavily forested area where rivers, streams and hiking trails meander through rifts and valleys. Spring and fall are special seasons here.

THE CUMBERLAND PLATEAU

The Cumberland Plateau lies in the extreme northwestern corner of the state. Here, two broad, flat-topped ranges, Lookout Mountain and Sand Mountain, are separated only by a narrow valley. Although the peaks here are similar in size to those of the Valley and Ridge, the rocks are horizontal, not bent and folded. The peaks rise from around 1,800 feet to more than 3,000.

Climate

The altitude, latitude and the proximity of the warm waters of the Atlantic Ocean and the Gulf Stream determine the climate of Georgia's various regions. The winters are generally mild and the summers warm and humid. The mountains and forests north of Atlanta are colder in winter and cooler in summer. Snow and ice turn them into a winter wonderland. In winter, temperatures range from an average of 44° in the northwest to 54° in the southeast. In July they range from an average of 78° in the northwest to 81° in the southeast.

Late winter and early spring rains often cause floods during March and April. Annual precipitation ranges from an average of 68 inches in the extreme northeast to 44 inches in the east. Along the Atlantic coast the average is 52 inches. October and November are the driest months.

People

The first European explorers found several major Indian tribes living in what was soon to become Georgia. By the turn of the 19th century the only Native Americans remaining in Georgia were the Cherokee, who had become assimilated into the European culture. For a while they managed to co-exist with their white brothers, but it was not to last. Greed soon played a heavy hand in the destiny of the Cherokee. Because of the Europeans' desire for land, the Cherokees were forced to give up their holdings and move to Indian Territory (now Oklahoma) during the 1830s. They were gathered together by an army under the command of General Winfield Scott and force-marched more than a thousand miles westward to the reservations. More than 13,000 of them died along the way. The Cherokee called their hard journey the Trail of Tears.

Today, the population of Georgia is a little more than 6.5 million, of which roughly 20% are African Americans. Georgia was one of the fastest-growing states during the 1980s, and in 1986 Gwinnett County (metropolitan Atlanta) became the fastest-growing county in the nation.

When Georgia came under direct rule of the British government in the 1750s, there were only 3,000 inhabitants, most of them either English or of African descent. Irish, German and other Europeans arrived in great numbers during the early 19th century, but their effect on Georgia was minimal, and by 1910 only about 15,000 foreign-born whites resided in the state. Each decade from 1870 to 1960, Georgia lost more people than it gained, but the total population increased steadily due to high birth rates.

Recreation

Outdoor Georgia from Cohutta in the northwest to St. Mary's Island in the southeast is a vast adventure playground. There's so much to see, do, experience and enjoy here, one hardly knows where to begin.

The beaches, wetlands and wild scenic beauty of the Golden Isles in the southeast present endless opportunities: fishing, hiking, swimming, sailing and cruising. The Golden Isles, St. Simons Island, Sea Island, and Jekyll Island, offshore from Brunswick, are reached by causeway and bridge.

One of the most interesting areas is the Okefenokee Swamp in the southeast, and across the state line into northern Florida. Its unique character is preserved through the administration of the Okefenokee National Wildlife Refuge, as well as the Stephen C. Foster and Laura S. Walker State Parks. The Georgia section covers 700 square miles, a vast wetland area of islands and prairies, interlaced with waterways, where hundreds of species of wild animals and birds make their homes. Boat trails lead into the wilderness, but there are no highways. If you feel uncomfortable traveling by boat, you can view the swamp from wooden walkways and an 80-foot observation tower.

The Chattahoochee National Forest, in the north-central part of the state, covers more than 700,000 acres. Here, the great rivers offer more opportunities for outdoor adventure: rafting, canoeing, fishing, hiking and camping.

From Chattanooga to Atlanta to Savannah and beyond, Georgia's American Civil War battlefields are preserved at Pickett's Mill, Kennesaw Mountain, Chickamauga and Chattanooga National Military Park, Andersonville, Fort Pulaski and Fort McAllister, with a number of smaller, but no less interesting sites scattered all across the state.

America's early history is preserved through the old towns and historic sites scattered along the coast from Savannah to St. Mary's – Brunswick, Darien, Fort George, Fort Frederica, and many more. Savannah itself is one of the nation's oldest and best-preserved cities.

For the spectator, Georgia has three professional sports teams, all based in Atlanta. They are the Braves, in baseball; the Hawks, in basketball; and the Falcons, in football.

History

Long before Europeans came to North America, the region that is now Georgia was occupied by the peace-loving Cherokee and Creek Indians. The Yamacraw branch of the Creek lived along the coast. By the 17th century, French, Spanish and English explorers were seeking to establish themselves in the area.

In 1540 the Spaniard Hernando de Soto, lured by tales of wealth in the New World, passed through the region on his way to the Mississippi River. As a result of his travels, Georgia became part of the territory claimed by Spain.

In 1732 George II, for whom the state was named, granted a charter to a group of wealthy Englishmen headed by James E. Oglethorpe. Under this charter they planned to found a colony as a haven for imprisoned debtors, the poor and unemployed, and persecuted Protestants from Germany and Austria. Such a colony would also serve as a defensive buffer against the Spaniards in Florida and the French in Louisiana.

In February 1733, Oglethorpe, with 120 followers, sailed up the Savannah River to Yamacraw Bluff, where he and his people were welcomed ashore by Tomochichi, chief of the Yamacraw. Oglethorpe's first priority was to establish a settlement. This he did at Savannah, soon to become the first city in the new colony of Georgia; it was to be the last of the 13 original English colonies. Word of the new colony spread quickly, and Oglethorpe's group was soon joined by other adventurers, mostly Protestant and Jewish refugees.

In 1734 Oglethorpe went back to England for supplies and more settlers. When he returned to Georgia he had tools, seeds and other essentials, as well as more colonists. He also brought with him a full regiment of soldiers. In 1736 Oglethorpe looked to the south and the ever-present threat of a Spanish invasion from St. Augustine. His explorations took him to St. Simons Island, where he built Fort Frederica to help defend Savannah from the Spanish. The Spanish, however, were not to be denied. In 1742 they set out from Florida with a fleet of more than 50 ships and landed 3,000 men on the east coast of St. Simons Island. Their plan was to destroy the settlement at Frederica. They advanced overland almost to the fort itself, but Oglethorpe and his troops were waiting. The Spanish were soundly defeated at the battle of Bloody Marsh, and Spain's hold on the land north of Florida was broken.

Following the fighting on St. Simons Island, life in Savannah, Frederica and the surrounding countryside went on quietly. Silkworms, hemp, grapes and olives were cultivated, but the colonists didn't thrive. Restrictions on size and a prohibition on the importation of slaves made it difficult for the small coastal farms to compete with the large, slave-worked plantations of nearby South Carolina. Many colonists were stricken with malaria, but rum, which was used as a medicine, was prohibited. To induce settlers to remain in Georgia, the trustees gradually lifted the restrictions against slavery.

Georgia's Native Americans remained friendly until 1751, when Mary Musgrove, an Indian woman who had acted as an interpreter for Oglethorpe, marched into Savannah with a large band of Indians to demand the return of certain lands. The uprising was quickly put down by William Stephens, Oglethorpe's successor.

After the trustees surrendered their charter, the colony became a royal province in 1754. During the American Revolution, Georgia was a major battlefield. In 1778 the British routed the Americans under General Robert Howe and seized Savannah. The city was the headquarters of the British in the South until General Anthony Wayne's offensive of 1782 forced them out. The years that followed were, for the most part, peaceful. Then came the Civil War.

After Abraham Lincoln was elected president, the pot began to boil. Georgia voted for secession on January 19, 1861, and declared itself a free republic. Alexander H. Stephens, a native of Georgia, became vice-president of the Confederacy.

For most of the war Georgia saw little fighting; then, in 1864 General William T. Sherman cut and burned his way across the state, captured Atlanta, and marched on to Savannah and the sea.

Georgia recovered slowly from the war. Occupation and reconstruction brought hard times, and the Cause never really died; even today, the Confederate battle flag flies over the state capitol. Georgia was readmitted into the Union on July 15, 1870. The glittering skyline of its capital, Atlanta, is a symbol of the prosperous New South. The city played host to the 1988 Democratic National Convention, the 1994 Super Bowl and, of course, was the site for the 1996 Olympic Games. Georgia's capital is only the third American city to be honored with the Summer Games.

Georgia's coastal areas long remained undiscovered by the vacationing public, at least by those from other states. But that's changing rapidly. Savannah and the Golden Isles to the south have become some of the most popular destinations north of Florida. Even so, you can still find a secluded spot, if you've a mind to, and get away into the great outdoors.

For those who like things a little more lively, there's plenty to see and do: shopping, sightseeing, fishing, all sorts of watersports, wining, dining – there's even a resort area or two where you can join the crowds on the beach.

Getting Around

While one or two rural areas are still not easy to reach, especially in the north, getting around in Georgia is relatively simple because four major routes – Interstates 16, 20, 75 and 85 – open up the entire state, connecting Atlanta with all points of the compass. Interstate 16 connects with Interstate 75 south of Atlanta and provides the quickest and most direct route to Savannah and the east coast; Interstate 75 is the most direct route north and south; Interstate 20 runs east and west and connects Atlanta with Birmingham and Augusta; Interstate 85 runs northeast and southwest, connecting Atlanta with Greenville, South Carolina; Columbus and Montgomery, Alabama. Other major routes include US Highways 82 and 19, which connect Albany with the rest of the world. Georgia's main ancillary roads are, for the most part, well planned and maintained. In the more rural areas, however, they often deteriorate.

AIRPORTS

All roads in Georgia lead to Atlanta, and that's where you'll find its key airport. There's also a regional airport at Savannah, another at Albany, one at Augusta, and the northwest can be accessed through Chattanooga in east Tennessee.

BUS LINES

Service into all of Georgia's major metropolitan areas and most of the smaller cities is provided by Greyhound/Trailways Buslines, ☎ 1-800-231-2222.

RENTAL CARS

The five major airports are served by most of the national car rental companies, including Hertz, Alamo, National, Thrifty, Enterprise, Dollar and Avis.

RV & CAMPING TRAILER RENTALS

Cruise America has a fleet of trailers and RVs that range in size from 15 to 36 feet. In the low season, you can rent a 23-foot RV to sleep five people for as little as $650 per week, including insurance. A 31-foot, top-of-the-line luxury motorhome to sleep six will cost you about $765 per week. You'll be required to leave a refundable deposit, depending upon the rental package you choose, of either $100 or $500. Cruise America has branches in most major cities throughout the country. ☎ 1-800-327-7778.

Safety

PERSONAL SECURITY

Personal security is very much a matter of common sense. Mugging and other crimes of violence are as common as they are in any major city. Stay alert. If you need to ask directions, go to a gas station or convenience store. It's a good idea to carry one of the proprietary personal protection systems: mace, pepper spray, a personal siren. Firearms are prohibited in most national and state parks, but are permitted, provided you have the proper licenses, in the national forests.

Many areas of Georgia are still very primitive – especially in the mountainous areas to the north. Keep in mind that homeowners in isolated areas can be suspicious of strangers.

Car-jacking is a growing and all-to-real problem, especially in the big cities. Keep your vehicle doors locked at all times, especially at stop lights. Never pick up hitchhikers. At rest stops and welcome centers, keep a sharp lookout for suspicious characters; stay securely locked inside your car until they are gone. If you have a cellular phone, it's a good idea to keep it handy. Emergency 911 service is available almost everywhere.

Be careful inside public restrooms. Don't leave purses, pocketbooks, bags or any other tempting articles beside the washbasins.

It's a good idea to invest in traveler's checks and leave jewelry at home, preferably in a bank.

ANIMALS

Wild animals should not be a problem, if you stay away from them and don't feed them. Of the bigger and more exotic animals, only the alligator, black bear and wild boar are really dangerous – bears and boars are found mostly in the forests and mountains in the north. The alligator rarely ventures north of Albany and Waycross.

To see a bear, even at a distance, is a rare delight. To see one close up and angry is something else. The cubs are delightful little creatures. Playful, full of fun and curiosity, they will often wander up close. But wherever there's a cub, you can be sure mama bear is close at hand with her ears cocked, and she will defend her young with her life.

Though rarely seen during daylight, even in the wild, the wild boar is a long-time resident of the great national forests, the Cherokee, Nantahala and Chattahoochee. Hunters track them down with handgun and rifle, but they will tell you that the boar is a fierce and ferocious adversary, apt to charge when cornered, and its tusks are certain to inflict a nasty wound if it gets close enough.

Don't feed wild animals, and don't give them the opportunity to feed themselves – a scrounging bear is a clever and resourceful creature. Somehow, they can identify a brightly colored backpack and will have no hesitation about raiding yours if you leave it within easy reach. Hang packs and food containers from a high branch, at least six feet off the ground, and make sure that the branch will not support the weight of even a baby bear. Small animals, too, will invade your pack or food supply if you leave it lying on the ground.

The alligator, found mostly in southern Georgia, is not a picky eater and will attack almost anything that moves, including turtles, snakes, raccoons, fish, deer, other alligators and humans. They often appear lazy and sluggish. In reality they are always on the alert and can move like lightning on land or in the water. The jaws of a full-grown alligator are extremely strong and can easily crush the shell of a large turtle. Males can grow to 11 or 12 feet, and specimens in excess of 17 feet are not unknown. A running alligator can easily reach a speed of more than 20 mph.

If you swim in wilderness lakes and rivers, be sure to keep a sharp lookout. You might not be able to see a lurking 'gator, but you can bet he sees you. Never swim alone or without a companion keeping watch from the riverbank or lakeshore.

Always remember, the woods and forests are their home, not yours. You are the visitor.

INSECTS

Insects are naturally attracted to the flowers and foliage of the forests, rivers and lakes. Unfortunately, they will also be attracted to you. Check with your doctor or pharmacist for any allergy medication or insect repellent you may need.

Mosquito concentrations are heavy during the summer months, especially during the evening hours. Wear a lightweight, long-sleeved shirt or blouse and pants along with your insect repellent and you should stay free of mosquitoes and other nighttime pests.

Other venomous insects you're likely to encounter are the fire ant, the honeybee, the yellow jacket and the hornet. Only in cases where there's an allergy will emergency room treatment be required; calamine lotion will usually help ease the pain.

More annoying than dangerous are the deerflies that live in the forests; chiggers, the nasty little red bugs that inhabit the dense bushy areas in the summertime; and the horseflies that seem to live everywhere, especially in the open woods and grasslands.

TICKS

Unfortunately, ticks are common in Georgia's woodlands, forests and wetlands. Even worse are the diseases that some of them carry and can inflict upon humans.

Lyme disease is rapidly becoming a problem, and Rocky Mountain spotted fever has been around for a long time. Both are carried by ticks, and both can have a devastating effect. Anyone venturing into heavily wooded areas needs to be extremely careful.

Rocky Mountain spotted fever is the result of toxins secreted during the bite of the American dog tick, one of the family of wood ticks found throughout the area. It can be fatal if not treated quickly.

Lyme disease is a tick-borne viral infection for which there is no cure or vaccination. It need not, however, be fatal. A program of antibiotics will keep the disease in check until the immune system can build up antibodies to cope with it.

The symptoms of lyme disease are similar to many other illnesses: low-grade fever, fatigue, head and body pain. The tick bite itself may at first go unnoticed but, within a month of being bitten, a red rash may appear around the bite. Sometimes the rash is a solid red, sometimes it has a brighter outer edge with little or no color in the middle. Although the rash can vary in size and can cover an entire arm or thigh, it usually is about four inches in diameter.

A blood test will usually confirm the disease by detecting antibodies in the immune system, but it can take as long as two months before those antibodies begin to appear.

The deer tick lives in wooded areas, and that's where you're most likely to get bitten. Unfortunately, however, that's not the only source: your pet, good friend that he is, can bring the tick to you. You can decrease the chances of this happening by using a tick spray, dip, powder or collar to keep them off your pet.

- Wear proper clothing when venturing out into the forests or woodlands: long-sleeved shirts, long pants and, especially, a hat. Use repellents and tuck your pants into high socks to keep ticks from crawling under your clothes.
- Keep shoes and boots tightly laced.
- Wear light-colored clothing. It will not only be cooler, but also will make it easier to spot ticks before they can crawl into an open neck or buttonhole.
- Wear collared shirts to help stop ticks crawling onto your neck.
- Check your clothing after an outing. The deer tick is small, often no bigger than a large pinhead, and can be difficult to see.

If you find a tick attached to your skin, don't try any of the old wives' remedies for removing it. The application of a lighted cigarette may cause it to regurgitate fluid back into your body, thus causing all sorts of infection.

Use fine-jawed tweezers and grip the tick as gently as possible, and as close to your skin as possible. Do not squeeze the tick's body; you will inject its fluids into the bite.

There are many good repellents on the market, but the strongest contain an agent called DEET. However, it is suggested that you use only repellents with a DEET content of less then 20%; in stronger concentrations it can cause itching and burning.

Best of all are the proprietary brands of skin softener, such as Avon's Skin-So-Soft, a product that was used extensively against all sorts of flying bugs and pests during the Gulf War. It smells nice and won't cause burning or itching.

SPIDERS

There are only two venomous spiders you'll need to watch out for: the brown recluse and the black widow. Although most spider venoms are not harmful to humans, those of these two nasty little critters are, and the brown recluse is the deadliest of all North American spiders.

The black widow's venom contains neurotoxins that affect the transmission of nerve impulses. That produced by the brown recluse is necrotic. It causes local swelling and death of tissues around the area where the poison was injected.

The black widow lives in old wooden buildings, on dead logs, wooden benches and picnic tables. They are easily recognized by their jet black color, large bulbous body and a distinctive red, hourglass-shaped mark on their underside.

The brown recluse makes its home in out-of-the-way nooks and crannies; dusty places, in the roofs of old buildings, garages, shelters, outhouses and such. It's slightly smaller than the black widow, but has the same characteristic long legs. Its color varies from a light fawn to a dark chocolate brown.

If you are bitten by either spider, you should go immediately to the nearest emergency room for treatment. Many national park and forest ranger stations can offer immediate first aid, but expert treatment is essential.

SNAKES

You should be aware of and stay away from the pit vipers: the copperhead, water moccasin, cottonmouth, eastern diamondback rattlesnake and the timber rattlesnake. The copperhead, diamondback and the timber rattlesnake are fairly common and found throughout forests in Georgia. The cottonmouth can also be found almost everywhere, but it also likes the water and can sometimes be found in the swamps, on the riverbanks and close to the lakes, where you'll also find the water moccasin.

To avoid a snakebite, watch where you step. Never put your hands into nooks and crannies or other rocky places; never go barefoot; sleep up off the ground.

If you or someone in your party is bitten, administer first aid (do not apply a tourniquet) and transport the victim immediately to the nearest hospital emergency room. If you are by yourself, go immediately for help, but try to avoid exerting yourself.

PLANTS

There are a great many poisonous plants indigenous to Georgia. At least a dozen of them, including some species of mushroom, are deadly if ingested; a great many more will cause nasty skin rashes. Especially deadly is the jimson weed, which can cause coma and even death, and, of course, most members of the nightshade family. All grow profusely throughout the forests to the north.

Poison oak and poison ivy, along with several other varieties of poisonous creeper, grow everywhere throughout the state. They can cause a nasty, inflamed rash. Some people are more sensitive to the stinging plants than others; some can handle them without any problems. If you're venturing out into the woodlands, you should learn to identify them. Their most distinctive feature is a characteristic three-leaf arrangement.

To avoid problems, assume that everything is poisonous. Don't put anything into your mouth, not even if you're sure you know what it is. Don't touch plants you can't identify. Don't pick flowers.

A victim of poisoning should quickly drink two or three glasses of water to dilute the poison, then vomiting should be induced – syrup of ipecac works well – and the victim transported to the nearest emergency room along with a sample of the poisonous plant.

BOATING

There are literally hundreds of accessible lakes and rivers in Georgia. It's no wonder that boating is one of its most popular pastimes. But it's also the one in which the most accidents occur. So it's imperative you obey all boating regulations, speed limits and motor restrictions when on the water, especially when traveling around other boats.

- Always handle and store boat fuel and oil properly.
- Never drink and drive on the water. The laws that apply on the road also apply on the water. More than 50% of all boating fatalities are alcohol-related. Unfortunately, a six-pack seems to be an essential part of many people's boating equipment.
- Always wear a life jacket. Four out of five deaths on the water are caused by drowning. Federal law now requires that every boat carry one personal flotation device per passenger. It takes only one unexpected wave from the wake of another boat, or a waterlogged branch, to throw you into the water. A bang on the head or the sudden shock of cold water can render you helpless.
- Clear water weeds from boats, motors and trailers immediately after returning to the ramp so that you won't spread them to other lakes and rivers.

FORESTS

Streams & Creeks

Georgia is a land of a thousand beautiful streams, creeks and rivers, every one of them a delight. But after a rainfall water levels rise quickly and can turn a shallow stream into an impassable torrent. Remember that water-worn rocks are always smooth and slippery, often overgrown with a fine layer of moss or algae, slimy and treacherous. One false step and you're in the water.

Here are a few tips that will help keep you out of trouble when crossing:

- Always test the water before your party attempts to cross. Either do it yourself or, if you can't swim, have some other sure-footed member of your party do it. If you can, use a rope. Loop members of the party together and cross one at a time.
- Stay away from large rocks in the middle of rushing waters; the water around them is often deep and the currents strong.

If someone does take a bath, especially in winter, dry them off quickly and have them change into dry clothing. Many mountain streams and creeks are icy cold, even during the summer months, and hypothermia can be deadly.

Forest Fire

Forest fire is a big problem in forests everywhere, but especially so in northern Georgia. Each year, thousands of acres of woodland are lost to fires. Some are the result of arson, some of lightning strikes, but most are caused by careless adventurers. A campfire left smoldering, or a carelessly tossed match or cigarette, can do an untold amount of damage. So, make sure fires are dead. Dowse them with water and then cover them with dirt. Also, it's better not to smoke at all in the forest, but if you must, use a cigarette lighter and carry your butts out with you.

Thunderstorms

Lightning is something everyone should be concerned with, especially in the forests. If you find yourself caught in a storm in open country, keep moving; don't stand still. Static electricity can build in your body. Remove exposed metal objects from your body. Never shelter under a large tree, and never in a metal-roofed shelter.

HIKING

Although hiking is often a delightful experience, it can also be a hazardous one. The wilderness areas covered in this book, especially in the mountains and forests of northern Georgia, are often vast, forested regions. So vast that it's not unusual for hikers to get lost, and stay lost for days on end, especially in winter.

And, while a vacation in the wilderness will take you far from civilization and bring you close to nature, it's important that you behave responsibly. Not only must you exercise basic common sense for you own safety but also for the sake of all who might follow you.

If you're new to hiking, there are a number of excellent books that will help you get started. Several come readily to mind, including *The New Complete Walker III*, by Colin Fletcher; *Backpacking, One Step at a Time*, by Harvey Manning; and *Walk Softly in the Wilderness*, by John Hart. In the meantime, here are some basic rules and hints that even the most experienced hiker would do well to remember.

- Most of your hiking will be done either on state or national park or national forest property; all are controlled and maintained by park or forest rangers. Before you begin your hike, establish your presence at the ranger station; let them know you're there, and exactly what your plans are. Don't forget to call and let them know you've arrived at your destination; if not, they'll be out looking for you.

- **Maps:** Never leave home without a map. Maps of the better-known hiking trails are available almost everywhere: at ranger stations in the national forests, state parks, book stores and gift shops.
- **Stay on the trail.** True, the well-maintained trails are well marked and easy to follow. Even so, it's easy to take a wrong turn onto a smaller trail, and then onto something that's barely a trail at all. Always plot your progress as you go, take notes, and try to remain aware of your position on the map at any given time. If you wait until you're lost, it will be an almost impossible task to re-establish your position.
- **The Compass:** If you should happen to lose the trail, you might have to go five or six miles before you stumble onto another one, and that only if you walk in a straight line. Maintain your sense of direction in relation to your position on your map at all times.
- **If you do get lost, don't panic.**
- **First Aid Kit:** Keep it simple – band-aids, elastic bandage, butterfly closures, adhesive tape, aspirin or something similar, antihistamines for bee stings, bug repellent.
- **Knife:** Take along a good hunting knife with either a fixed or folding blade. Buck makes some great outdoor knives, as does Schrade and Case. Forget the much vaunted, but basically useless Swiss Army knives with all their bits and pieces. A fixed-blade or folding knife with a strong, sharp, four- or five-inch blade is all you'll need. The so-called survival knives – à la Rambo – while extremely useful, are heavy and, after a mile or two, tend to weigh you down. Leave the machete at home; you won't need it.
- **Flashlight:** Who knows what can happen in the wilderness. Make one wrong turn, and a four-hour hike can quickly turn into an all-night experience. The woodland grows dark much more quickly than does open terrain and the trails will become difficult to see, let alone follow.
- **Batteries:** Never assume that batteries are good. Always carry at least one spare set.
- **Wet Weather Gear:** No, you don't necessarily need to carry a full set of rain gear, especially if you're only going on a half-day hike. A large, three- or four-ply garbage bag will do quite nicely in an emergency, and will fold almost to nothing. It might look a little strange, but it's better to stay dry than to struggle through the undergrowth soaked to the skin, and suffer even further when the rain stops and the sun comes out to turn your wet clothing into something a medieval torturer would have been proud to own. For extended hikes, take along a poncho or a

lightweight rain suit. In the winter you'll need to dress appropriately.

- **Matches:** You'll need waterproof matches in addition to your cigarette lighter. Lighter flints sometimes get wet and refuse to work. A small fire, especially in winter, can save your life.

- **Hats:** Always wear a hat, a good hat. It will keep the bugs out of your hair and your body heat in. You lose up to 35% of body heat through your head. In winter a good warm hat could save your life.

- **Snacks:** Rarely regarded as an essential, an extra snack or two can do wonders for your disposition. A candy bar will give you extra energy and a feeling of well-being. Take along more than you think you'll need; you won't be sorry.

- **Water:** It's always a good idea to carry plenty of water. Many wilderness streams look pure and inviting, and so they often are. Some, however, can be polluted. It's best not to take chances.

- **Camp Stove:** If your hike is an extended one, you should avoid lighting fires where you can. Forest fires are a real problem in the mountains, often destroying thousands of acres at a time. Almost all are started by careless hikers, campers or tourists.

- **Waterfalls:** As beautiful as they are, they can be deadly if you don't watch your step. The rocks are smooth, worn away by millions of years of fast-flowing water, covered in algae or moss, and thus extremely slippery. One wrong or careless step can send you plummeting to the rocks below. View waterfalls from the bottom, if possible, and stay off the rocks at the head of the falls.

- **Sunburn:** It's essential that you carry a good sunscreen. Check with your pharmacist to ensure the proper SPF for your type of skin.

The Adventures

Sightseeing

Georgia is rich in history, much of it preserved for you to see through its many historic sites. There are tiny cabins, once the homes of famous (some not so famous) people who made a significant contribution to the development of the state; living history communities where you can view life as it was centuries ago. There are museums full of artifacts and memorabilia; old buildings and historic downtown districts; and several major Civil War battlefields. The stories of the battles are described in detail, along with a guided driving or walking tour.

Camping

Hundreds of campgrounds – commercial, state and national forests or parks – offer a range of facilities. Many are located on the banks of the great rivers, some are on the shores of vast lakes or the ocean, others are deep in the forest far away from civilization. Camping is very much a part of the Georgia experience.

First, there are the commercial campgrounds. They vary in size, quality of service, and amenities from one operator to another. Then there are the state and national park campgrounds. While most of these may not offer the level of luxury available at the large commercial operations, some do provide facilities and recreational opportunities that rival those offered by many of their privately owned competitors, including some extra opportunities, such as group camping, youth camping and primitive camping. The state and national parks are the places to go if you really want to try something different. Some are tiny, with maybe only a half-dozen sites; some are so far away from the beaten path you'll have to hike for miles to reach them.

You'll find listings throughout the book, by region and destination, of all three types of campground. Meanwhile, here's a run-down of what you can expect to find.

COMMERCIAL CAMPGROUNDS

Profit, obviously, is the motivating force at all commercial campgrounds. Large or small, they are all in business to make money, and that's good for the camper. Competition – and there's more than many of them want – means the commercial campgrounds are constantly striving to improve facilities, services and recreational opportunities. In the main, the commercial campgrounds are clean, tidy and well cared for. Security in the smaller campgrounds often leaves a lot to be desired, but it's taken much more seriously at the larger establishments where gates are manned 24 hours a day and on-site personnel patrol the grounds.

Most of the larger campgrounds are self-sufficient, offering all sorts of amenities from laundries to full-service shops and stores, to marinas and restaurants. Some do not allow tents, catering only to campers with RVs or trailers. Many have rental RVs, trailers, and cabins available. Many more offer rental bicycles, boats, paddleboats and canoes. Larger campgrounds will have staff on hand to look after your needs around the clock; smaller ones might have employees available only for checking in during the daylight hours. Most will have a list of rules and regulations that restrict pets, noise and activities after dark.

KOA KABINS

There are rustic wooden cabins at most KOA campgrounds that provide some of the comforts of home and all the fun of camping out. Each Kabin sleeps at least four, and has an outdoor grill and picnic table. Campers have full use of the campground's amenities and services: hot showers, flush toilets, laundry, convenience store and recreational facilities.

NATIONAL FOREST CAMPGROUNDS

There are a great many campgrounds located in the national forests. Facilities, at most, are rarely as extensive as they are at their sister state park units; some are downright basic – no hookups, hand-pumped water, and so on. All are far away from civilization, and are surrounded by spectacular countryside and wildlife.

Most of the campgrounds are fairly small, but they are well kept and clean. Fees are very reasonable and, if you don't mind roughing it a little, the national forest campgrounds offer great value for money. Be sure to take all you need with you; service outlets can be many miles away from your campground.

STATE PARK CAMPGROUNDS

There are more than 60 state parks, historic sites and forests scattered throughout Georgia. Each is unique. No matter where you might be, there's always at least one close at hand.

The state of Georgia has gone to great lengths to make its state parks as attractive as possible to visitors. Facilities at many are extensive: Some parks can legitimately lay claim to resort status, while others are just as remote and primitive as their national park and forest competitors. Few commercial operations can compete with the best of Georgia's state park system, which includes a half-dozen championship golf courses. Some of Georgia's state parks have resort inns that rival even the finest of those found at the nation's hot-spots; excellent for those whose idea of camping is nothing less than a king-size room complete with mini-bar. There are also several hundred vacation cabins and chalets available to campers who like to keep a roof overhead; all are equipped with the comforts of home: air-conditioning, kitchen, etc. For the real camper, even if you do drive a luxury motor home, there are more than 2,900 camping sites, most of which are fully developed to provide all the modern conveniences: water and electric hookups, sewage disposal, etc. Many of Georgia's state parks offer a range of recreational facilities that rival those offered by many of their privately owned competitors; almost all offer extra camping opportunities that the commercial establishments don't: primitive camping, hiking trails, lakes, fishing and boating. Although many state parks are located close to major cites, their campgrounds are usually set far away from civilization.

Restrooms and hot showers are conveniently located and most are handicapped-accessible.

Group camping and youth camping are offered at most state parks in designated areas for youth organizations, groups of families, or gatherings of friends. Facilities in group camping areas vary throughout the park system, from full-service group cabins to limited accommodations.

Primitive camping is also available at most state parks. Overnight backpacking and canoeing into these areas is strictly for the physically fit, experienced and self-contained outdoor enthusiast.

Cabins are for the camper who likes a roof overhead. Many of the state parks offer a variety of rustic cottages and cabins that sleep from four to six persons. These locations are identified in the individual park listings. Some of the cabins have the rustic appeal of the original Civilian Conservation Corps construction, while other contemporary cabins feature modern amenities.

"Vacation Cabins" are a little more luxurious than the camping cabins. Usually, they provide all the comforts of home, including private baths and kitchens. The facilities in these cabins vary from park to park, but typically they sleep six, and may offer fireplaces and/or air conditioning.

"Private Cabins" offer private sleeping quarters that are sometimes convenient to other park facilities.

"Group Cabins" offer sleeping facilities in groups of units, or in large, single-unit sleeping quarters. They usually feature fully equipped kitchens, dining rooms, and/or meeting spaces.

Reservations for cabin rentals usually will be accepted up to one year in advance, and a deposit equal to a two-night stay is required for a confirmed reservation. Calls for reservations should be made between 8 am and 5 pm, Monday through Friday.

Like camping fees, cabin rental fees vary from park to park, according to season and the type of facilities offered, and are subject to change.

ACCESSIBILITY

Most of the campgrounds are easily accessible. Reaching some of the more primitive locations does, however, require lengthy and often strenuous hikes. Campers going primitive should be sure they are in the best physical condition.

AVAILABILITY

At times, the availability of some sites can become scarce, especially in the spring and early fall. Be sure to book far enough in advance to ensure your stay at the campground of choice.

The high season for camping on the East Coast seems to begin when the first blooms of spring appear and ends when the last leaf has fallen in early November, although die-hard campers can still be found roughing it out when the snow is two feet deep in the forests.

The most popular campgrounds stay heavily booked throughout spring, summer and fall. When the schools are out, and on most major holidays, especially Easter, Labor Day and Christmas, it's almost impossible to find a berth at any of the larger commercial grounds. And you can bet the choice sites at the state parks, allocated either by reservation or on a first-come, first-served basis, will almost always be occupied.

If you're looking for a cabin, you should choose your location as far in advance as possible, and then book your reservation immediately; many are reserved up to a year in advance.

COSTS

Commercial Campgrounds: Costs vary from campground to campground over a range that starts at around $16 per night for a basic site with few frills to a high, depending very much upon location, of $50 for a site with all the amenities, including private deck, table and chairs.

National Forest Campgrounds: Fees for camping depend upon the individual locations but are generally low.

State Parks: Camping fees generally range from $9.50 to $14 per night for RV sites, and from $6.25 to $9.50 per night for tent sites. A non-refundable deposit of $5 may be required in order to reserve a site. Campsites may be reserved by telephoning the park of your choice directly.

Resort Hotels: For current rates and reservations you should call the resort of your choice directly.

Vacation and Rustic Cabins: Again, you need to call your resort for reservations and current rates. Typically, however, the rates range from $40 per night during the week, and $60 per night on weekends, with a two-night minimum stay.

Picnic Shelters: Reservations must be made directly with each park, or may be used on a first-come, first-served basis. The daily fees charged vary from park to park.

Group Lodges: Reservations must be made directly with each park. The fee depends upon the location, size, and availability.

Credit Cards: Credit cards are accepted at most commercial and some state park campgrounds throughout Georgia.

LENGTH OF STAY

Commercial: There are no restrictions at commercial campgrounds. You can visit for as long as you like, or for as long as you have money to pay the bill.

State Parks: Maximum of two weeks.

National Forests and Parks: Maximum of 14 days at any location in any one 30-day period.

PETS

Pets are not permitted in the camping areas at most state parks, but are welcome in national park campgrounds as long as they are quiet and on a leash. Pets are welcome at some commercial campgrounds. Check individual listings. It is unlawful in Georgia to leave pets in your vehicle, locked or not.

SECURITY

Most of the campgrounds listed in this book maintain good security and have the safety of their guests very much in mind, especially at the state parks, most of which are gated and locked at night.

Many commercial campgrounds are not gated. Usually, however, they have on-site staff working security around the clock. Even so, it pays to be extra careful.

Spring Wildflowers

Spring, like autumn, brings something special to the Peach State. Each year, from late March through early June, the forests, parks, rivers, lakes and woodlands burst into new life in a riot of pink and white. The air fills with the scent of dogwood, honeysuckle, foamflowers, trillium, lady's slipper and a thousand others. Highland places such as Bald Mountain, Lookout Mountain, Cloudland Canyon, Black Rock Mountain, Fort Mountain and hundreds of other sites across the southern Appalachians put on spectacular displays of color as nature spreads a breathtaking blanket of pastel shades.

There are a number of places where the colors of spring can be observed at their best, and you'll find them individually listed by location throughout the book.

Birdwatching

More than 140 species of birds make their homes in Georgia. Bird lovers can expect to see red-tailed hawks, ruffed grouse, wild turkey, five types of owl, vultures, ravens, blue herons, a wide variety of warblers and seven species of woodpecker. If you're lucky, you may see such rare birds as the eastern screech owl, the endangered red-cockaded woodpecker, the hooded warbler, golden eagle, osprey, roseate spoonbill, egret, peregrine falcon or even a bald eagle.

Birding is best done in the early morning. Find a spot, then remain still and quiet. Be sure to take along a good field guide, binoculars and a notebook. The best times are said to be during April and May, and September and October; May is best of all.

Photography

Photography is an adventure? For most of us it surely is. Rarely do we have any idea exactly what we are putting on film, or how it will turn out when we get it home. A photograph can be many things: a simple record of a visit to a particular attraction, a very personal souvenir of a visit to a special place, even a work of art. And these days you don't have to be an expert to obtain consistently good results. Modern automatic-everything cameras – auto-focus, auto-exposure, etc. – have brought good photography to almost everyone, not just the pro. And you don't need to spend the earth on your equipment either. Experts say a nice point-and-shoot 35mm camera, available at most large stores for around $60, will do just as good a job in the right hands as will the mighty Nikon F4 that costs a couple of thousand dollars. But here are some tips and simple techniques to help make your adventures in photography a little more successful, a little more pleasing, and ensure you won't be disappointed when you get your photos back from the lab.

- First, film is not expensive. So carry plenty with you and shoot lots of frames.
- Be sure to carry a spare set of batteries. Although they are readily available almost anywhere, there's nothing more annoying than to have your camera quit, and then have to go in search of batteries.
- If you're flying, don't be afraid to put your film through the airport security machines. Unless it's a very high-speed film, the machine won't hurt it.
- Use a low-speed film. The fine-grain film of 50 or 100 speed will produce the best results. The lower the speed of the film, the sharper the image will be. True, a low-speed film is not always the most practical. In the interest of great pictures, however, it's the one you should use whenever you can, especially on bright sunny days. Use a high-speed film only when low light or a telephoto lens makes it a necessity.
- If you have the option, shoot at the highest possible shutter speed. This will reduce camera shake. Often, you'll hear people bragging about how they can hand-hold a 200mm lens with the shutter set to 1/30th of a second, and they probably can, sometimes. The rule is, "the longer the lens, the faster the shutter speed." You should never hand-hold a camera and shoot at a shutter speed slower than the focal length of the lens. For example, you would only hand-hold a camera fitted with 180mm lens when the shutter speed is set to 1/250 of a second or more; never slower. Likewise a 50mm lens could be hand-held with the shutter set to 1/60th of a second, but no slower.
- The best light for photography is in the early morning and late afternoon. The colors are warmer and the shadows deeper. At noon, when the sun is overhead, the lighting is flat and uninteresting.
- Good composition means good photographs. Dull days and skies without detail mean dull photographs. Such situations call for a little thought before you shoot. A technique called "framing" will eliminate large, detail-less areas from your pictures: shoot from beneath tree branches, through doorways and windows, and include odd sections of wall and pieces of furniture in the picture. Walk around the subject until you find something, anything, you can place in the picture that will break up those large, uninteresting areas of sky. Use the following "Rule of Thirds." Never place a dominant point of interest in the center of your picture; move it up or down a third, or place it a little to one side. Be sure to think it through. Make sure you have the shot framed properly: don't cut the tops off heads and buildings. Finally, look around. Make sure there is no trash lying around to spoil an otherwise special picture.

- Never shoot into the sun. For the best effect, the sunlight should be coming from behind one shoulder or the other, and never, unless you're looking for silhouettes, from in front.
- If you can, take notes. Memories can be short, especially when there are lots of images to consider – was that really Christ Church or was it the one on Main Street in Brunswick? There's nothing worse than getting a half-dozen rolls of film back from the lab and not knowing what it is you're looking at.
- Don't miss the opportunity to shoot under water. Even if you don't intend to go diving, you should take a camera to the beach; the fish in the shallow waters are colorful and abundant. Purchase one of those neat little ready-made underwater cameras that come ready to shoot. You simply take it into the water, shoot until it stops, and then take the whole thing in for processing. The second option is to rent a more sophisticated underwater camera from one of the many dive shops.

PHOTO OPPORTUNITIES

The coastal regions of Georgia, with their lush scenery and unique culture and history, make them a photographer's dream. Farther inland, the opportunities are even more extensive. Here are some ideas to get you started.

The historic homes dotting the hills and valleys, the crowded streets of the old cities, and the fine old churches, mansions and plantations provide endless opportunities to be creative. Take a moment to compose your shots. Use a long lens and group sections of several roofs or different-colored corners of the cottages together; try cropping in only small sections of a building, say a shutter or a door; and you'll be able to create some remarkable images.

The ribbon of green that stretches the entire length of the coastline encompasses thousands of acres of reserves, parks and beaches, offering a wide variety of wildlife, lush landscapes and unforgettable views. Try low angle shots, from right down at ground level across the flower beds, the sun shining through a palmetto fan or Spanish moss, the gnarled and twisted shapes of the live oaks you'll find almost everywhere, or close-ups of the flowers themselves. You'll have little trouble finding subjects for your camera among the rocks, dunes and reserves.

The Civil War sites, forts and batteries present opportunities of a slightly different kind. The great stone structures, earthworks and trenches are, in themselves, impressive, and make great pictures, but you can do even better. Once again, a little time taken to compose the shot will make all the difference. Try to isolate sections of the old structures for an arresting look – a flight of stone steps; a view of the ocean, beach or city framed by a gun port; or use a long lens across the battlements to draw it all together.

Churches and graveyards, too, offer unique and interesting opportunities. The churches themselves (and there are some of great historical significance) can be the focal point of your efforts and will provide you with many hours of pleasure. The headstones and tombs in the churchyards, some with the strangest epitaphs, can be even more fascinating.

In the cities of Atlanta, Savannah, Augusta, Albany and a hundred other less well-known towns and villages, the homes and gardens are always impeccably groomed.

Amid the lakes, forests and mountains, the opportunities are endless, especially in the spring and fall. Rise early and stay late. The early morning mists that surround the valleys and canyons can make for very special images. The reflections on the still surface of a lake, always there but rarely noticed, show up spectacularly in a well-composed photograph. Woodland paths, rocky gorges, fallen trees, wetlands, all provide unique opportunities.

Finally, always be on the lookout for that little something with a difference. After all, art is in the eye of the creator as well as the beholder. Don't be afraid to take pictures in the rain; afternoon showers don't last long and the results as the sun breaks through the clouds can often be spectacular. Of course, you'll need to protect your camera from water, but don't let that put you off. Taking pictures of the people bustling about the crowded streets of Atlanta or Savannah in the rain can be fun and very productive. Good luck and good shooting.

Boating

Boating is allowed on most of the larger lakes throughout the state, and, to a lesser extent, on smaller lakes where motor restrictions may apply.

CANOEING

Georgia offers a number of paddling opportunities. These range from quiet mountain lakes to wide rivers or fast-running whitewater.

WHITEWATER CLASSIFICATION CHART

CLASS	WATER CONDITION	HUMAN REACTION
I	Calm, moving water with occasional riffles	Chuckles
II	Little bursts of bouncing rapids in clear, wide channels between long stretches of calm	Squeals of delight
III	Irregular waves through narrower channels where maneuvering around rocks is required	Screaming time! Tonsils may be visible during more difficult maneuvers
IV	Rapids are intense, loud, and long, with complex, rocky obstacles in the way	Level eight on the scream scale; jaws start to ache from extended periods of screaming
V	Rapids are long, loud, narrow, and violent, following one after the other without interruption	The top of the scream scale; you begin to make terrifying animal noises

Some of the routes pass through state and national parks, some through the great forests. Some are in controlled waters where the levels rise and fall at the whim of the TVA or the Army Corps of Engineers. Almost all of the canoe trails described in this book are in scenic country.

Canoes and kayaks, along with a certain amount of basic instruction, are available for rent at most whitewater outfitters. Many offer vacation packages that include not only rafting or kayaking, but horseback riding and hayrides too. You'll find a list of outfitters, with a brief description of the services offered, by location, in the *Information Directory* under *Whitewater*.

While the lakes, streams and rivers offer hundreds of miles of canoeing possibilities, most of the waters open to canoes are also open to other users as well, including anglers, motor-boaters and waterskiers. In most areas, the waterways are publicly owned, but in some the riverbanks belong to private individuals and are not open to public use. Canoe and adventure outposts throughout each region will equip you for a canoe trip, pick you up at your exit point, and shuttle you back to your car (see *Information Directory*). Before you attempt canoeing a river, always check that you are experienced to handle the conditions. Use the chart on the previous page to help you.

Fishing

Freshwater fishing is the sport of choice in the Peach State. The great lakes and rivers across the state provide innumerable opportunities to hunt trophy-sized bass – smallmouth, largemouth, white and striped – sauger, walleye, muskie, crappie, bluegill and, of course, catfish, the staple in many a backcountry restaurant.

Trout fishing in Georgia, not too popular with local sportsmen, is at its best in the mountains to the north and east. If you're one of those strange creatures who like to take to the waters encased in thigh-length rubber boots, festooned with brightly colored fluffy hooks, fly rod in hand, you'll find plenty of opportunities.

From Savannah to St. Mary's Island, the saltwater fishing along the East Coast is extremely good; in many places, excellent. The beaches provide a popular platform, but there are literally hundreds of fishing piers and docks scattered all along the coast. Some you can fish for free; some will cost you perhaps a couple of dollars for a whole day.

Freshwater fishing licenses are required for all persons aged 16 and older. They can be obtained at any local bait or tackle shop, and at any State Wildlife Resources Agency Office. It's also a good idea to check for specific local regulations that may be in effect.

The fishing spots listed in each section of the book have been selected because they are areas where we think you will do well. Some are easily accessible; some are off the beaten path. There are a great many more places to fish in Georgia, but to find them you'll have to do some exploring. Rarely will you find a local fisherman willing to give away the location of his favorite fishin' hole.

DEEP-SEA FISHING

An expensive pastime, but exhilarating, deep-sea fishing is a popular sport in coastal Georgia. Boat captains from Savannah to Jacksonville stand ready to take you on board and whisk you out to sea, often 20 miles or more, in search of the big one. And the big one is no more prolific anywhere than here. Among the species that populate these waters are the mighty tarpon, sharks of every shape and size, including the hammerhead and tiger shark, tuna, blue marlin, dolphin (the fish, not Flipper), barracuda, amberjack, cobia, black sea bass, king mackerel, swordfish and, the most spectacular of all, the sailfish. Charters are readily available and you can head out for a half-day, full day, or you can charter for several days. Rates, depending upon the location and season, run from $250 for a four-hour trip to as much as $600 for a full 12 hours. Check individual listings in the various sections throughout this book.

FISHING THE COASTAL WATERS

From Savannah to Jacksonville, more than 120 miles of coast, not to mention the shores of the barrier islands that protect them and the streams that meander through almost a million acres of coastal salt marshes, provide some of the most prolific coastal fishing waters in the United States. Within these waters, inshore and offshore, anglers can expect to enjoy their sport at its very best. Aside from the excitement of deep-sea charter fishing, the cost of which can be prohibitive, you can hit the surf, marsh creeks, salt river inlets and streams almost anywhere along the coast and have a good day out. So, what can you expect to catch?

Atlantic Croaker: This smaller member of the drum family is one of the most abundant coastal fishes. It takes the hook readily, and is a good table fish. Why croaker? There are 13 species of drums and croakers found in these coastal waters; all have the ability to makes sounds, and they typically grunt or croak when taken out of the water. The sounds are produced by a pair of muscles located next to the swim bladder, an air-filled sac just below the backbone inside the body cavity. Croakers are bottom feeders that live on small crustaceans, clams, snails and other little critters they consider delicacies. The adult croakers found in these waters are usually 9 to 15 inches and weigh up to a couple of pounds.

Black Drum: This species is found along the Atlantic coast from Massachusetts to Argentina, but is most abundant in the warmer waters from the Carolinas to Texas. Like the Atlantic croaker, it's a bottom feeder with small sharp teeth in the jaws and large flat teeth on the floor and roof of the mouth for crushing clams, snails, crabs and the other hard-bodied, bottom-dwelling animals. The black drum is the largest of the bony fish you're likely to encounter inshore, and fish in the range of 10 to 40 pounds are not uncommon; the largest on record was taken off the coast of Florida and weighed in at 146 pounds. Its color is usually an even black, with an overall glossy appearance, and it has numerous sensory chin barbels (whiskers). It's not a good table fish.

Flounder: Both the summer and southern flounder are abundant in these waters. The two are so similar in appearance that most anglers cannot tell them apart. Like most flatfish, both are adept at changing color to match the bottom on which they happen to be. The eyes at birth are positioned on both sides of the head. During early development, however, one eye migrates from its normal position to join the other on one side of the head, at which time it begins swimming with eye side up. Both species have large mouths with a single row of sharp teeth in both jaws. They are bottom feeders, living on small crustaceans and fish.

Kingfish: Three species of kingfish (whiting, as they are known locally) are found here, all closely related: southern, northern and gulf kingfish. When they are young, the three are difficult to identify, but larger fish can be easily distinguished. The gulf kingfish is a plain gray or silver, while the other two have dark bars on their sides; the bars on the southern kingfish are usually less distinct than those on the northern kingfish. These are small fish, reaching a maximum length of about 17 inches and rarely weighing more than three pounds; those you are likely to catch will be smaller, in the range of ½ to 1½ pounds. Small though they are, they are tough fighters, abundant along the beaches and especially so on the barrier islands. They are great table fish, with a distinctive flavor. Lightly sprinkle fillets with salt, pepper and garlic powder and poach gently in white wine and butter.

Red Drum: This fish is found along the Atlantic and Gulf coasts from Massachusetts to Texas and, while it does have some commercial standing, it's sought mostly by anglers as a sport fish. Adult fish are most abundant during the summer months in or just beyond the surf line along the beaches, especially on the barrier islands. During the colder months, the fish move offshore and are no longer available to surf casters. Adult fish are easily identified by the large eyespot – usually one on each side, but sometimes several – located just in front of the tail, and by its lack of barbels (whiskers). Specimens of five feet and 75 pounds or more have been recorded. Those you are likely to catch will be much smaller, around 10-15 pounds, but you might get lucky and hook one as big as 40 pounds.

Sheepshead: This species belongs to a large group called porgies. Several more species of porgies are found in these waters: the scup, pin fish, spotted tail pinfish and the white bony porgy. All are usually found close to the shore, and often in schools. The sheepshead shares many of the porgy characteristics. It stays close to the bottom, feeding on small crustaceans and fish, is laterally compressed, flattened on both sides and has a steep forehead. It is easily distinguished from its brother species by seven vertical black bars along the length of the body, and differs from the young black drum in its lack of barbels. The biggest porgies found in these waters are around 20 pounds, but those you are likely to catch will weigh in at around 5 to 10 pounds. Small crabs are often used for bait. The sheepshead is a delicious table fish.

Spotted Sea Trout: This is the most sought after sport fish in the southeastern United States. It's a true estuarine fish, living all of its life in the river inlets, bays, sounds and creeks along the coastline. Its abundance in the small tidal creeks and rivers makes it available to anglers with small boats. Like the red drum, black drum, kingfish and Atlantic croaker, the spotted sea trout is a member of the drum family; only the male of this species, however, is able to croak. The spotted sea trout is one of three species that can be found in these waters; the silver sea trout and the weakfish are the other two. All three are easily distinguished from other local fish by slender, streamlined bodies, projecting lower teeth, and from one to three sharply pointed teeth projecting downward from the upper jaw. The spotted sea trout is easily distinguished from the other two by the round black spots scattered all over the upper fins and body. Although all three species are quite good table fish, the spotted sea trout is the most popular with anglers. Adult fish are at least a foot long, growing up to two feet, and can weigh from two to five pounds; two to three pounds being the mostly likely catch size.

Striped Bass: The "striper" is equally at home in salt or fresh water, leaving the coastal waters and moving upriver only to spawn; it rarely strays far from land. These fish grow to considerable size: The largest – taken in North Carolina – weighed 125 pounds. Such fish are rare. But fish weighing 50 to 60 pounds are not unusual. Distribution along these coastal waters is somewhat spotty. They seem to be confined to the major rivers and the estuaries and are rarely caught from the beaches.

Shell Collecting

Has there ever been a visitor to any beach who hasn't wandered the water's edge, gaze locked on the sand, looking for shells? Surely not. The best time for shelling is just after high tide. The best places are those where people rarely go. So, what can you find? Most common are the tiny bivalves: small animals with a shell consisting of two more or less equal valves (sides), joined together by a hinge. These two valves are opened and closed by powerful muscles, but after the animal has died, they often become separated or spread out. Next, there are the whelks, members of the gastropod family. These animals have a single large shell, spirally coiled into a helix. Several whelks are fairly common on the east coast and barrier islands: the channeled whelk, as its name suggests, has deep grooves at the joints; the lightning whelk has a row of knobs on the shoulder of the body whorl; the whitish knobbed whelk has knobs on the shoulder of the body and an orange mouth. The moon shell is the home of another gastropod, a snail that feeds on clams which it digs out of the sand. Usually white or pale yellow in color, the empty shells can often be found just beneath the surface of the sand, left behind by the receding tide. Other nice shells you can find are the glassy lyonsia, coquina shell, blue mussel, Atlantic bay scallop, eastern oyster, giant Atlantic cockle, northern softshell clam, angel wing, Atlantic surf clam, Atlantic jackknife clam, stiff pen shell and numerous other small bivalves and gastropods.

Hiking

Hiking is a major pastime in Georgia, especially in the northern mountains and Chattahoochee National Forest. Literally hundreds of hiking and nature trail systems meander the length and breadth of the state. Thousands of miles of foot trails lead through rolling pine forests, beside fast-moving mountain rivers, waterfalls and along hundreds of miles of country lanes and backroads. All are available for backpacking, nature watching, and all are open year-round for public use. In the cities, the downtown streets, historic districts and parks provide a different sort of walking opportunity. In this book you'll find most popular trails, as well as some of the smaller ones, along with their locations, lengths, entry and exit points, and their degrees of difficulty.

Horseback Riding

Horseback riding is available throughout the Chattahoochee National Forest and in most state parks. Well-marked equestrian trails take riders through some of the most scenic portions of the state, and there are staging areas or corrals and overnight camping for horses and riders in many of the parks. Be sure to call ahead when planning your ride, especially when organizing a group event. Contact the appropriate state park, the National Park Service or the National Forest Service to learn about trail conditions and any special regulations that may be in effect.

The following rules and regulations for equestrians are in effect throughout the year in Georgia:

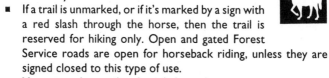

- Horse trails are marked with a horse-use sign like the one you see here.
- If a trail is unmarked, or if it's marked by a sign with a red slash through the horse, then the trail is reserved for hiking only. Open and gated Forest Service roads are open for horseback riding, unless they are signed closed to this type of use.
- You must obey trail and road closures.
- You are required to stay on the trail. Taking shortcuts causes erosion and skirting wet areas widens trails.
- You should travel in small groups, preferably six or fewer.
- Do not tie horses to trees, even temporarily. Use a highline.

- Plan your trip to avoid the spring thaw and extended wet weather.
- Pack it in, and pack it out. In other words, leave no trash in the forest.
- Communicate with other trail users, and tell them how to pass your horse safely.
- Hikers and mountain bikers should yield to horses, unless riders have a better place to pull off.
- When camping, use a highline with tree-saver straps to tether your horse.
- Highline your horse 100 feet away from streams, creeks, trails and campsites, if possible.
- Pack some grain, since grazing is limited.
- Break up and scatter manure.
- Fill in pawed holes when breaking camp.
- Horses are not permitted in developed campgrounds and picnic areas.

Northern Georgia

Northern Georgia is a vast outdoor adventure playground, most of which lies within the foothills of the southern Appalachians and the Great Smoky Mountains. The area covered in this section is considered the best for adventuring in Georgia and is primarily found within the perimeter of the Chattahoochee National Forest – a strip that also includes some half-dozen counties lying on the Georgia/North Carolina border. To the west, it includes Lookout Mountain as far south as Lafayette; to the east, most of Rabun County.

Once you leave the main arterial highways, with the exception of the Greater Chattanooga area to the west, Northern Georgia contains vast tracts of mountainous wilderness, forests, a large number of lakes, wild and scenic rivers, and tiny mountain creeks and streams. Georgia is proud of its wilderness areas and has gone to a great deal of trouble to ensure their preservation. At the same time, these regions have been opened up for outdoor recreation on a grand scale.

Within the Chattahoochee National Forest, there are hundreds of miles of hiking trails, dozens of backcountry campgrounds, several whitewater rafting and kayaking rivers, and vast lakes for fishing, boating, sailing, waterskiing or swimming.

There are a dozen or so state parks scattered throughout the area. These, too, have received a great deal of money and attention from the powers that be in Atlanta. Some have purposely been maintained as primitive backcountry parks; others have been developed to a point where they rival even the finest of holiday resorts.

Within the Chattahoochee National Forest itself, the Forest Service has not been idle. Compared with other national forests in the east, it's blessed with superior recreation areas, wilderness campgrounds, and well-marked trails.

And then there are the tiny mountain communities. Towns like Ellijay, the Apple Capital of Georgia; Helen, a tiny tourist town that might have been lifted right out of Germany's Black Forest; Clarksville; Dahlonega; Chattsworth; Blue Ridge; Blairsville and Clayton. All have unique attractions.

Northern Georgia and its rivers and mountains were the subject of James Dickey's novel, *Deliverance*, subsequently turned into a major motion picture. You'll remember the story was about four men from Atlanta and their terrifying experiences running the rapids.

With the exception of Helen, Northern Georgia is not favored or, as some would say, cursed with the tourist magnets, such as Gatlinburg, that one finds in some sections of the Great Smoky Mountains. There are no flashing colored lights, no fairyland-like attractions, no theme parks, and certainly no clogged and crowded roads – at least, not yet. And Helen itself is a very poor cousin when compared to Gatlinburg. Northern Georgia is a kinder, gentler place, packed with adventuring possibilities – a place where the pace is slow, the people friendly, the accents soft and lilting.

How To Get There

BY AIR

You have a couple of options here. The easiest way is to fly into Atlanta's **Hartsfield International Airport** ("You can't go anywhere in the South without flying into Atlanta"), then rent a car or RV and drive north. You can also fly into Chattanooga, even though that probably means changing planes in Atlanta, then drive south or east. Atlanta is the headquarters for Delta Airlines and the city is served by almost every other major carrier as well. Chattanooga, having recently lost its Delta jet service to Atlanta, is well served by USAir, ASA, Comair, and other small carriers.

BY ROAD

From Atlanta

Driving out of Atlanta, depending upon the time of day, can be the easiest of experiences or hell on earth. The city is served by a 16-lane (eight in either direction) super-highway, and several four-lane arterial highways. On weekdays from 7 to 9 am, and 3:30 to 7 pm, all roads in and out of the city turn into one solid mass of barely moving vehicles. If you arrive between those hours, you'd be well advised to take time out, eat some breakfast, and then sally forth when the congestion has eased.

Once you do get out onto the highways, you'll have several choices. You can take I-75 and travel north toward Chattanooga, either branching off on any one of a dozen minor state roads that lead into the forests and mountains; you can take Highway 19 north to Dahlonega and Brasstown Bald; or you can take Highway 23 northeast through Gainesville to Toccoa and the Tallulah Gorge. A fourth option is drive north on I-75 to its intersection with I-575, and from there to its intersection with Highway 76, then on to Blue Ridge and McCaysville.

From Tennessee

If you're driving in from Chattanooga, you also have a couple of options. Both revolve around I-75. You can drive south on I-75 to Dalton and then take Highway 76 through Chatsworth, Ellijay, and all the way to Brasstown. You'll find it a very beautiful drive through the mountains. The other option is to drive south on I-75 to Ressaca, turn east on Georgia 136, and then proceed to its junction with Highway 76 via Carter's Lake. Either way, you're in for a treat.

From North Carolina

From western North Carolina and the Great Smoky Mountain National Park, you really only have one viable option, Highway 19. From Cherokee, the road runs all the way southwest to Murphy, and from there into Georgia, where it joins Highway 129 and heads on down to Dahlonega and Atlanta, with side roads branching east and west into the mountains along the way.

When You Get There

Here, at the southern end of the chain, the Appalachians are smoothing down – settling, if you will. The mountains are not as sharply defined as they are in North Carolina, nor are they as high. The hiking trails are, for the most part, just a little easier here than they are farther to the north. The rivers are not as fast-moving or wild. The lakes are surrounded by forests and mountains; the scenery is often spectacular. The Chattahoochee National Forest is just as magnificent and just as well managed as are its more famous cousins to the north. Perhaps the best way to enjoy these southern mountains is to rent an RV or camping trailer, maybe even a tent, and venture out into the wilderness on your own, making a base for yourself at any one of the many well-developed state parks in the area; good hotels are few and far between.

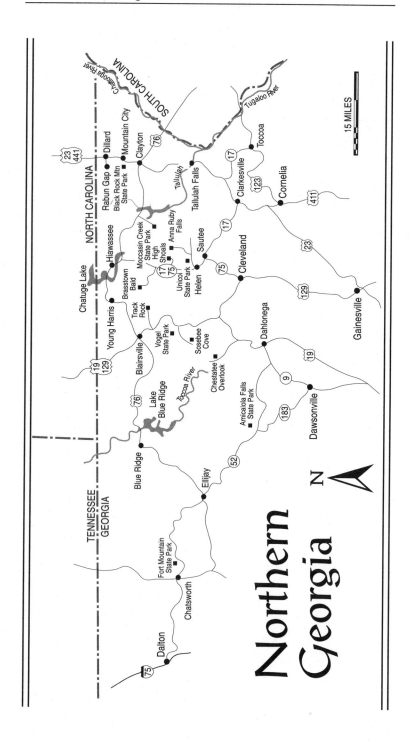

WHERE TO STAY

Other than in Helen, this region is poorly provided with accommodations. The best hotels are located on the perimeter of Northern Georgia in Chattanooga and Atlanta, and at one or two of the larger state parks. You'll find listings under individual headings throughout the following text.

The authorities in Atlanta have long recognized that the forests and mountains to the north are among the state's most important resources. If you want to try a state park or wilderness campground, you won't find a better place to get started.

As to the commercial campgrounds in the area, those listed are considered to be among the best. This is not a recommendation for any or all of them, but you won't be disappointed by the facilities or the service you receive.

ACTIVITIES

Boating

Northern Georgia is a happy land for boaters, with 1,000 lakes and more than 100 rivers, streams and creeks. Access ramps are provided in most public areas and at some of the commercial lake and riverside campgrounds. Most of the public areas are very busy throughout the warmer months, but it's still possible to find a secluded spot or two. Boating is at its best in the early morning or late afternoon.

☞ Be careful on the big rivers, and below the weir gates of the big dams; the waters there are subject to rapid changes in depth and speed.

Shopping

Other than the usual malls, or Wal-Mart and Kmart, Northern Georgia is not a center for shopping. Helen does offer some unique opportunities, but for fine goods, top-notch stores and variety, the locals go to either Atlanta or Chattanooga. Here and there, however, you will find out-of-the-way antique stores and specialty outlets.

Touring

Amicalola Falls State Park

In the language of the Cherokee Indian, Amicalola means "Tumbling Waters." No other word could better describe the spectacular falls that plunge 729 feet in seven cascades, making it the highest waterfall in Georgia.

The Park Service has a year-round program of special events, including Spring Wildflowers in April; an extensive schedule of Naturalist Programs during the summer; Summer's End Trading Days in August; an Overnight Backpacking Trip in October; and the Fall Leaf Displays, also in October. Other popular activities

Amicalola Falls State Park.

include fishing, camping and hiking, nature study, birdwatching, wildlife photography and picnicking. There are three playgrounds, five picnic shelters and a rustic walk-in lodge.

Take Highway 53 west out of Dawsonville, and then Highway 183 to Highway 52 east. The park, 15 miles northwest of Dawsonville, is open from 7 am to 10 pm, and the park office is open from 8 am to 5 pm.

Amicalola Falls State Park and Lodge, Star Route, Box 215, Dawsonville, GA 30534. ☎ 706-265-8888.

CAMPING

Camping facilities here are limited to 17 tent and trailer sites, but there are 14 rental cottages and a 57-room lodge with a restaurant and meeting rooms. There is a comfort station with hot showers, flush toilets and laundry.

HIKING

An eight-mile trail meanders through the 1,020-acre park, leading first to the falls and then on to Springer Mountain and the southern end of the 2,150-mile Appalachian Trail that runs from Georgia to Maine. There are three excellent hiking trails, one of which intersects with the southern end of the 2,150-mile Appalachian Trail.

Appalachian Trail Approach: This is an eight-mile trail that meanders through the 1,020-acre park from the visitor center, northward to a scenic overlook of the falls, and then on to Springer Mountain and its intersection with the southern end of the Appalachian Trail (AT). The hiking is fairly easy for most of the way, with odd sections where the going can be a little strenuous.

Amicalola Falls Trail: At just over a quarter-mile, this is perhaps the most scenic walking trail in Georgia. It leads from a parking area beside the creek, near the Reflection Pool at the end of the park road, to a steep and rocky path that climbs uphill alongside the cascading waterfalls, ending at an observation deck. Magnificent – a must for photographers.

West Ridge Loop: From the parking area near the visitor center, take the scenic trail beside the creek to its intersection with the loop, a distance of about 350 yards. From there you can turn either left or right and walk the mile-long trail through some of Georgia's loveliest parkland. This pleasant walking trail is suitable for everyone.

Black Rock Mountain State Park

This park lies atop the Eastern Continental Divide close to the Georgia/North Carolina border. At an altitude of more than 3,600 feet, it's the highest state park in Georgia. The 1,500-acre park, named for its great granite cliffs and peaks, offers some of the most spectacular views of the southern Appalachian Mountains. On a clear day, it's possible to see for more than 80 miles, and even as far as Atlanta, from its seven scenic overlooks.

The Park Service offers a schedule of activities and programs that include Spring Wildflowers in May; Overnight Backpacking in the fall; and a variety of other events and mountain culture programs. There's a visitor center where you can find nature guides, raised relief maps, and hiking and trail guides. Park Service Rangers ready to answer your questions and help you make the most of your visit.

The park, three miles north of Clayton, via US Highway 441, is open from 7 am to 10 pm and the park office from 8 am to 5 pm.

Black Rock Mountain State Park, Mountain City, GA 30562. ☎ 706-746-2141.

CAMPING

This is state park camping at its best. The views are spectacular, the terrain wild and desolate, and the facilities excellent.

There are 53 tent and trailer sites, 11 primitive walk-in campsites, 10 rental cottages, a comfort station with modern restrooms and hot showers, a visitor center, two picnic shelters, and a 17-acre lake, all set on more than 1,500 acres of mountain parkland.

HIKING

Three challenging trails of varying difficulty – the **Tennessee Rock Trail, Ada-hi Falls Trail**, and the **James E. Edmonds Trail** – put this park high on the hiker's list.

Blairsville

This tiny community is situated right in the heart of the Chattahoochee National Forest. The Old Court House contains a small but well-stocked museum; Brasstown Bald, with its panoramic views, is nearby; and the Richard Russell Scenic Highway offers more than 14 miles of peaks, trails and overlooks.

WHERE TO STAY

Best Western Milton Inn, 222 Highway 515, Blairsville, GA 30512. ☎ 706-745-6995. This is a nice motel located in Blairsville's commercial district. There's a pool and a restaurant nearby. No pets. $.

CAMPING

Canal Lake Campground

A small but scenic lakeside commercial campground with 24 semi-shaded sites on level ground and good recreational facilities. Of the 23 sites, 14 have water and electric hookups, 10 have no hookups and there's only one pull-through. The comfort station has flush toilets, hot showers and restrooms for the handicapped. There's also a small grocery store where you can purchase a limited range of supplies.

Recreational facilities include a pavilion, recreation room, a boat dock and the opportunity to go swimming, boating, waterskiing or fishing. There are also horseshoe and volleyball courts.

Rates start at around $10 per night per vehicle.

Canal Lake Campground, 1035 Canal Lake Road, Blairsville, GA 30512. ☎ 706-745-1501.

From the junction of Highways 76 and 19, go north for two miles on 19, then turn left onto Pat Colwell Road and drive on for another mile to Canal Lake Road. Go for about a half-mile on Canal Lake Road to the campground.

CRAFT HUNTING

The **Blairsville Sorghum Festival** in early October focuses not only on the production of molasses, but also features a number of mountain crafts exhibitors from around Northern Georgia, along with square dancing, rock throwing and greasy pole climbing. Call ☎ 706-745-5789.

Blue Ridge

Blue Ridge is a small mountain community at the southern end of the Appalachian Mountain chain. With a population of under 1,400, it's barely a spot on the map. It is, however, set right at the heart of some of the most spectacular country in all of Georgia: the Cohutta Mountains in the Unaka Range and the Murphy Syncline, a great depression in the mountains that runs northward from Tate, through Ellijay, to Blue Ridge and beyond.

It's a rural community, devoted mostly to farming and, lately, tourism. It's also steeped in Native American history and folklore, being one of the last strongholds of the Cherokee Nation before its removal to Oklahoma.

Blue Ridge is inside the Toccoa Ranger District of the Chattahoochee National Forest, just to the east of the vast Cohutta Wilderness, a wild and woolly area with a great deal to offer outdoor enthusiasts. (See Cohutta Ranger District in the section on the Chattahoochee National Forest.)

DINING OUT

Forge Mill Crossing Restaurant, Forge Road. This is a busy little place, so it might be a good idea to make a reservation, especially on weekends. Open from 11 until 2 and from 5 until 9. You can enjoy good Southern cooking and the unusual hilltop location. ☎ 706-374-5771.

Carters Lake

This is a 3,500-acre man-made tract of quiet water 12 miles south of Chatsworth off Highway 411.

BOATING

Unlike most of the great lakes in the region, Carters Lake was constructed by the Army Corps of Engineers. It's a very pleasant stretch of water, popular not only with the boating fraternity, but with anglers, too. It can get very crowded during the summer, but the scenery more than makes up for the crush. Early mornings and late afternoons are the best times because they are less crowded. A large area near the dam has been developed as the **Blue Ridge Mountain Marina Resort**. It has boat launching facilities, and you can purchase boating and fishing supplies. Contact the Resource Manager at Carters Lake, PO Box 86, Oakman, GA 30732. ☎ 706-334-2248.

CAMPING

There are four campgrounds at Carters Lake, all quite small, and they include a range of facilities: primitive, group and full-service camping.

Carters Lake

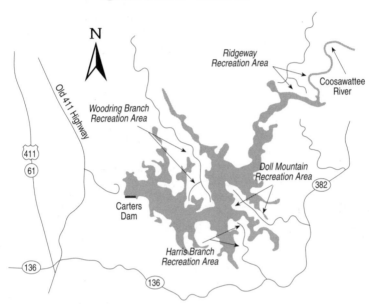

Harris Branch Park

Group camping only. There's a shelter with six tables and a large grill, 10 tent sites, fresh water and two comfort stations. There's also a public beach on the lakeshore. Gates open from 9 until 9. Closed October through March. Call for rates.

Doll Mountain Park

Lakeside camping on 65 sites, 28 of which have water and electric hookups. There are two comfort stations with flush toilets, hot showers and a dumping station. At the time of writing, the fee for a site with hookups was $9 per night, $7 without. Gates open 9 until 10. Closed October through March.

Ridgeway Park

A small, primitive campground. There are 22 sites with pit toilets, and two boat ramps. Accessible by dirt road only. No Charge.

Woodring Branch

A smaller campground than Doll Mountain, but better developed. All 31 campsites have water and electric hookups; there's also a comfort station with extensive facilities and a boat ramp. At the time of writing, the fee for a site with hookups was $9 per night, $7 without. Gates open 9 until 10. Closed October through March.

For additional information and reservations, contact the Resource Manager's Office listed above.

FISHING

The fishing here at Carters Lake is considered good, but you'd better go in the early morning on weekdays; it gets very crowded with recreational craft during the summer, especially on weekends. Lots of small fish, some bass and catfish.

HIKING

Hidden Pond Trail: A short trail of about a half-mile that crosses the creek by way of a 20-foot bridge and traverses a large beaver pond via a structure that's more than 200 feet long. There's an observation platform at the end of the trail suitable for bird and beaver watching. The trailhead is located near the entrance to the Carters Lake management area off Highway 136 and Highway 441.

Chatsworth

Chatsworth lies at the heart of an important talc-mining region. Talc is found in the mountains in layers at depths ranging from five to 50 feet. It's blasted out of the rock, then transported to a mill where it's ground into fine powder. Carters Lake is just to the south, and Fort Mountain State Park is just a few miles away to the east.

SIGHTSEEING

Chief Vann House State Historic Site

The Vann House is a classic, two-story brick mansion built in 1804. Called the "Showplace of the Cherokee Nation," it was built by

Chief James Vann and is decorated with magnificent hand carvings painted in natural colors of blue, red, green and yellow. Of the house's many features and antiques, perhaps the most outstanding is the fine cantilevered stairway.

Chief Vann is remembered for his contribution to the education of the Cherokee. He was responsible for bringing the Moravian missionaries to teach the children the Christian way of life. But Vann was still a Cherokee Indian and a polygamist. He had three wives and five children. When he came to a violent end in 1809 for killing his brother-in-law in a duel, the house, along with his other possessions and business interests, passed to his son, Joseph.

In 1834 the government seized the house when "Rich Joe" Vann unknowingly violated state law by employing a white man. The house passed into the hands of white owners by way of a land lottery.

Chief Vann House State Historic Site, Route 7, Box 7655, Chatsworth, GA, 30705 (One mile south of Highway 76 on State Route 225.) ☎ 706-695-2598. Open year-round, Tuesday through Saturday, from 9 until 5; Sunday, from 2 until 5. Admission is $2; children 6-18, $1.

CRAFT HUNTING

Vann House Days is a festival held in Chatsworth annually in mid-July. It features demonstrations and exhibits of Indian crafts, including Indian finger weaving, carding and spinning. ☎ 706-695-2598.

Chattahoochee National Forest

This is one of the most visitor-oriented national forests in the southern United States. Now a part of a single forest system that includes the Oconee National Forest to the south, the Chattahoochee stretches across Northern Georgia like a great ribbon of green velvet. The two forests together are administered through eight National Forest Service Ranger Districts. They are responsible for more than 860,000 acres – 750,000 of which are within the boundaries of the Chattahoochee. Also within its boundaries lie more than 500 developed campsites, 200 picnic sites, 10 wilderness areas, six swimming beaches, the Chattooga Wild and Scenic River, several hundred lakes, rivers and streams, and more than 500 miles of hiking trails, including 83 miles of the Appalachian Trail. The following is an overview of the seven Ranger Districts, with some of the most popular attractions and recreation areas included. More information can be obtained by contacting the district offices listed in each section.

The US Forest Service in the Chattahoochee has made an effort to develop its wilderness camping areas, while still maintaining fees at "reasonable levels." The facilities are extensive and, for the most part, less primitive than in other southern national forests. One campground, Rabun Beach, even has water and electrical hookups. But camping in the Chattahoochee is still very much a wilderness experience.

ARMUCHEE RANGER DISTRICT

Headquartered in Lafayette, this office is responsible for the far western reaches of the forest that run from Summerville in the south all the way to Ringgold, just outside of Chattanooga, in the north. Armuchee Ranger District, 806 E. Villanow Street, PO Box 465, LaFayette, GA 30728. ☎ 706-638-1085.

There are three popular recreation areas within the district:

Hidden Creek

The main feature here is a small creek that's sometimes there, but often isn't. When it does run, the waters are crystal clear. It's a popular spot for hiking, picnicking and camping.

Take GA 156 southwest from Calhoun for 7½ miles and turn left onto Everatte Springs Road. Drive two more miles, then turn right on Rock House Road and go for three miles to Forest Service Road 955. Turn right there and drive about 1.3 miles to the entrance.

Forest camping on a small, secluded campground. Facilities are sparse – just 16 sites, and no flush toilets or showers. Vault toilets and fresh drinking water are available, and there are several hiking trails. Free.

Keown Falls & Scenic Area

The focus here is the small but scenic waterfall from which the area gets its name. There's a small recreation area (no camping), with flush toilet, and a picnic site with tables and grills.

Take GA 136 east from Lafayette and drive for 13½ miles, past Villanow, and turn right on Pocket Road. From there, drive about five miles to the entrance.

Pocket

This is a small wooded glen surrounding a large spring and a small creek. It was the site of a Civilian Conservation Corps Camp during the 1930s. Today, it's a nice, quiet place where you can go camping, hiking and picnicking.

Take GA 136 east from Lafayette and drive 13½ miles, past Villanow, and turn right Pocket Road. From there, it's seven miles to the entrance.

Forest camping in a small wooded glen that surrounds a large spring and a small creek. A nice, quiet developed campground, with lots of possibilities for hiking and picnicking. There are 27 sites, flush toilets and fresh drinking water, but no showers. Free.

BRASSTOWN RANGER DISTRICT

Lots to see and do here. Centered on Blairsville, this district includes some of the forest's most scenic areas, including the Brasstown Wilderness Area and Brasstown Bald, Georgia's highest mountain.

High Shoals Scenic Area

Two waterfalls, several crystal-clear mountain creeks and a profusion of wildflowers, rhododendron and mountain laurel make up a mountain landscape you just have to see. The scenic area covers some 175 acres, with a mile-long hiking trail from a parking area on Forest Road 283 to the falls. Day use only. No camping.

From Cleveland, take GA 75 north for 22 miles. Turn right onto Forest Road 283 and drive a mile to the trailhead that will take you to Blue Hole Falls.

Russell/Brasstown Scenic Byway

This is a 38-mile driving loop. Along the way, there are several scenic overlooks with views of the mountains and valleys. Begin your tour at Helen by taking GA 17/75 and driving north. Turn left on GA 180, and then left again on GA 348. Drive on and turn left on GA 74ALT, then proceed back to Helen.

Brasstown Bald

This is Georgia's highest mountain; it's also one of its most popular. From the summit, some 4,800 feet above sea level, there are breathtaking panoramic views across four states. Although the

Brasstown Wilderness is a section of the Chattahoochee National Forest, the mountain itself is not inside the wilderness area. This is a beautiful region, where the upper slopes are covered with spectacular displays of wildflowers, rhododendron, mountain laurel and azaleas in the spring. The foothills glow with color in the fall.

The **Brasstown Bald Visitor Center** helps you understand the mountain and forest ecosystems. This is done through a series of interpretive programs and exhibits, such as one aptly called "Man and the Mountain," which traces both the human and natural history of the Southern Appalachians. Within the complex, the Mountaintop Theater offers a series of continuously running video programs, and there are a number of interesting artifacts on display. Perhaps the center's best feature is its outside observation deck, where you can experience the chill winds of the mountaintop and enjoy a 360° view. It's an awesome experience. You'll be expected to pay a small parking fee (at the time of writing it was $1), but entrance to the center, its theater, observation deck, and bookstore/gift shop are all free.

The center is open daily from 10 until 5:30, Memorial Day through October, and, depending upon the weather, on weekends during the spring. (It's best to call first, ☎ 706-896-2556.) The observation deck is open year-round. Brasstown Ranger District, 1881 Highway 515, PO Box 9, Blairsville, GA 30512. ☎ 706-745-6928.

From Cleveland, take GA 75 north and drive through Helen to GA 180. Turn left there, and then go six miles and turn right onto the GA 180 Spur. Three miles farther is the Brasstown Bald parking lot. From there, you can hike up the steep, half-mile trail to the center, or you can take the shuttle bus to the top. The hiking trail leads upward through some stunning countryside.

Sosebee Cove Scenic Area

This is a 175-acre tract of hardwood forest, set aside as a memorial to Arthur Woody, who served as Ranger from 1918 to 1945. Known universally as the "Barefoot Ranger," he loved this peaceful cove and spent much of his spare time here before negotiating its purchase for the Forest Service. Along with its wonderful displays of wildflowers, the cove has some of the best second-growth yellow poplars in the nation.

From Blairsville, take Highways 19 and 129 south for 10 miles. Turn west on GA 180 and drive two more miles.

Lake Winfield Scott

This is a beautiful 18-acre lake set high among the mountains of northeast Georgia. Located only 10 miles from Blairsville to the north or Helen and Cleveland to the east and south, it's no wonder that the lake is a popular spot for outdoor lovers of all types. Hiking, picnicking, swimming, boating (electric motors only) and, of course, fishing are all popular here.

Camping: Featuring mountain and lakeside sites, this is one of the best-developed recreation areas in the Chattahoochee system. There are 36 developed campsites, a comfort station with flush toilets, hot showers and fresh water, and a picnic area with tables and grills.

From Blairsville, take Highways 19 and 129 south for 10 miles, then turn west on GA 180 and drive seven more miles.

From Cleveland, take Highways 19 and 129 north to GA 180. Turn left there and drive seven more miles.

Coosa Bald Scenic Area

This 7,100-acre scenic area lies in both the Brasstown and Chestate Ranger Districts. It's an area full of botanical diversity, an area where many species of endangered plants grow and where great boulders are evidence of the last great glacial retreat. And it's filled with wildlife: black bears, deer, wild hogs, birds of prey. There are no facilities here, just the natural terrain, some remote streams where the trout fishing is supposed to be good, and one or two primitive trails. If you're looking for solitude, you'll find it here.

From Blairsville, take Highways 19 and 129 south for about 10 miles and then turn west on GA 180. The scenic area borders 180 for the next seven miles.

Lake Chatuge

Lake Chatuge is know locally as "The Crown Jewel of the TVA Lakes." It was designed and built to produce energy. But the by-product of the lake is a vast outdoor playground that is maintained in pristine quality. Easily accessible by a network of free-flowing highways, it's a popular outdoor center, not only for northern Georgia, but for most of southwestern North Carolina as well.

The facilities here are extensive: hiking trails, picnic areas, boat ramps, marinas and campgrounds. From Hiawassee, take Highway 76 north and drive two miles. Make a left on GA 288 and drive about a mile.

Boating: You'll appreciate the stretches of open water, some almost two miles across, and the hidden nooks and crannies where you can drive your boat far away from the maddening crowds. The great lake has more than 132 miles of scenic shoreline backed by forest-covered mountain peaks and, in the spring, a profusion of color from the wildflowers blooming on the mountain slopes. Public-access boat ramps are available.

Camping: Lakeside camping with 30 developed campsites, a comfort station with flush toilets, hot showers and fresh water.

INFORMATION

Forest Supervisor, US Forest Service, 508 Oak Street NW, Gainesville, GA 30501. ☎ 404-536-0541.

Oconee Ranger District, 348 Forsyth Street, Monticello, GA 31064. ☎ 706-468-2244.

CHATTOOGA RANGER DISTRICT

This district is responsible for six national forest recreation areas. Chattooga Ranger District, PO Box 196, Burton Road, Clarksville, GA 30523. ☎ 706-754-6221.

Anna Ruby Falls

Perhaps the biggest attraction in the Chattooga District is Anna Ruby Falls, two waterfalls that together drop more than 150 feet. In the summertime it's a cool and inviting place; in winter the entire area turns into a wonderland of ice and snow, making it one of the most photographed spots in the state. The recreation area itself features a visitor center and craft shop, two interpretive trails and a scenic picnic area. There's a small parking fee ($1 at the time of writing). You'll find it extremely busy at times, especially on summer weekends.

From Helen, take GA 75 northeast for one mile to Robertstown. Turn right onto GA 356 and drive 1½ miles, where you turn left to drive through Unicoi State Park. Follow the signs for 3½ miles to the parking area.

Chattahoochee River Recreation Area

Located close to the headwaters of the Chattahoochee and adjacent to the beautiful Horse Trough Falls and the Mark Trail Wilderness

Area, this area is packed with outdoor opportunities – camping, hiking, canoeing, picnicking and fishing.

From Helen, take GA 75 north for about 1½ miles, then turn left on GA 356. Cross the river and turn right on the paved road next to the Chattahoochee Church and follow it, beyond the point where the pavement ends, for nine miles to the campground.

Camping: Wilderness camping at its best near the headwaters of the Chattahoochee River. There are flush toilets, but no showers. Can be busy in season.

Dukes Creek Falls

The falls here plummet more than 300 feet into a scenic gorge and can be viewed from a number of strategically located observation points, most of which are reached via a mile-long hiking trail through the forest. Aside from the falls, Dukes Creek itself is a place of great natural beauty, a must for naturalists, birdwatchers, and wildlife photographers. Fishing is available, too, and there's a gift shop and a nice, quiet picnic area.

From Helen, take GA 75 north for 1½ miles, then turn left on GA 356. Drive on for 2½ miles.

Andrews Cove

A very small **campground** in the forest beside a beautiful, crystal-clear mountain stream. Just 10 campsites, flush toilets, fresh drinking water, hiking trails and opportunities for trout fishing. No showers.

From Cleveland, take GA 75 north for 14 miles.

Lake Russell

Lakeside camping with a large, grassy beach and great views over Chenocetah Mountain. One of northern Georgia's best developed campgrounds, and one of its busiest. There are 42 campsites, a comfort station with flush toilets, hot showers and fresh drinking water. There's also a large group campsite (reservations only). Lots to see and do, with access to a number of nearby hiking trails, opportunities for boating, swimming and fishing. Altogether a very pleasant campground. For group camp reservations, ☎ 706-754-6221.

Take Highway 441/GA 365 north from Cornelia to the Clarksville exit on GA 197. Turn right onto old 197 and right again at the second stop sign onto Dick's Hill Parkway. Go just under a mile and turn left onto Forest Road 59 (Lake Russell Road). Then drive two more miles to the lake.

COHUTTA RANGER DISTRICT

This district takes in the area north of Chatsworth on the North Carolina and Tennessee borders. Most easily accessed via GA 52, the Cohutta Wilderness is a wild, heavily forested area that provides a natural habitat for the black bear, as well as a number of other exotic species, including wild boar, deer and eagles. It's also the location of a small, scenic river – the Conasauga. There are just two recreation areas in the district, only one has camping facilities. National Forest Service, Cohutta Ranger District, 401 Old Ellijay Road, Chattsworth, GA 30705. ☎ 706-695-6736.

Lake Conasauga Recreation Area

At an elevation of more than 3,100 feet, near the top of Grassy Mountain, Conasauga is Georgia's highest lake. The name comes from an old Indian word, "kahnasagah." Loosely translated, it means sparkling water. And sparkle the waters do. Set among the peaks and forests of the Blue Ridge, the lake is beautiful. It's also one of the most popular recreation areas in the Chattahoochee. With a well-developed campground, public-access boat ramps, good fishing and excellent picnic facilities, it's no wonder that people from miles around flock to the lake, mostly on summer weekends, but also through the spring and fall to see the color.

If you are coming from Ellijay, you'll take Highway 52 west for seven miles to FSR 18, where you'll find a sign pointing the way to Lake Conasauga Recreation Area.

If you're a **birdwatcher**, you'll love it here. More than 100 species make their home around the lake. These include several species of hawk, owls, woodpeckers, cuckoos, flycatchers, chickadees, titmice, nuthatches, tanagers, grosbeaks, buntings and crossbills.

Lake Conasauga is one of Georgia's most popular **boating** lakes, and it can become very congested on summer weekends, especially during spring and fall when visitors arrive by the thousands to see the color.

Set among the peaks and forests of the Blue Ridge, this is one of the Chattahoochee's most beautiful **campgrounds**. Well developed, it has 35 sites and a comfort station with flush toilets and fresh drinking water, but no showers. Free.

This is also a very popular **fishing spot**, and not only for anglers. Unfortunately, its popularity also makes it one of the most heavily fished lakes in northern Georgia. But it's kept well-stocked, so you should be able to enjoy some fine sport. Tales are told of some very large bass that are supposed to lurk in the deepest areas. Walleye, crappie, bream, catfish and rainbow trout are also present in good numbers.

From Chattsworth, take Highway 441 north for four miles into Eton; turn right at the red light. Follow that road until it becomes an unpaved road, FSR 18 (Forest Service Road 18), then turn right onto FSR 68 and drive 10 miles more.

Hiking

There are more than 95 miles of hiking trails within the Cohutta Wilderness. All are well maintained, well blazed and easy to follow. In some areas, however, bad weather can make hiking very difficult, if not impossible. Heavy rains can cause water levels to rise quickly and turn the Jacks and Conasauga rivers into raging torrents, often impossible to cross. If you're planning to walk in the rain or snow, be sure to file a route plan with someone. Take along plenty of fresh water and something to eat, just in case. Camping is permitted throughout the wilderness, except on the trails themselves and at the trailheads. Here's a sample of what's available.

Conasauga River Trail: From a trailhead at Betty Gap to a parking area on FSR 17, the trail winds its way through the Cohutta Wilderness, following the Conasauga for a little more than 13 miles. This is a great hike, very picturesque and quite popular. There's a large tent campground along the way at Bray Field, just beyond the trail's junction with the Panther Creek Trail.

From Ellijay go west on GA 52 for two-thirds of a mile to FSR 90 and onto FSR 68. Turn north and go to the intersection with FSR 64 at Potato Patch Mountain; turn right and drive to the trailhead at Betty Gap.

Chestnut Lead Trail: From a trailhead on FSR 68, Chestnut winds northward through the forest for almost two miles to intersect the Conasauga River Trail, at which point you have several options. You can return the way you came; turn right and hike to the Conasauga Trailhead on FSR 64 and then turn west and return to FSR 68; or turn left and hike on along the Conasauga to its end at FSR 17.

From Ellijay go west on GA 52 for two-thirds of a mile to FSR 90 and onto FSR 68. Turn north and go to the intersection with FSR 64 at Potato Patch Mountain. Bear left on 68, drive on to the trailhead and continue for 1½ miles to the trailhead on the right.

Panther Creek Trail: Panther Creek can only be accessed by hiking into the wilderness on one of the other trails. The shortest route is from the Crandall Access on FSR 17. From there, you'll follow the Conasauga River Trail to its intersection with the Panther Creek Trail just south of Bray Field. The trail then heads east to a junction with the East Cowpen Trail. It's a popular trail that takes in a high waterfall along the way. Be sure to bring your camera.

From Ellijay go west on GA 52 for two-thirds of a mile to FSR 90 and onto FSR 68. Turn north and go to the intersection with FSR 64 at Potato Patch Mountain. Bear left on 68, drive on to FSR 17 and turn right. From there, it's 2½ miles to the parking area at the end of the Conasauga River Trail.

East Cowpen: From a trailhead in a parking area at Three Forks, Cowpen meanders northward to another trailhead on FSR 51. The route follows Old GA 2, now closed, up hill and down dale, with several interesting stops along the way. It's a great hike and highly recommended.

From Ellijay go west on GA 52 for two-thirds of a mile to FSR 90 and onto FSR 68. Turn north and go to the intersection with FSR 64 at Potato Patch Mountain. Turn right onto 64 and drive four miles to the trailhead on the left.

Jacks River Trail: Dedicated hikers should put this trail on their "must do" list. It's a hike to remember. For more than 16 miles the Jacks Trail follows the river, crossing and recrossing it some 40 times, through the Cohutta Wilderness, past Jacks River Falls, through Horseshoe Bend to its end on FSR 221 near Conasauga. Often wet, always picturesque, sometimes difficult, this is one of the most popular trails in the wilderness. Be sure to wear appropriate hiking gear, especially shoes, and take along your camera.

From Chattsworth, take Highway 441 north to Cisco and turn right at Greg's General Store. Go east until you hit FSR 16. Turn left there and follow 16 to the Tennessee state line. You'll find the trailhead just over the line on your right.

From Blue Ridge at the intersection of Highway 76, take note of your mileage and drive north on GA 5 for 3.2 miles to the intersection with Old FSR 2. Turn left onto Old 2 and drive on until your odometer reads 13.3 from the intersection of Highway 76 and the pavement ends. You should be able to see a Cohutta Wildlife Management Area sign for Watson's Gap. Turn right there onto FSR 22 and drive on to the trailhead at Dally Gap.

Conasauga River

The Conasauga has its origins deep in the Cohutta Wilderness. It's a crystal-clear mountain river that winds northward through a series of gorges into the Alaculsy Valley, eventually joining the Jacks River. The upper section of the river flows through some very scenic country. If you are a canoeist of some ability, you'll want to give it a try. If you're a hiker, you'll also want to investigate the Conasauga. The fishing is good, too.

From Atlanta take I-75 north to its intersection with Highway 411. Turn north on 411 and drive all the way to the Conasauga Bridge, just a couple of miles across the Tennessee border. Continue for a short distance and turn right onto Sheeds Creek Road (the first paved road past the bridge next to a gas station). From there, drive for about seven miles to a small valley where you'll find the river, several campgrounds and a number of hiking trails. The road is unpaved for most of the way.

Canoeing: Most of the rapids on the Conasauga are designated Class I and Class II, with one section designated Class III (see page 35 for classification chart). The river is usually runnable for most of the winter and spring months when the water levels are at their highest. During summer, however, there's often not enough water in the river to maintain even a rubber raft. In the depths of winter the waters are icy; a full wet-suit is essential. The river is also quite remote, and therefore help is not likely to happen along just when you might need it. Don't venture onto the waters alone.

Fishing: Although the river is inaccessible over much of its length, where you can get to the water, there's some good bank fishing to be had. If you like solitude along with your sport, this is the place for you.

Fort Mountain State Park

High on the top of the mountain, in the heart of the Cohutta Ranger District, is an ancient, 855-foot-long stone wall from which the park gets its name. No one knows for sure how the wall came to be, but some believe it was built in prehistoric times by Indians for protection against other more hostile tribes. Some think it might have been built as a place to carry out ancient tribal ceremonies. We'll probably never know. Today, the ancient wall adds an air of mystery to this magnificent mountain park.

With its abundance of wildlife, and the surrounding Chattahoochee National Forest, Fort Mountain is a place of outstanding natural beauty, and well worth a visit. The wall is reached by hiking up a long, very steep set of steps and a trail to the top of the mountain. The Park Service puts on several annual events, including Spring Wildflowers, Fort Mountain Mysteries in August, and overnight backcountry trips in October and November.

The park covers more than 1,900 acres and has an extensive range of facilities. There's mountaintop **camping** in a secluded, but well-developed campground with lots of facilities, including 70 tent and trailer sites, 15 rental cottages, a comfort station with hot showers and flush toilets, more than 12 miles of mountain hiking trails (see below), a swimming beach and a miniature golf course. This is a very popular campground, almost always fully booked, so be sure to make your reservations as early as possible.

There are four **hiking trails** within the boundaries of Fort Mountain State Park. You can obtain detailed maps with directions at the park office.

Old Fort Trail: This is the most popular of the four trails. From the park entrance, take the park road all the way to the picnic area at the north end; the trailhead is just to the right. From there, the trail leads upward, via a series of wooden steps and earthen plateaus, to the top of the mountain and the remains of the old wall from which the park takes its name. The view from the top is outstanding and well worth the long and strenuous climb. If you're taking children, be sure you keep an eye on them once you arrive at the top. There are a number of rocky outcrops that are very tempting to small and inquisitive minds.

Big Rock Nature Trail: This is a small, attractive trail just to the west of the park lake. For about three-fourths of a mile it loops through the rugged terrain on the slopes of the mountain. Be sure to take along your camera, for the trail leads past an overlook with a magnificent view of Gold Mine Creek, which cascades down the mountain more than 400 feet.

Lake Loop Trail: A really nice, easy walk of a little more than a mile and suitable for almost everyone. It leads around the shores of the 17-acre Fort Mountain Lake.

Gahuti Trail: A long, looping trail of more than eight miles that takes you round the outer perimeter of the park to a number of scenic overlooks. They offer spectacular scenic overlooks of the surrounding countryside and the Cohutta Wilderness. There are a number of primitive and limited-use campsites along the way. The trail is an excellent backpacking experience that never takes you too far from Park Service personnel and help if you need it. The trailhead is in a parking area at the north end of the park.

Fort Mountain State Park, Route 7, Box 7008, Chatsworth, GA 30705. ☎ 706-695-2621. The park, seven miles from Chatsworth on GA 52, is open from 7 am until 10 pm daily.

TOCCOA RANGER DISTRICT

This Ranger District has nothing to do with the town of the same name. It centers instead upon the forest in and around the Toccoa River, with its focal point at Lake Blue Ridge. Toccoa Ranger District, E. Main Street, Box 1839, Blue Ridge, GA 30513. ☎ 706-632-3031.

There are seven recreation areas in this section of the forest, which covers a large mountainous region in north-central Georgia to the east of Blue Ridge and south of the Tennessee/North Carolina border. Six of the areas have camping facilities.

Lake Blue Ridge

This great, man-made lake in the heart of the Chattahoochee National Forest, just to the west of Blue Ridge on GA 60, stretches for more than 10 miles along the Toccoa River. The Toccoa flows north through the lake to Copperhill, Tennessee, where it changes its name and becomes the mighty whitewater river and 1996 Olympic kayak venue, the Ocoee.

Lake Blue Ridge is a popular spot for anglers and boaters alike, but never quite as busy as one might expect. It's a fairly remote location compared to the great lakes farther to the south, Alatoona and Lanier, but it's something of an open secret among watersports afficionados. Even on its busiest days, there's plenty of room for everyone to do their thing, be it skiing, swimming or fishing.

Lake Blue Ridge is blessed with two national forest recreation areas: Lake Blue Ridge and Morganton Point. Both have boat ramps and well-developed campgrounds. Lake Blue Ridge offers **lakeside camping** in a large, well-maintained area within the confines of the Chattahoochee National Forest. Although there's no dumping station, the 55 sites are provided with a comfort station that has flush toilets and hot showers. Trailers and RVs are permitted, but there are no water or electric hookups. Facilities include a boat ramp, four picnic areas and several hiking trails. Morganton Point Recreation Area offers similar lakeside facilities. There are 37 sites with access to a comfort station, flush toilets and fresh drinking water, but there are no hot showers.

The **Fannin County Fair** is held in mid-August in Blue Ridge. This annual fair features all the traditional country exhibits including mountain crafts, livestock, local produce and country foods.

This is one of the Tennessee Valley Authority's finest **fishing** lakes, and one of its best managed. Blue Ridge is a mecca for sport fishermen, and the only lake in Georgia where anglers can hunt the mighty muskellunge. The "muskie" is a fierce member of the pike family that can grow up to four feet in length. For those who have the patience to hunt the muskie, the rewards can be great; some of the largest on record have been caught in the area. As for the rest, you'll find there are plenty of smallmouth bass in the lake, and bluegill, crappie, walleye and catfish are also present in good quantities. The fishing is considered good to excellent.

To reach the Lake Blue Ridge Recreation Area, drive east from Blue Ridge on Highway 76 to its junction with Dry Branch Road and then turn right. From there, you'll drive on for about three miles to the entrance to the recreation area.

To reach the Morganton Point Recreation Area, drive a little farther on along 76 to its junction with GA 60 and then turn south. From there, drive on for about three more miles, through Morganton, and look out for the white and green signs that point the way. You'll then turn right onto County Road 616 and drive for about a mile.

Cooper Creek Scenic Area & Recreation Area

Cooper Creek is a remote recreation area with plenty to see and do adjoining the Cooper Creek Scenic Area, a 1,240-acre tract of forest with a number of hiking trails, some of which follow the progress of the Cooper Creek and its tributaries. The recreation area has a partially developed campground, and more opportunities for hiking, fishing and picnicking. It's a very beautiful area with lots of sparkling water and plenty of trout.

The area offers remote, **riverside and forest camping**. The campground is adjacent to the Cooper Creek Scenic Area. There are 17 campsites with access to flush toilets, fresh drinking water and hot showers. Free.

From Dahlonega, take GA 60 north for 26 miles. Turn right onto FSR 4 and continue for six miles more.

From Blue Ridge, take Highway 76 east to its junction with GA 60 at Morganton, then go south for 17 miles. Turn left onto FSR 4 and continue on for six miles.

Deep Hole

This is another mountain recreation area set beside the Toccoa River, not far west of Cooper Creek Scenic Area. It's a fairly remote spot, still not quite as popular as many wilderness sites have lately become. It has a nice campground, numerous opportunities for hiking, and some very good river fishing.

Deep Hole offers **mountain and riverside camping** on the banks of the Toccoa River. Deep Hole is quite remote, with just eight campsites. Even so, there's a comfort station with flush toilets and fresh drinking water. Unfortunately, there are no showers.

From Dahlonega, take GA 60 north for 27 miles. An alternative route is to take Highway 76 east from Blue Ridge to its junction with GA 60 at Morganton, then go south for 16 miles.

Frank Cross

This creekside recreation area is near the Chattahoochee National Fish Hatchery on Rock Creek. It has a small campground, and the fishing on the creek is good. Lovely country and sparkling waters. If you like to get away from the crowds, this one will suit you fine.

There's just a small **campground** with 11 campsites and access to flush toilets and fresh drinking water. Sorry, there are no hot showers.

From Dahlonega, take GA 60 north for 27 miles. Turn left onto FSR 69 and go for five miles.

From Blue Ridge, take GA 76 to its junction with GA 60, then drive south for 15 miles to GA 69 and turn right. Drive on for five miles more.

Mulky

Mulky has another small creekside campground on the banks of Cooper Creek. Only 10 campsites, but they do have access to flush toilets and fresh water; no hot showers. There are good opportunities for hiking and picnicking, and the trout fishing is great.

From Dahlonega, take GA 60 north and drive for about 26 miles, then turn right onto FSR 4 and continue about six miles more.

From Blue Ridge, take Highway 76 east to its junction with GA 60 at Morganton, then go south for about 17 miles, where you turn left onto FSR 4 and continue on for six miles.

CHESTATEE RANGER DISTRICT

This district is centered on the old gold mining town of Dahlonega. It was during the years 1828-1829 that white settlers first began pouring into the area searching for the yellow metal. And there was so much of it here that the Federal Government built a mint to process it. From 1838 to 1861, more than 1.3 million gold coins were struck. The Civil War soon brought an end to that, but gold can still be found in the area. Chestatee Ranger District, 1015 Tipton Drive, Dahlonega, GA 30533. ☎ 404-536-0541.

There are three campgrounds, one in the Desoto Falls Recreation Area.

Dockery Lake

Wilderness camping beside a three-acre trout lake. Not much in the way of facilities; just 11 campsites, several picnic sites, flush toilets and fresh water; no hot showers. There are some nearby hiking trails and the lake is open for fishing.

Take GA 60 from Dahlonega and drive north for 12 miles. Turn right onto FSR 654 and drive one mile to the campground.

Waters Creek

Creekside forest camping on a very small, rather primitive campground. Nice and secluded with good fishing and hiking. Just eight sites with access to flush toilets and fresh water, but no showers.

From Dahlonega, take Highway 19 and drive north for 12 miles. Turn left onto FSR 34 and drive another mile to the campground.

Desoto Falls Recreation & Scenic Areas

This scenic area covers some 650 acres of rugged, mountainous country ranging in elevation from 2,000 to 3,500 feet. It's an exceptionally beautiful area with magnificent views, several lovely waterfalls and a number of crystal-clear streams and creeks. Desoto Falls offers scenic **mountain camping**. The campground is small, secluded, and well developed. There are 24 campsites with a comfort station, flush toilets, hot showers and fresh water. A half-dozen picnic sites, several hiking trails, and lots of good fishing provide plenty of recreation.

From Dahlonega, take Highway 19 and travel north for about 18 miles, or you can take Highway 129 north from Cleveland for 15 miles.

TALLULAH RANGER DISTRICT

This district covers a large tract of wilderness at the northeastern corner of the Chattahoochee. It's an area with extensive opportunities for outdoor recreation. The Appalachian Trail, the Chattooga River, the southern section of the Elliott Rock Wilderness Area, and some of the most beautiful mountain scenery in Georgia all lie within its boundaries. Of its nine recreation areas, five have camping facilities. Tallulah Ranger District, 825 Highway 411 South, PO Box 438, Clayton, GA 30525. ☎ 706-782-3320.

Chattooga Wild & Scenic River

The Chattooga is one of the longest free-flowing rivers in the southeastern United States that remains relatively primitive and undeveloped. "Wild and Scenic" is an official designation awarded by the Federal government to certain unique rivers, just as "National Park," "National Forest," and "National Recreation Area" are designations given to certain areas in order to preserve and protect them. For more than 40 miles, the Chattooga serves as the border between Georgia and South Carolina. Wild and Scenic applies in more ways than one. It's one of the most beautiful rivers in northern Georgia, but it also can be dangerous. It's a center where the rafting companies ply the waters with their great rubber boats and is also a popular kayaking destination, and therein lies the danger. Only canoeists of considerable experience should venture out onto the waters, and then never alone. (See page 80 for more information.)

The river is most easily reached by traveling northeast on Highway 23. Maps of the river are available from the National Forest Service.

Tallulah Falls & Gorge

Unfortunately, the falls that once tumbled into the Tallulah Gorge, and from which the little mountain community takes its name, are no longer there. They dried up when the Georgia Power Company dammed the river to create Tallulah Lake. The great gorge, however, still remains as the center of the Tallulah Basin, which is rapidly becoming one of Georgia's great outdoor recreation areas. For years hunters have known about Tallulah, and for years they've hunted the black bear, wild hog and white-tailed deer that make the Basin their home. Today, it's not quite the secret locals and dedicated hunters have tried to keep it.

An experienced canoeist enjoying the whitewater at Tallulah Gorge.

There is a terraced **mountain campground** in the Tallulah Gorge area; very appealing with lots to see and do. Terrora Park has only 50 sites. None have full hookups, but they do have water and electric; 12 are pull-throughs. The bathhouse has flush toilets, hot showers, handicapped-accessible restroom facilities, and there's a laundromat. There is no store as such, but ice is available, and there are shops not too far away in Tallulah Falls. Sewage disposal facilities are available too. From the gorge bridge on Highway 441, go north on 441 for about a half-mile, then southeast for a half-mile more on Rock Mountain Road.

Aside from the obvious attractions of the wilderness, the falls and Tallulah Gorge, the campground offers a pavilion, lake swimming, fishing, a playground, hiking trails and court games.

Tallulah is a land of deep ravines, sparkling rivers and creeks, waterfalls, threaded throughout with hiking and horse trails, many of which connect with the Appalachian Trail.

To visit, take Highway 23 from Atlanta, through Gainesville, and on to Tallulah Falls.

Rates start out at around $12 per vehicle. ☎ 706-754-6036.

Tallulah River & Coleman River

Tallulah River is a forest recreation area; Colman River is a forest scenic area. They are close enough together to be counted as one, at least for the purposes of this book. It's an area of old-growth timber, rugged scenery and tumbling waters, with lots of hiking and fishing opportunities, plus a small, secluded campground. Never very busy, it's one of those quiet places where you can go to relax and perhaps enjoy fresh trout cooked over the grill or a romantic outdoor picnic.

There's **forest camping** in a small, secluded area that's never too busy. There are 17 campsites, no water, no electric hookups or showers, but there are flush toilets and fresh drinking water. Trout fishing is a popular activity.

Take Highway 76 west from Clayton for eight miles, then turn right onto an unpaved road for four miles more. Turn left on FSR 70; the campground is a mile farther on.

Willis Knob

Rugged mountain country near the South Carolina state line and spectacular scenery make this recreation area quite popular with outdoor enthusiasts, especially those who enjoy horseback riding.

The **campground** here is very small – only eight sites – but there's good fishing on the Chattooga River, lots of hiking and horse trails, and the campground itself is never very busy.

From Clayton, go east on Warwoman Road for 11.6 miles. Turn right on Goldmine Road – it's a gravel road – and look for signs indicating Woodall Ridge Day Use Parking Area on the left.

Rabun Beach

Situated on the edge of 940-acre Lake Rabun, this area offers some of the most spectacular mountain scenery in northeast Georgia.

The main feature of the lake is its spectacular mountain scenery, which provides for a very pleasant, though often crowded, **boating** experience.

This is the most developed **camping** site of all the national forest recreation areas in the Chattahoochee. Facilities include 80 campsites with water and electric hookups, a comfort station with flush toilets, fresh drinking water and hot showers, four picnic sites, several hiking trails and a boat ramp. Rabun Beach is also one of the busiest national forest campgrounds, so be sure to book your site well in advance.

Good **fishing**, along with numerous **hiking trails, boating** and **watersports** opportunities, make this a very popular and often congested outdoor destination. Unfortunately, it's too small to get away from the crowds. Anglers will only find peace and quiet in the early mornings and, perhaps, on weekdays. Fishing is said to be good, with bass, crappie, bream and catfish all present in fairly good numbers.

Take Highway 441/23 south from Clayton for seven miles. Turn right on an unnumbered county road, drive one-tenth of a mile and turn left onto GA 15. After two miles, make a right onto County Road 10 and go five miles more.

Rabun Gap

This small spot on the map in northeast Georgia is famous for the Foxfire books, a product of Rabun Gap Nacoochee School. A young English teacher not long out of Cornell University, Elliott Wigginton, was unable to make much impression upon his students. Exasperated, he set aside the school textbooks and asked the children if they would like to publish a magazine. Soon the children were out interviewing parents and neighbors about local culture, history and living. The first edition of *Foxfire* magazine sold out all 600 copies. From that small beginning came the books and, eventually, national attention for Wigginton and his school. But there the story ends. There are no souvenirs to buy or sights to see. Rabun Gap is a sleepy little community set deep in the heart of the Chattahoochee National Forest, surrounded by lakes, mountains, creeks, state and national parks, and some fine scenery.

From Atlanta, take Highway 23 north.

Hambridge Center: A community for the arts, the Hambridge Center is a 600-acre estate where qualified artists, composers and writers can go to pursue their craft in peace and quiet. Visitors are welcome. It's on Batty's Creek Road in Rabun Gap, three miles west of Highway 23/441. ☎ 706-746-5718.

Rabun Gap Crafts: An interesting little craft shop operated by the Rabun Gap-Nacoochee School, featuring wood carvings, pottery and hand-made dolls and toys. Open Monday through Saturday, March through December. Highway 23/441.

Tate Branch

Tate Branch offers a remote, secluded **campground** at the junction of the Tallulah River and Tate Branch. Exceptional fall color and mountain scenery. There are 19 campsites with access to flush toilets and fresh water. Unfortunately, there are no hot showers, but there are a number of hiking trails, and the river offers exceptional fishing.

From Clayton, take Highway 76 west for eight miles. Turn right onto an unnumbered county road and drive four more miles. Turn left onto FSR 70 and go another four miles to the recreation area.

Sandy Bottom

This area has a small forest recreation area with a few undeveloped **campsites** and access to flush toilets and fresh water. There are no showers, but there are a number of picnic sites and opportunities for good fishing.

From Clayton, take Highway 76 west for eight miles. Turn right onto an unnumbered county road and drive four more miles. Turn left onto FSR 70 and go four miles to the recreation area.

Chickamauga National Military Park

The Civil War battle of Chickamauga was the climax of the Union's first invasion of Confederate territory.

Confederate General Braxton Bragg had retreated from Murfreesboro on January 2nd, 1863, after the battle of Stones River, and by September his 43,000-strong Army of Tennessee was defending the key railhead and river crossing at Chattanooga. Union General William S. Rosecrans with his Army of the Cumberland knew that Chattanooga was the key to the invasion. If he could take the city, he would throw open the gates to the heart of the Confederacy. Rosecrans arrived in Chattanooga on September 9th. By then Bragg had concentrated his forces at Lafayette, Georgia, some 26 miles to the south; a major confrontation was inevitable.

The battlefield at Chickamauga has changed very little over the last century and a half. The open fields were much the same then as they are today, and dense woods still cover most of the area.

As you tour the battlefield, located at strategic positions all over the battlefield, you'll find hundreds of cast-iron tablets. These describe the precise movements of every brigade and division that fought here during the two days of September 19th and 20th.

Your tour of the battlefield begins at the visitor center, where you can get a free map from the information desk, then continues through more than seven miles of park roads and trails. Be sure to visit the museum, then drive left on Highway 27, go to the traffic signals and turn right on Reed's Bridge Road to stop 1A, where you will find a monument to the Tennessee Artillery. From there you proceed along the road to stop 1B at the northern end of the battlefield, the site of what was once Jay's Mill, starting point of the battle.

Stand for a moment or two on the roadside and look across the small field in front of you toward the woods – the field was much bigger then. Let your imagination wander back to the morning of September 19, 1863. The time is about 7:30; there's a light ground mist over the forest; the weak sunlight is just beginning to filter through the treetops. The field in front of you is swarming with Confederate horse-soldiers, some on foot tending to their mounts, some still on horseback after returning from an early morning patrol. The whole area is filled with the hustle and bustle of a thousand men preparing to do battle.

Through the woods behind you a full division of General George Thomas' Federal infantry is making its way quietly through the trees. Their boots make little noise on the soft surface. Only the soft whisper of sporadic conversation disturbs the early morning stillness. Then, as they break out of the trees, they find they've run slap into a division of Confederate cavalry commanded by Nathan Bedford Forrest himself.

Both forces are taken by surprise. Confusion reigns as troops on both sides rush around in all directions, soldiers on each side falling over one another as they try to take advantage of what little cover there is. There's no time for the Federals to retreat back into the woods, and there's no time for Forrest's Confederates to organize and get mounted. Within seconds the air is filled with the crash of gunfire, the screams of wounded men and dying horses, and the yells of officers trying to manufacture order out of chaos. Suddenly, in the midst of the confusion, a tall, bearded man appears in the Confederate ranks. He wears a belted, knee-length Confederate coat and carries a cavalry saber in one hand, a pistol in the other, and there's a second pistol stuck in the belt at his waist. Within minutes, by the sheer weight of his personality, General Forrest has restored order to his beleaguered cavalry. His men lie face down in the dew-sodden grass and steadily return the Federals' fire. But the Confederate losses are heavy. In less than an hour, Forrest has lost more than a quarter of his command. And so the Battle for Chickamauga had begun.

The battle raged on as the two great armies clashed again and again all day long on Saturday, then on into the night. It resumed again at first light on Sunday and continued under a hot sun until at last the superior striking power of the Confederate force began to take its toll. By mid-afternoon General Longstreet had broken the Union line, and Rosecrans and the bulk of his army were streaming from the field in headlong flight. Only General George Thomas was able to hold his ground on Snodgrass Hill; he is

Chickamauga Battlefield

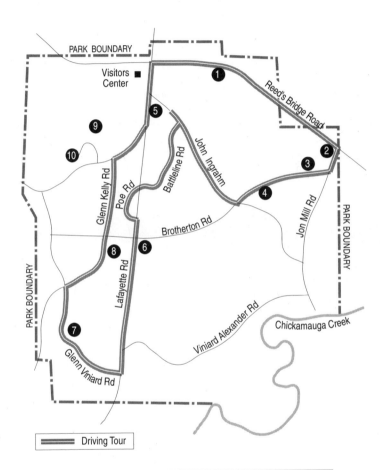

Driving Tour

1. Tennessee Artillery
2. Jay's Mill Site
3. Bragg's Headquarters
4. Winfrey Field
5. Battleline Road
6. Brotherton House
7. Wilder Tower
8. Rosecrans' Headquarters
9. Snodgrass House
10. Snodgrass Hill

credited with saving the Federal army from destruction that day and, in doing so, earned the sobriquet, Rock of Chickamauga.

The Battle of Chickamauga, an outstanding victory for the South, was one of the bloodiest of the Civil War. Combined casualties totaled more than 34,000. The Union lost more than 16,000 men, 57 pieces of artillery and 24,000 stands of arms.

Chickamauga National Battlefield is close to the city of Chattanooga, Tennessee, at Fort Oglethorpe in northwest Georgia on Highway 27. It can easily be reached from either I-24 going west from Chattanooga toward Nashville, or I-75 going southeast from Chattanooga toward Atlanta. It can also be reached going north toward Chattanooga from Lafayette on Highway 27. The park is open daily from 8 am to 4:45 pm during the winter months and from 8 am to 5:45 pm during the summer. Admission is free. Horses and bicycles can be rented locally and picnicking is allowed in the park.

Clarksville

A tiny mountain community on Highway 441, just west of Highway 23, with a delightful downtown square surrounded by all sorts of little shops and stores selling gifts, crafts, art and antiques. A nice stop-off on your way through the Chattahoochee National Forest.

DINING OUT

Try **Adams Rib** on Route 5. They are open for lunch and dinner, do a great prime rib, barbeque ribs, and they have an oyster bar. ☎ 706-754-4568.

CAMPING

Appalachian Camper Park

A well-managed campground on rolling woodland with 48 shaded sites, of which 15 are pull-throughs, 10 have full hookups and 38 have water and electric hookups only. Facilities include flush toilets, hot showers, sewage disposal, a laundromat, and a convenience store where you can get ice and wood.

For recreation, there's a swimming pool, a playground, lake fishing, hiking trails and the usual court games.

Rates start at around $12.50 per night per site.

From the junction of Alt Highway 17/US 441 Bypass, drive one mile north on US 441. ☎ 706-754-9319.

CRAFT HUNTING

Mark Of The Potter is northern Georgia's oldest craft shop. Housed in a 66-year-old grist mill, it showcases the works of more than 40 southeastern artists and crafters. The scenery around the old mill is spectacular. You can feed the trout in the stream, browse through arts and crafts ranging from ceramic jewelry to handblown glass and contemporary pottery. Open daily throughout the year. North of Clarksville on Route 3. Box 3164, Clarksville, GA 30523. ☎ 706-947-3440.

Serendipity. This is a stained glass studio and shop where customers can choose from a variety of ready-made art-glass, or order custom pieces: lamps, windows, etc. Highway 69, ☎ 706-947-3643.

Chattahoochee Mountain Fair is an annual event held on the Habersham County fairground in August. Basically a country fair, it features all sorts of agricultural exhibits, along with a large number of crafts and carnival rides.

Cleveland

The little town's main claim to fame is its **Babyland General Hospital**, home of the world-famous Cabbage Patch Kids. The hospital is housed in a medical clinic from the early 1900s, where you can witness the birth of the hand-sculpted kids and even adopt one if you like. Open Monday through Saturday from 9 until 5, and from 10 until 5 on Sunday. Free. Babyland General Hospital, 57 West Underwood Street, Cleveland, GA 30528. ☎ 706-865-2171.

CAMPING

Turner Campsites

A level campground on the banks of a mountain stream. Facilities include 120 sites, of which 52 are pull-throughs, 115 have full hookups, and five have water and electric only. There are flush toilets and hot showers, and campers have access to a laundry and sewage disposal.

For recreation, there's a fully equipped pavilion and opportunities for river swimming and fishing, boating and hiking. There's also a playground and a sports field.

No pets. No tents.

Rates start at around $15 per night for two persons. From the junction of Highways 75 and 129, drive 10 miles northwest on 129 and turn onto Highway 129. The campground is 200 feet south of the intersection. ☎ 706-865-4757.

Clayton

This small community is set deep in the heart of the mountains of northeast Georgia and the Chattahoochee National Forest. As such, it has become a center for outdoor activities that run the gamut through hiking, boating, canoeing, whitewater rafting, fishing, rock climbing and camping.

CRAFT HUNTING

Granny's Hilltop Crafts. You'll find this neat little shop on Highway 441 three miles south of Clayton. It's jam-packed full of hand-crafted goodies from toys to textiles to food, including jams and jellies.

Homemakers' Harvest Festival. Held annually in Dillard over three weekends in October, the festival is a showcase for mountain arts and crafts and good Southern cooking.

WHITEWATER SPORTS

Chattooga Wild & Scenic River

This river cascades from its headwaters in the mountains of North Carolina southward for more than 57 miles to Lake Tugaloo on the Georgia/South Carolina border. The scenery along its banks is magnificent, often spectacular, with gorges, waterfalls, rocky peaks, and unusual natural formations. The river provides for a number of activities, including canoeing, rafting, fishing and hiking. Take Highway 76 and go southeast from Clayton.

Rubber rafts offer thrills and spills on the Chattooga River.

SOUTHEASTERN EXPEDITIONS

This company offers whitewater rafting trips on the Chattooga. Kayaking and canoeing are also available. You'll ride a large rubber raft which carries up to eight people and an experienced guide. The ride is exciting, wet, and often bumpy. Wear old clothes and a strong pair of shoes or boots. Open Monday through Saturday from March through October. The rates vary from around $55 to $90. Allow for a full day out. Often very busy, so call ahead and make reservations. ☎ 800-969-7238.

Cloudland Canyon State Park

Cloudland Canyon State Park is situated high on the western edge of Lookout Mountain and is the westernmost state park covered in this book. It's also one of the most scenic parks in northern Georgia. Everywhere, an abundance of wildlife and wildflowers make the park a mecca for the naturalist, especially in the spring and fall. The canyon itself, a great gash cut into the earth by Sitton Gulch Creek, varies in elevation from more than 1,800 feet at the highest point to a low of less than 800 feet. Overlooks on the canyon rim provide breathtaking views, and a wooden walkway offers an exciting, though somewhat long and strenuous, climb down to the foot of the waterfall and the canyon floor. The climb can be hazardous in winter.

Cloudland Canyon is one of Georgia's busiest parks. Its magnificent views and close proximity to Chattanooga make it attractive, not only to outdoor adventurers, but also to casual day-visitors and tourists. Nature lovers flock to the mountaintop park in the spring for the annual show of wildflowers; hikers, with more than six miles of backcountry trails available, are especially well cared for. In the fall, the canyon is a blaze of color. The park is also a popular picnic spot (there are lots of tables and an open-air pavilion with grills).

The Park Service provides several annual special events, including Crafts in the Clouds the third weekend in May (subject to change), a wildflower program during May, and an overnight backpacking trip in October.

Cloudland Canyon State Park is on Lookout Mountain about 10 miles south of Chattanooga on Georgia Route 136, eight miles east of Trenton and I-59 and 18 miles west of Lafayette. Open daily from 7 am until 10 pm; the park office is open from 8 until 5.

Cloudland Canyon State Park, Route 2, Box 150, Rising Fawn, GA 30738. ☎ 706-657-4050.

CAMPING

Mountain camping on the rim of the gorge. Magnificent views, lots of wildflowers, rhododendrons and azaleas, and lots of facilities. Very busy from spring through fall (be sure to book well in advance).

Facilities include 75 tent and trailer sites, a 40-bed group camp, 16 rental cottages, a winterized group shelter, a swimming pool, tennis court, and 30 walk-in campsites.

HIKING

Cloudland Backcountry Trails: Backpacking is the way to go in Cloudland's backcountry. More than five miles of trails, each one intersecting another, through some beautiful wilderness territory. Lots to see and enjoy: views, wildflowers and birds. Camping is allowed on the trail, but you'll need to obtain a permit from the park office.

West Rim Loop Trail: For almost five miles this trail winds along the canyon rim and then back again. In the spring the way is lined with rhododendrons and azaleas, in the winter the views overlooking three gorges are breathtaking. When the early morning mist lies low in the rift and the tips of the mountains show above it like rocky islands in a sea of white cotton wool, it bestows an aura of magic. The going is fairly easy for most of the way.

Waterfall Trail: Just a third of a mile long, this is a pleasant walk through the woodland to two lovely waterfalls. The hike is a little strenuous in places, but woth the effort.

The waterfalls are one of many attractions at Cloudland Canyon State Park.

Dahlonega Gold Museum & Historic Site

For more than 30 years the gold towns of Dahlonega and Auraria thrived as a river of yellow metal flowed in from the mountains. Gold was discovered in the region in 1828, some 20 years before the great finds in California. From all points of the compass, thousands of hopeful prospectors headed for the diggings located deep in the heart of the Cherokee Nation. It was the beginning of the gold rush.

A Federal Branch Mint was established in Dahlonega, and from 1838 to 1861 the plant turned out more than $6 million in gold coins. Today, the old Lumpkin County Courthouse is a museum dedicated to the good old days of the nation's first major gold rush. A wide range of exhibits, including a gold nugget that weighs more than five ounces, a 30-minute film show entitled *Gold Fever*, and a series of special events, give a unique look into the lives and times of the pioneering families that lived, toiled and fought for their very existence in the gold fields.

The museum, on the Public Square in Dahlonega, five miles west of Georgia 400, is open all year, Monday through Saturday from 9 to 5, and on Sunday from 10 until 5; closed Thanksgiving and Christmas Day. Admission, $2; children 6-18, $1.

Dahlonega Gold Museum State Historic Site, Public Square, Box 2042, Dahlonega, GA 30533. ☎ 770-443-7850.

Dalton

Dalton is one of northern Georgia's industrial centers, famous for its carpet industry. Located on I-75, it's a great jumping-off point for day-trips into the forests and mountains.

WHERE TO STAY

Best Western, 2106 Chattanooga Road, at the Rocky Face exit on I-75. ☎ 706-226-5022. Typical of the chain, the motel has all the usual facilities: pool, playground, restaurant, meeting rooms, etc. Easy access to the mountains via Highways 76 and 441. $.

Holiday Inn, 515 Holiday Drive, at Exit 135 on I-75. ☎ 706-278-0500. One of the nicer examples of the chain; quiet, almost elegant, with a nice restaurant, pool, exercise room and conference facilities. Access to the mountains via Highways 76 and 441. $.

DINING OUT

The Cellar Restaurant, in the Dalton Shopping Center, just off I-75 at Exit 136, is open for lunch and dinner. Upscale (gentlemen will need to wear a jacket), with a menu that features lots of seafood dishes, Black Angus steaks, and an extensive range of specialty desserts. Often quite busy; best to make a reservation. ☎ 706-226-6029. $$.

Dillard

CAMPING

Dillard's Resort

A scenic campground, close to the mountains, with wonderful views. Not too big, but has good facilities and some opportunities for recreation. Facilities include 58 sites, of which 30 have full hookups and 28 have no hookups. There are flush toilets, hot showers and a laundromat. Tents are available. For recreation, there's the river and a pond, both good for fishing, several hiking trails, and the usual court games. Rates start at around $12 for two persons.

From the junction of Highways 246 and 23/441, go south on 23/441 for three-quarters of a mile. ☎ 706-746-2714.

Ellijay

This little mountain community is Georgia's Apple Capital and home of Carter's Lake. Apple houses are open to the public from late summer through December. The prices are reasonable and the fruit is exceptional.

CRAFT HUNTING

Possum Holler Country Store is located east of Ellijay on GA 52. This neat country store is packed with interesting goodies, especially locally made crafts, and antiques.

Held the second week of October, the **Apple Festival** is the highlight of Ellijay's year. The fair, one of the largest in Northern Georgia, features more than 100 craft exhibitors from as far away as Tennessee and Kentucky.

Hart State Park

Situated as it is on the banks of Lake Hartwell, this park is one of Georgia's most popular outdoor centers. The fair-weather crowd makes it somewhat congested at times, but the fishing is excellent and anglers come from miles around for the largemouth and smallmouth bass, black crappie, bream, rainbow trout and walleye. If it's boating, waterskiing, or swimming that you like, there's no better place for it than on the sparkling waters of the great reservoir.

Several boat ramps and docks offer easy access to the 56,000-acre lake and it's a rare day in summer when the park and lake are not busy. Even so, it's just the place to enjoy an afternoon on the beach with a picnic.

Lakeside camping on a 145-acre park beside vast Lake Hartwell. Extremely busy during spring and summer, but lots of facilities, including 65 campsites, a comfort station and two rental cottages. Campers also have access to the park's beach and picnic shelters.

Lots of facilities for outdoor recreation, including fishing and hiking, swimming, fishing and boating. The 146-acre park has its own swimming beach and three picnic shelters. There's also a small theater where you can enjoy live music programs.

The Park Service puts on a number of annual events, including the Labor Day Music Festival in September, the Memorial Day Weekend Craft Show, and the Hot Rods of Hart Car Show on the first Sunday in November.

Hart State Park, 1515 Hart Park Road, Hartwell, GA 30643. ☎ 706-376-8756.

The park, open daily from 7 am until 10 pm, is east from Hartwell on Highway 29; turn left on Ridge Road and then go two miles to the park.

Helen

No coverage of northern Georgia would be complete without a look at the Alpine village of Helen. Known throughout the Southeast, much to the locals' displeasure, as the Gatlinburg of northern Georgia, the little mountain town has long struggled to establish an identity of its own. It's inevitable, however, that Helen should be compared with the much larger mountain city in Tennessee. Both have striven to achieve an Alpine facade, but that's where the similarities end. Small as it is, Helen really does have something different to offer, and its visitors remain remarkably faithful, returning year after year. For the past several years, commercialism has been steadily on the increase – it's said there are more hotel rooms in Helen than there are permanent residents – but the garish colored lights and high-tech attractions so characteristic of Pigeon Forge and Gatlinburg have not yet made their appearance. Helen is, for the most part, a quiet little town with pleasant views of the surrounding countryside, the inevitable gift shops, factory outlets, and some very nice country restaurants and cafés. If you're visiting the mountains, stop by; you'll find this side trip an enjoyable one.

CAMPING

Sleepy Hollow Campground

A small campground, close to Helen, with level sites in a nice country setting on the lakeshore. Facilities include 67 sites, of which 30 have full hookups and 17 have water and electric. The bathhouse has flush toilets and hot showers, and there's a limited grocery store when you can purchase the essentials, including groceries and some camping supplies. Sewage disposal is also available.

The campground, for its size, has extensive recreational opportunities, including a pavilion, boat dock and ramp, a sports field and several hiking trails. All of the usual court games are available, as well as badminton and basketball. There's also a playground for the kids.

Rates begin at around $14 per vehicle.

Sleepy Hollow Campground, Route 1, Box 1324, Sautee, GA 30571. ☎ 706-878-2618.

From the junction of Highways 17 and 255, drive 2½ miles north on 255, then turn north onto Skylake Road and drive 2½ miles more to the campground.

CRAFT HUNTING

The Country Store is not exactly a craft shop, but is well worth a visit. This old, lovingly restored drugstore features an ice cream parlor and original soda fountain. It's on Skylake Road, off GA 255.

Tekawitha is a neat shop on South Main Street in Helen, it's a member of the Indian Arts and Crafts Association and, as such, is packed with all sorts of interesting Native American handcrafted bits and pieces: wall hangings, carved goods, jewelry, etc.

The Helen Arts Council Craft Show is held annually the last weekend in October in the Helen Pavilion. It features the works of local and regional crafts people. Demonstrations, exhibits and sales.

WHERE TO STAY

Comfort Inn, 101 Edelweiss Strasse, Helen, GA 30545. ☎ 706-878-2271. Typical of the chain, but has few advantages other than clean, comfortable rooms and easy access to the town and surrounding mountains. $.

Valley Haus Motel, 75 South Main Street, Helen, GA 30545. ☎ 706-878-2111. A small motel, clean, comfortable and close to the town center. No pets. $-$$.

DINING OUT

Hofbrauhaus Inn, 1 Main Street, is a German restaurant open for dinner from 5 until 10. Better make a reservation if you want to eat on Saturday. ☎ 706-878-2248. $$.

Hiawassee

A small mountain town on the banks of Lake Chatuge, and surrounded by the Chattahoochee National Forest. The tail-end of the Blue Ridge Mountains provides a dramatic backdrop, topped by Brasstown Bald. Rock hunting is a popular pastime, including hunting the prized amethyst.

CAMPING

Bald Mountain Park

A very large, well-appointed campground beside a mountain stream, with good facilities and even better recreational opportunities. There are 400 sites, of which only 12 are pull-throughs, 63 have full hookups, 337 have water and electric hookups only. Cable TV and telephone hookups are available at extra cost. Other facilities include flush toilets, hot showers, laundromat and sewage disposal. There's also a grocery store where you can obtain the essentials, as well as RV and camping supplies. For recreation, there's a restaurant, a fully-equipped pavilion, an Olympic-size swimming pool, boat dock, rental pedal boats, mini-golf, a playground, fishing, hiking and planned group activities. Some of the above activities may involve an extra charge. Rates start at $12.50 per night.

Bald Mountain Park Campground, Hiawassee, GA 30546. ☎ 1-800-253-6605. From the junction of Highways 76 and 75/17, go northwest on 76 for about a quarter-mile, then west on Highway 288 for a quarter-mile. Turn south onto Foudder Creek Road and drive four miles to the campground.

Brasstown Village Resort

A smaller campground with excellent facilities on a shaded, level site beside a mountain creek. There are only 40 sites, eight of which have full hookups and 23 have no hookups. There are flush toilets, hot showers, a laundry, tables, patios, grills and sewage disposal. For recreation, you'll have access to Brasstown Bald and the wilderness, as well as a recreation hall/pavilion. There are opportunities for creek fishing, hiking, field sports and the usual court games.

Rates start at around $14 per vehicle.

From the junction of Highways 76 and 17/75, go south on 17/75 for 6½ miles to Highway 180. From there go 2½ miles west on 180 to the campground. ☎ 706-896-1641.

Georgia Mountain Campground & Music Hall

Another large, well-appointed campground in a county park. Facilities include 226 sites, of which only 11 have full hookups; the rest have water and electric only. There are flush toilets, hot showers, a boat ramp, a playground, six tennis courts, a sports field and several hiking trails nearby. Sewage disposal is also available. Most important is the fact that the campground is gated and there's a guard on duty.

For recreation there's a pavilion, lake swimming, boating, planned group activities through the services of an on-site recreation director, and the usual court games. The Music Hall features live entertainment, with stars coming in from Nashville.

Rates are available if you call the office.

Georgia Mountain Park Campground & Music Hall, PO Box 444, Hiawassee, GA 30546. ☎ 706-896-4191.

From the junction of Highways 76 and 75/17, go northwest on 76 for a quarter-mile, and west on Highway 288 for a quarter-mile. Turn south onto Foudder Creek Road and drive three miles to the campground.

CRAFT HUNTING

The Georgia Mountain Fair is a 12-day event held the first Wednesday in August. It brings some 200,000 visitors to Hiawassee. More than 75 crafts people display and sell their goods, which include everything from hand-made pottery to country furniture. In addition, live bluegrass music, country dancing, demonstrations of soap making, blacksmithing, rope making, quilting, and board splitting make the two weeks interesting for everyone. Held at the Hiawassee fairgrounds.

WHERE TO STAY

Fieldstone Inn, three miles west of Hiawassee on Highway 76. ☎ 706-896-3943. This is a very nice inn on Lake Chatuge, with easy access to the surrounding mountains. Complimentary coffee in the lobby; a restaurant next door; pool, playground, lighted tennis courts, lakeside picnic tables and lawn games. $$.

James H. "Sloppy" Floyd State Park

This state park was named for one of Georgia's most distinguished State Representatives. Sloppy Floyd served in the Georgia House of Representatives from 1953 until his death in 1974. The 250-acre park is adjacent to the Chattahoochee National Forest and hiking and fishing are the popular activities. You can take along your boat if you can get by with an electric motor, or you can rent a pedal boat and spend an afternoon on the quiet waters of two small managed lakes. Beyond that, there are a couple of picnic shelters and a playground.

The park offers **lakeside camping,** with 25 tent and trailer sites with water and electric hookups, a pioneer campsite with fresh water and pit toilets, two lakes totaling about 51 acres, a playground, two boat ramps, pedal boat rentals and two picnic shelters.

Aside from its 250 acres of parkland on the edge of the Chattahoochee National Forest, the park has two small lakes totaling about 51 acres and two boat ramps. The lakes are kept stocked with bass, crappie, bluegill, bream and channel catfish. You can use your own boat, but will only be allowed the use of an electric motor. The fishing is fair.

The park, open daily from 7 am until 10 pm, is three miles southeast of Summerville on Marble Springs Road via Highway 27.

James H. Floyd State Park, Route 1, Box 291, Summerville, GA 30747. ☎ 706-857-5211.

Moccasin Creek State Park

This is affectionately known as "the place where spring spends summer." And it's true, for here on the shores of magnificent Lake Burton, among the hills and valleys of northeast Georgia, the unspoiled countryside is literally covered by a blanket of greenery and wildflowers. It's an enchanted setting, threaded throughout with tiny trout streams and backcountry trails. It's the perfect starting point for high country exploration or a place where you can simply enjoy the peace and quiet of the mountains, leave your worries behind and relax. Boating and fishing are the popular activities here. There's a boat dock and ramp, a playground, a wheelchair-accessible fishing pier, and a fishing stream set aside for senior citizens and children. You can hike the Moccasin Trail and the nearby Appalachian Trail. You can also visit the trout-rearing station adjacent to the park.

There's **mountain camping** on 32 acres of quiet, secluded parkland, surrounded by the peaks, valleys and mountain creeks of the southern Blue Ridge. Facilities include 53 tent and trailer sites with water and electric hookups.

Annual Park Service events include the Georgia Mountain Trout Program and Contest in June, and the Lake Burton Arts & Crafts Festival in July.

The park, open from 7 am until 10 pm, is 20 miles north of Clarksville on GA 197.

Moccasin Creek State Park, Route 1, Box 1634, Clarksville, GA, 30523. ☎ 706-947-3194.

New Echota State Historic Site

The Cherokee Nation once covered almost all of northern Georgia, western North Carolina, eastern Tennessee and Northern Alabama. In 1821 the Cherokees made a remarkable step forward with the invention of a written form of their language. In 1825 they established their capital, New Echota, in northwest Georgia. By 1828 it had become a thriving community and government headquarters for the independent Indian nation, a city complete with a tavern and a bilingual newspaper, the *Cherokee Phoenix*. But this new-found prosperity was not to last. The Indians, who had tried to model their government and lifestyles after those of the white man, were gathered together in 1838 and herded westward along the Trail of Tears to the reservations in Oklahoma.

Today, New Echota is an historic site where visitors can tour the reconstructed buildings: the Print Shop, the Supreme Courthouse, Vann's Tavern, and the original home of missionary Samuel A. Worcester.

Annual events here include the Cherokee Festival, a New England Christmas, Artifacts Identification Day and Gold Panning.

New Echota State Historic Site, 1211 Chatsworth Highway NE, Calhoun, GA 30701. ☎ 706-629-8151. The site is open year-round, Tuesday through Saturday from 9 until 5, and on Sunday from 2 until 5.

New Echota is one mile east of I-75, Exit 131, on Highway 225

Ringgold

CAMPING

KOA-Chattanooga South

This KOA site is a wooded campground on rolling hills with lots of facilities, both for camping and recreation. There are 152 sites and seven Kamping Kabins. Of the sites, 60 have full hookups, 86 water and electric only, and six tent sites have no hookups; 67 of the sites are pull-throughs. Six of the Kabins are one-room units; one has two rooms. Other facilities include flush toilets, hot showers, a laundromat and sewage disposal facilities. There's also a store where you can purchase groceries, camping and RV supplies, ice and LP gas by weight or meter. Security is handled by on-site staff.

There's a recreation room, a pavilion, swimming pool, a playground and all the usual court games. The staff conducts a program of group activities.

Rates for campsites range from $14.50 to $19.50 for two persons; for a one-room Kamping Kabin the rate is $30 per night for two persons, and $35 per night for the two-room unit. The KOA discount card is honored. ☎ 706-937-4166.

From the junction of I-75 and Highway 2 (Exit 141), go one-tenth of a mile west on Highway 2.

Rossville

Best Holiday Trav-l-Park

Close to Chattanooga; a large campground with extensive facilities set on a level site with plenty of shade. Facilities include 171 campsites, 89 with full hookups, 64 with water and electric only, and 18 with no hookups; 130 are pull-throughs. The campground has a full-service store where you can buy groceries and camping supplies, as well as LP gas by weight or meter. There are also three bathhouses with flush toilets, hot showers, and sewage disposal facilities.

There's a recreation hall, pavilion with coin games, swimming pool, wading pool, playground, several court games, and planned group activities handled by an on-site recreation director.

Rates begin at around $16.50 for two persons.

From the I-75 Exit 1 in Chattanooga, turn right at the top of the ramp, then left at the second red light onto Mack Smith Road and drive a half-mile to the campground.

Traveler's Rest State Historic Site

Traveler's Rest was the center of Devereaux Jarrett's once-thriving plantation. Jarrett was the richest man in the Tugaloo Valley before the Civil War and, in order to accommodate the growing numbers of travelers to northwest Georgia, he expanded the structure and opened it as an inn. It soon became a popular watering hole, and the hotel register boasts many a famous name, including those of John C. Calhoun and Joseph E. Brown, the Civil War Governor of Georgia.

The Traveler's Rest of today is furnished much as it was back in Jarrett's day. Many of the antiques you'll see in the old house were made by local craftsmen. In 1966 the house, with its 90-foot-long porch, hand-numbered rafters, and 20-inch-wide paneling, was recognized as a National Historic landmark. A very special annual event at the Traveler's Rest is Old-fashioned Christmas, held on the second Sunday in December.

Traveler's Rest State Historic Site, Route 3, Toccoa, GA 30577. ☎ 706-886-2256. The site is open year-round, Tuesday through Saturday, from 9 until 5, and on Sunday from 2 until 5.

The Traveler's Rest is six miles east of Toccoa on Highway 123.

Trenton

CAMPING

Chattanooga West/Lookout Mountain KOA

This is another of those campgrounds right at the tail-end of the Smokies, but close enough to be included here. The campground is blessed with an exceptional view of the mountains, as well as excellent facilities and recreational opportunities. There are 150 sites and six one-room Kamping Kabins. Of the regular campsites, 45 have full hookups, 75 have water and electric, 30 have no hookups; 100 are pull-throughs. The bathhouse has flush toilets and hot showers, there's a laundry, sewage disposal facilities and a full-service store where you can purchase groceries, camping supplies, and LP gas by weight or meter.

There's a recreation room and pavilion, a swimming pool and playground, and all the usual court games.

Rates for campsites range from $15 to $19, and the Kamping Kabins are $28 per night for two persons; extra adults are $3 more per night. ☎ 706-657-6815.

From the junction of I-14 and 59, go south on 59 for two miles to Exit 3 at Slygo Road. Go west on Slygo for 2½ miles and follow the signs.

Tugaloo State Park

Tugaloo is an old Indian name for the river that once flowed freely through the valley. The river is gone now, covered by the great lake that is the result of the construction of Hartwell Dam. The 390-acre Tugaloo State Park occupies a rugged peninsula jutting out into the Hartwell Reservoir.

This is a very busy **boating** site, popular for all sorts of watersports, including waterskiing (private boats are allowed on the lake) and fishing. There are two boat ramps.

A busy lakeside **campground** here offers 120 tent and trailer sites, all with water and electric hookups, and comfort stations with flush toilets and hot showers. There are 20 rental cottages, tennis courts, nature trails, a swimming beach and bathhouse, miniature golf, and two boat ramps.

Hartwell Reservoir, the lake adjoining this park, is the result of Hartwell Dam's construction. Surrounded by spectacular scenery, it offers some of the finest year-round lake fishing in Georgia. It's kept well-stocked with bass, and you'll also find plenty of crappie and catfish. There are also two public-access boat ramps and a dock. The lake gets very busy at times, but the fishing is considered excellent.

Entertainment is provided, and includes frequent Mountain Music programs and an annual Harvest Festival held in October.

Tugaloo State Park, Route 1, Box 1766, Lavonia, GA 30553. ☎ 706-356-4362.

The park, open from 7 am until 10 pm, is two miles northeast of Lavonia, close to the South Carolina border. Take I -85 to Exit 58 and go north on Georgia 17; follow the park signs and turn right onto County Road 385. From there, go 1½ miles to Georgia 328 and turn left. Drive on for 3.3 miles to the park entrance on the right.

Unicoi State Park

Unicoi State Park is set deep in the mountains of northern Georgia only a couple of miles from the Alpine village of Helen. It's a fairly busy park, with spectacular views, rugged terrain, fine fishing, excellent watersports, and a year-round program of organized activities. It's also one of the most extensively developed state parks in Georgia.

There are more than 1,000 acres of unspoiled parkland, with a lake, a magnificent 100-room lodge, rental cottages and a campground, all of which offer visitors a wide range of vacation accommodations. There's also a swimming beach, four lighted tennis courts, a restaurant and a craft shop.

Because of its location only two miles from the popular tourist town of Helen, Unicoi State Park is a busy park. **Watersports** enthusiasts of all types come to enjoy the waters, the spectacular views and the rugged terrain. Thus, the lake is very busy during spring, summer and winter.

The lake, though almost always crowded, is well known for its bass, crappie, bluegill and catfish.

Unicoi offers **mountain and lakeside camping**. Facilities include 84 tent and trailer sites with water and electric hookups; a comfort station with fresh water, flush toilets and hot showers; 30 rental cottages. For corporate campers, if such a species exists, there's a 100-room lodge and conference center with a buffet-style restaurant, a swimming beach, four lighted tennis courts and a craft shop.

Unicoi Lodge: Double room/loft weekdays, December 1 through March 31, $30; April 1 through November 30, $50. Double room/loft weekends, December 1 through March 31, $40; April 1 through November 30, $50.

Lodge rates are based upon single occupancy and they are subject to change without notice. Each additional adult is $6. Children under 12 years of age stay free when accompanied by an adult in the same room.

Fireside Arts & Crafts: Held in mid-February, this festival features local crafts people and their goods. Demonstrations, workshops and sales. For more information, contact the park.

The Park Service provides a full schedule of annual and monthly programs for entertainment and education, including special Friday night and Saturday programs year-round.

Unicoi State Park & Lodge, PO Box 849, Helen, GA 30545. ☎ 706-878-2201. Unicoi, open 7 until 10, is two miles northeast of Helen via GA 356.

Victoria Bryant State Park

This is one of Georgia's smaller state parks. Set in the mountains, it offers excellent hiking, picnicking, swimming, golf and camping. There are more than five miles of nature trails that meander this way and that through the woodlands, and a well-stocked fish pond. There's also a small golf course with a pro shop, clubhouse and driving range.

Victoria Bryant has **mountain and backcountry camping**. Facilities include 25 tent and trailer sites with water and electric hookups, flush toilets, hot showers and fresh drinking water. For the dedicated camper, there are two pioneer campsites. There's also a dumping station, and campers have free access to the hiking trails, playgrounds, golf course, swimming pool, picnic shelters and fishing pond.

Special events include the Annual Jr.-Sr. Catfish Rodeo in April or May, the Independence Day Bluegrass Festival held over the July Fourth weekend, and Pioneer Skills Day the first weekend in November.

Victoria Bryant State Park, Route 1, Box 1767, Royston, GA 30662. ☎ 706-245-6270 (office) or 706-245-6770 (golf course).

Victoria Bryant, open 7 until 10, is two miles north of Franklin Springs on GA 327.

Vogel State Park

Vogel is one of Georgia's oldest state parks. Located in the Blue Ridge Mountains, deep inside the Chattahoochee National Forest, and close to Blairsville, the park is steeped in local folklore. Stories of Indian battles and buried gold tickle the imagination. Vogel, with its 280 acres of rolling parkland, forests and spectacular views, is one of Georgia's most beautiful state parks. There are more than 17 miles of hiking trails, extensive camping facilities, a number of rental cottages, a 20-acre lake, a miniature golf course, a swimming beach with a bathhouse, four picnic shelters, rental pedal boats and a group shelter.

Obviously, there are lots of opportunities for outdoor recreation. The park is a popular place for nature study and birdwatching, wildlife photography, picnicking, boating (pedal boats only) and, of course, hiking.

There's **mountain and forest camping**. Facilities include 110 tent and trailer sites, all with water and electric hookups, along with a pioneer campsite, comfort stations with fresh drinking water, flush toilets and hot showers. There are 36 rental cottages on the edge of the lake, and campers have free access to all the recreational facilities mentioned earlier.

The Park Service puts on an extensive program of annual events and nature-related programs, including a Wildflower Program in April and an Old Timer's day in August.

Vogel State Park, Route 1, Box 1230, Blairsville, GA 30512. ☎ 706-745-2628.

The park, open from 7 am until 10 pm, is 11 miles south of Blairsville on Highway 19/129.

The Piedmont Region

Georgia's Piedmont Region cuts right across the center of the state, taking in everything from Cedar Town in the east to Augusta in the West, including Atlanta. And, while outdoor adventure is still an important part of what goes on, the opportunities are not quite as extensive as they are to the north and southeast. Still, there's plenty to see and do if you know where to look for it.

Hiking trails are limited to state parks, state recreation areas, and Corps of Engineers recreation areas on and around its many lake projects. Some can be a little hard-going, but most are no more than pleasant walks in the country, of varying lengths up to seven or eight miles, along lake shores or through woodland and forest.

Boating is big in the Piedmont Region. There are a half-dozen very large, Corps of Engineers-operated dam and lake projects, and a hundred smaller lakes, along with several thousand miles of rivers, their tributaries and creeks. Water sports of all types, from swimming to skiing, to jet boating, windsurfing, sailing, and canoeing, are available all over the Piedmont. Rental boats are available almost everywhere. Even the Federal authorities have gotten into the business.

Fishing in Georgia is more than a pastime; it's a way of life, and nowhere more so than in the Piedmont region. The Corps of Engineers' lakes, the rivers, the creeks, streams and ponds are stocked with bass, bluegill, crappie, sauger, catfish, trout and more. Many of the lakes can be very busy at times, but you can always find a secluded spot where the action is hot and the fish good to eat.

There are hundreds of commercially operated campgrounds in this region, and they offer facilities that range from poor to luxurious. But this region is blessed with state and federal projects that can offer much more. Rarely are these campgrounds limited in size as are their commercial competitors. Most are situated on vast areas of parkland among some of the most stunning scenery in the South, and the fees are always much lower than at commercial facilities. If you haven't already tried one of these wilderness campgrounds, you're in for a very pleasant surprise.

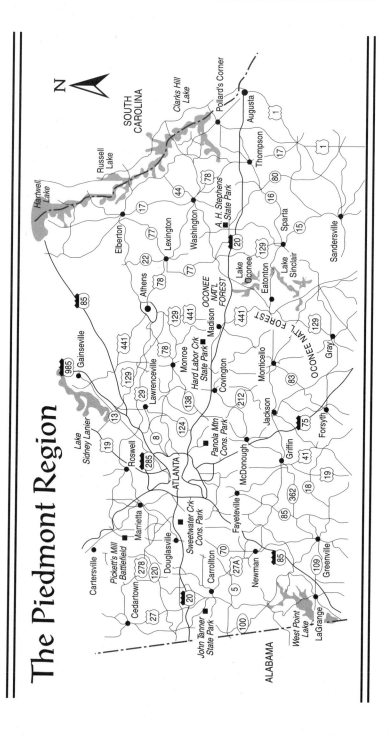

The Piedmont Region

Touring

Atlanta

Atlanta is all things to all people: its airport is the largest passenger terminal in the world; it has 130 retail centers, 41 public golf courses, 54 public parks, the tallest hotel in the Western Hemisphere, the tallest building in the southeast, and the list goes on. Perhaps the most vivid vision of the city is its torching during the American Civil War as it was re-created in the movie *Gone With the Wind*. Today, Atlanta is the crossroads of the southeastern United States; the capital of the South. The commerce of the region revolves around this city. When it was made the state capital in 1868, it became the symbol of the New South, but it still preserves the aura and traditions of the Old South.

Peachtree Street, Atlanta's central thoroughfare, follows the route of an old Indian trail. The dome of the Capitol is topped with native gold; it houses the State Museum of Science and Industry. Among the old homes on the 22-acre grounds of the Atlanta Historical Society are the restored Tullie Smith farmhouse and slave cabin dating from about 1840. On nearby Stone Mountain are carved the gigantic faces of Confederate war heroes Robert E. Lee, Stonewall Jackson and Jefferson Davis.

Atlanta is the cultural capital of the Southeast. The Atlanta Symphony Orchestra and the Alliance Theater Company perform in the Robert W. Woodruff Arts Center. The High Museum of Art, one of Atlanta's most recognized structures, houses more than 10,000 objects in its permanent collection. The 10-story, concrete Atlanta Public Library covers a downtown block.

The 1990s catapulted Atlanta into the limelight as an international sports city. In 1996 the city hosted the Centennial Olympic Games. The 85,000-seat Centennial Olympic Stadium is now the home of the Atlanta Braves baseball team. The Georgia Dome, adjacent to the World Congress Center, is the largest cable-supported domed stadium in the world, and home to the Atlanta Falcons NFL football team. Georgia's only NBA team, the Atlanta Hawks, call the Omni Coliseum home. Atlanta Motor Speedway is one of Georgia's best kept secrets. Just 30 miles south of the city, this 870-acre facility is the state's largest sports complex, and annually hosts two of the biggest events on the NASCAR

Winston Cup circuit. If that's not enough, Atlanta continues to play a role in the history and growth of the Southeastern Conference: SEC football and basketball championships are regularly held in the Georgia Dome, and the Georgia World Congress Center houses "SEC Fanfare," an interactive theme park for sports fans of all ages.

For the outdoor enthusiast, the mountains to the northeast and northwest are less than an hour away by car; the great lakes Lanier and Allatoona are even closer; the Chattahoochee National Forest is to the north; and heading south brings you to the Oconee National Forest. The city is surrounded by a ring of state parks that offer a range of outdoor experiences, from camping to hiking, rock climbing to fishing, and birdwatching to golfing. In the city itself, Zoo Atlanta offers a special experience, and numerous parks provide opportunities for tennis, hiking, boating, fishing and much more.

HISTORY

Atlanta was founded in 1837 at the end of the Western and Atlantic Railroad line, a site reflected in its first name, Terminus. In 1843 the name was briefly changed to Marthasville, after the daughter of the governor of Georgia. Two years later it was renamed Atlanta, supposedly a feminine form of "Atlantic," by an engineer of the Western and Atlantic Railroad.

By the outbreak of the Civil War in 1861, Atlanta was a major railroad hub, manufacturing center and supply depot. During the war, Confederate weapons were made and stored in Atlanta. In 1864 General William Tecumseh Sherman laid siege to the city for 117 days. After it surrendered, he ordered the city evacuated and burned. Of the 4,500 buildings in Atlanta at the beginning of the siege, only 400 survived the fire. But, like its symbol, the legendary phoenix of Egyptian mythology, Atlanta rose from the ashes to become the hub of the New South.

Within four years of Sherman's devastating visit, the Georgia capital was moved to the city from Milledgeville, and the drive to attract new business was underway.

Key events in the city's late-19th-century economic growth were the International Cotton Expositions of 1881 and 1895 and the invention of Coca-Cola, first sold in a drugstore on Peachtree Street in 1886.

By the late 1920s a downtown business center, ringed by residential districts, had taken shape, giving Atlanta the plan it maintains today. At about the same time, one of the city's aldermen,

William B. Hartsfield, was campaigning to turn an abandoned racetrack into an airport. His efforts were successful, and Atlanta's Hartsfield International Airport, the largest in the world, is the result of those efforts.

And Atlanta continues to make history. The 1996 Olympic Games and the Paralympic Games of the same year are already no more than a memory. Still to come: Superbowl 34 in 2000 and the NCAA Basketball Final Four in 2002.

An overview of Atlanta shows all the attractions.

HOW TO GET THERE

By Road

Three interstates provide access to Atlanta, which is ringed by I-285 (the Perimeter). I-75 (the Northwest Expressway) joins I-85 (the Northeast Expressway) just north of downtown to become the Downtown Connector, which passes just to the east of the city center.

From the southeast, I-75 becomes the South Expressway to a point just south of downtown, where it meets with I-20 coming in from the east and west (the West or East Expressway).

I-85 also approaches the city from the south, joining with the South Expressway at the Perimeter.

Other roads leading into Atlanta include SR-400 (toll 50¢) from the north; US-41 from the northwest; and US-19, which becomes Roswell Road, then Peachtree Street, and finally Spring Street.

By Air

Hartsfield International Airport, nine miles southwest of downtown, boasts the largest passenger terminal in the world, and is one of the busiest in the country. Thus Atlanta is served by every major domestic airline, most of the smaller ones, and many international airlines.

Rapid rail transportation is provided from the airport by the **Metropolitan Atlanta Rapid Transit Authority** (MARTA). The fare is $1.25.

Limousine service operates between the airport, business district, and many of the major downtown hotels. The fare is $8 each way, or $14 round-trip.

Taxis are plentiful. The fare begins at $15, but can increase significantly if traffic is heavy – and it almost always is, especially during rush hours.

By Bus

Greyhound/Trailways, 81 International Boulevard NW. ☎ 404-522-6300, or 1-800-231-2222.

By Rail

Amtrak, Brookwood Station, 1688 Peachtree Street NW. ☎ 800-USA-RAIL.

WHEN YOU GET THERE

Most of Atlanta's attractions are open daily, although a few do close on Monday, and some open late and close early on Sunday.

To make the most of your time in Atlanta, you should start at the visitors center where you can get detailed maps, brochures and other useful information.

Getting Around

Atlanta can be easy to get around in or, during rush hours, hell on earth. The great highways leading into and out of the city (some have as many as 16 lanes) feed traffic smoothly during off-hours, but turn into massive parking lots from 6:30 to 9 am, and 3:30 to 7 pm. Try to avoid travel during those hours.

Downtown is known as the Five Points Intersection. This is where Peachtree Street, Marietta, Decatur, Whitehall and

Edgewood converge, and the point where the four geographic regions of the city (NW, NE, SW, and SE) meet.

Downtown Atlanta.

Atlanta is not laid out in the traditional grid system, so finding your way around can become a little confusing. There are few square blocks or intersections.

Peachtree, running north and south through the city center, is the main street, which is also a little confusing because some 35 other streets and avenues also include the word "Peachtree." Peachtree Street is not to be confused with Peachtree Memorial Drive, Peachtree Circle, Peachtree Heights, or West Peachtree Street. Ponce de Leon and North avenues run east and west. The Downtown Connector bypasses the business district, while the East and West Expressways carry traffic directly into the city center.

All major **car rental** companies are represented at the airport. There is almost no on-street parking in the downtown business district, but garages and parking lots are plentiful throughout the city.

The rates run from 75¢ for the first 30 minutes to $7 or $8 per day, depending upon the location, and rates at such attractions as the CNN Center, World Congress Center, or the Omni Coliseum can be much more. Metered parking is available in outlying districts, but is strictly enforced; cars are often towed.

MARTA's 37-mile rapid rail service and connector bus routes provide quick and inexpensive access to most of greater Atlanta, while regular bus service is available between the Avondale Station and Stone Mountain.

Only exact fare or tokens are accepted at rail transit stations. Bus drivers will accept $1 bills, but no change is given.

Special seasonal buses are provided to many of Atlanta's major attractions, such as Six Flags. They leave from Hightower Station; the fare is $1.85 each way.

For information about bus or rapid rail transit routes and services, call ☎ 404-848-4711 between 6 am and 10 pm, Monday through Friday.

Climate

Atlanta lies among the rolling hills of northwestern Georgia, some 1,000 feet above sea level. As a southern city, it enjoys mild winters, but its altitude protects it from extreme heat. The average temperature is 61° Fahrenheit, and temperatures rarely rise above 90° for more than three days in a row.

DINING OUT

To fully describe Atlanta's culinary scene would take a bigger book than this one. The cuisine of almost every country in the world and every region of the United States is represented. Even so, most offerings will have a distinctly Southern flavor. In fact, Southern cuisine is available everywhere in one form or another, from family-style to old-world, antebellum luxury. You might like to try one or two of the following:

Bone's Restaurant, in the Buckhead area at 3130 Piedmont Road NE, is open for lunch and dinner from 11:30 until 2:30, and 6 until 11. This restaurant features good, traditional American cuisine: aged prime beef, fresh seafood, lamb chops and veal in a New York-style club. ☎ 404-237-2663. $$$.

Nikolai's Roof, high atop the Atlanta Hilton at Courtland and Harris streets, is open for dinner from 6:30 each evening. The restaurant features fine dining and elegance. Formal attire is required. The cuisine is Russian and features such specialties as wild game and lamb. The service is outstanding; the waiters are dressed in traditional Cossack attire. Reservations are required. ☎ 404-659-3282. $$$$ and up.

Panos' and Pauls, at 1232 W. Places Road in North Atlanta, is open from 6:30 for dinner. The emphasis here is on Old World elegance and fine dining. The cuisine is continental. Gentlemen will need to wear a jacket and tie. Call ahead and make a reservation. ☎ 404-261-3662. $$$.

Pittypat's Porch, 25 International Boulevard NW, is open for dinner Monday through Saturday from 5 pm. The decor and cuisine are decidedly Southern. Very busy over the weekend. Call ahead and make a reservation. ☎ 404-525-8228. $$$.

Partners, a morningside café at 1397 North Highland Avenue, is open for dinner from 5:30. The menu is American and features a variety of beef and seafood dishes. Can be very busy at times. ☎ 404-876-8104.

The Savannah Fish Company, in the Westin Peachtree Plaza at Peachtree and International Boulevard, is open for lunch and dinner. If you're a seafood lover, you won't want to miss this one. They have a fresh seafood market and oyster bar; specialties include sautéed, broiled or blackened fish, steamed vegetables and fish stew, as well as a variety of dishes for the health-conscious. Very busy most of the time, so it's best to make a reservation for dinner. ☎ 404-589-7456. $$$.

WHERE TO STAY

There must be a thousand hotels and motels in the Greater Atlanta area, at least a half-dozen at every exit on all roads leading into the city. Rarely are any of them full, only during very special events, and even then a diligent search will find a room somewhere. So extensive is the choice you will probably do best by calling the reservation number of the chain you prefer and let them do the searching for you. Here are a few to help you get started:

Best Western Hotels	☎ 800-528-1234
Choice Hotels	☎ 800-424-6423
Courtyard by Marriott	☎ 800-321-2211
Days Inn	☎ 800-DAYS-INN
Hilton	☎ 800-445-8667
Holiday Inns	☎ 800-HOLIDAY
Howard Johnson	☎ 800-446-4656
Hyatt Hotels	☎ 800-233-1234
Marriott Hotels	☎ 800-228-9290
Ramada	☎ 800-228-2828
Radisson Hotels	☎ 800-333-3333
Scottish Inns	☎ 800-251-1962
Stouffer Hotels	☎ 800-468-3571

For further details – hotels, motels, camping and other visitor information – contact the Atlanta Area Convention and Visitors Bureau, 233 Peachtree Street, Atlanta, GA 30303. ☎ 404-521-6600.

Atlanta itself does not have many camping opportunities. There are, however, any number of smaller cities, state parks, and wilderness areas within a 40-mile radius that offer camping.

TOURIST INFORMATION

Atlanta Chamber of Commerce, 235 International Boulevard NW, PO Box 1740, Atlanta, GA 30301. ☎ 404-880-9000.
Atlanta Convention and Visitors Bureau, 233 Peachtree Street, Atlanta, GA 30303. ☎ 404-521-6600.

SIGHTSEEING IN TOWN

Atlanta's Botanical Gardens, in midtown's Piedmont Park, contains more than 30 acres of landscaped vegetable, herb, Japanese rock and rose gardens; more than 15 acres of hardwood forest with walking and nature trails, and a glass-enclosed conservatory for tropical, desert and endangered plants. The gardens are open Tuesday through Sunday from 9 until 7, the Conservatory from 10 until 7. Admission is $6; children under 6, free. ☎ 404-876-5859.

Atlanta Cyclorama, 800 Cherokee Avenue in Grant Park next to Zoo Atlanta, is home to one of our national treasures – the 42-foot by 358-foot painting in the round, "The Battle of Atlanta." With the latest in sound and light technology, this magnificent painting comes to life, creating a virtual reality setting where you'll step back in time to July 22, 1864, and become a part of the Battle of Atlanta. You'll sit on a revolving platform as the action is narrated in five languages; 3-D figures heighten the experience. The museum features all sorts of Civil War artifacts, uniforms and weapons, even a locomotive. There's also a bookstore and theater. Open daily, 9:30 until 5. Admission, $5; military and seniors, $4; children 6-12, $3. ☎ 404-658-7625.

Atlanta Heritage Row, 55 Upper Alabama Street, is the Museum at Underground (the below-street-level area of Atlanta, accessed by stairways and escalators), an interactive history museum that traces the history of Atlanta through photography, videos and a walk-through exhibition. You can witness the drama of the Civil War while huddled in a replica bomb shelter, board a turn-of-the-century trolley, listen to the famous words of Dr. Martin Luther King Jr., and pilot a plane into Atlanta's Hartsfield International Airport. Heritage Row is an experience you shouldn't miss. It's open Tuesday through Saturday from 10 until 5:30, and on Sunday from 1 until 5. Admission, $3; children 6-17, $2. ☎ 404-584-7879.

Metro Atlanta

1. Botanical Gardens/Woodruff Arts Center
2. Kennesaw Mountain Nat'l Battlefield Park
3. Stone Mountain State Park
4. Atlanta Cyclorama/Zoo Atlanta
5. Atlanta History Center
6. CNN Studios/World of Coca Cola
7. The Herndon Home
8. Oakland Cemetery
9. High Museum of Art
10. Wren's Nest
11. Six Flags Over Georgia

Atlanta History Center, 130 West Places Ferry Road NW, offers a comprehensive interpretation of Atlanta's history through two National Register Historic Houses – the 1840s Tullie Smith Farm and the 1928 Swan House. There is also a museum and an extensive research library, all set on more than 33 acres of beautifully landscaped period gardens. The exhibits trace Atlanta's development from its beginnings as a railroad junction to the present day, including an extensive Civil War exhibit. There's also a museum shop and café. Open Monday through Saturday from 10 until 5:30, and on Sunday from noon until 5:30. Admission, $7; children 6-17, $4; seniors and students with identification, $5. ☎ 404-814-4000.

CNN Studio Tour, at One CNN Center, Marietta Street and Techwood Drive, is a 45-minute guided walking tour of the news complex, including CNN Headline News, CNN International, the TBS Collection and the weather station. You'll see how the anchors and support staff prepare the programs and, from an overhead observation booth, watch them deliver the news. Tours start on a first-come, first-served basis at 8:30, and continue throughout the day at 15-minute intervals. Admission, $7; seniors, $5; children under 12, $4. ☎ 404-827-2300.

The Herndon Home, 587 University Place NW, was the residence of the famous Alonzo Herndon, a slave-born barber and founder of the Atlanta Life Insurance Company. Designed by Herndon and his wife, Adrienne, the 15-room mansion was built entirely by black craftsmen in 1910 and is on the National Register of Historic Places. The house is full of original antiques, works of art, original furniture, Roman and Venetian glass, and old silver. Open Tuesday through Saturday from 10 until 4; tours are conducted on the hour. Admission, free; donations are requested. ☎ 404-581-9813.

Martin Luther King Jr. Birth Home, 501 Auburn Avenue, is in the heart of the Martin Luther King Jr. National Historic Site. King was born in this house on January 15, 1929, and spent the first 12 years of his life here. Open daily from 10 until 5. Admission, free.

Martin Luther King Jr. National Historic Site, Auburn Avenue, is a 23-acre area that includes not only King's birthplace, but his grave and a large section of the surrounding residential and commercial section of Sweet Auburn, the center of Atlanta's black community during the 19th century. It also includes the Martin Luther King Jr. Center for Nonviolent Social Change housed in the Freedom Hall Complex. Open daily, 9 until 8 from early April through October, and from 9 until 5:30 the rest of the year. ☎ 404-524-1956.

Oakland Cemetery, 248 Oakland Avenue SW, is one of Atlanta's most beautiful and significant historic sites. Established in 1850, it is the final resting place of a diversity of Atlanta's citizens: paupers, mayors, governors and Civil War dead. They all rest together under a canopy of oaks and magnolias. Now on the National Register of Historic Places, it contains an incomparable collection of Victorian architecture on a rolling hillside just east of the state Capitol. You can visit the graves of Margaret Mitchell, author of *Gone With the Wind*, and legendary golfer Bob Jones. Open daily during the winter from 8 until 6, and during the summer from 8 until 7. Admission is free, but guided tours are available for $3; children, $1. ☎ 404-688-2107.

Old Courthouse on the Square, at Clairmont and Ponce de Leon Avenues, was DeKalb County's seat of justice until 1967. It's an historic building of Stone Mountain granite, now operated by the DeKalb County Historical Society, and offers a research library and archives, as well as a local history museum containing such exhibits as Chapman Powell's medicine still, Stephen Decatur's sword and DeKalb County's first electric light bulb. The courthouse grounds, a major Battle of Atlanta site, feature cannons, busts of Stephen Decatur and Baron DeKalb and the Confederate Memorial. Open Monday through Friday from 9 until 4, and the second Saturday of each month from 10 until 1. The archives are available by appointment only. Admission, free; donations requested. ☎ 404-373-1088.

Rhodes Hall, 1516 Peachtree Street, is one of the last great mansions on Peachtree Street, completed in 1904. It is reminiscent of a time when the street was a fashionable residential area and when Atlanta's first great fortunes were just beginning to be made. Its owner, Amos Rhodes, while on a trip to Europe during the late 1890s, was inspired by Germany's Rhineland castles. Thus, the home has towers, turrets and battlements, all built from Stone Mountain granite. Inside, you'll find one of Atlanta's finest existing Victorian interiors – ornate woodwork, murals, parquet floors, mosaics and a magnificent series of stained glass windows that surround a curved grand staircase. Open Monday through Friday from 11 until 4. Admission, $3; children under 12, $2. ☎ 404-885-7800.

Road to Tara Museum, Suite 600 on the concourse level of Georgian Terrace Hotel at 659 Peachtree Street, houses one of the largest collections of *Gone With the Wind* memorabilia in the country. Exhibits include a collection of dolls dressed as Scarlett O'Hara, original designer sketches and authentic reproductions.

Open Monday through Saturday from 10 until 6, and on Sunday from 1 until 5. Admission, $5; children 12-17, $3:50. ☎ 404-897-1939.

Woodruff Arts Center, 1280 Peachtree Street, is dedicated to the 122 members of the Atlanta Art Association killed in a Paris plane crash in 1962. The four-story center is dedicated to entertainment and education in the performing arts. Here you can enjoy works performed by the Atlanta Symphony and Alliance Theater. The center is also headquarters for the Atlanta College of Art, including the High Museum of Art. Open daily, 10 until 5. Free. ☎ 404-733-5000.

High Museum of Art, part of the Woodruff Art Center, is a modernistic building, four stories high, built of steel and sheathed in white ceramic panels with great windows and an atrium lit by skylights. Permanent exhibits include Italian art from the 14th through the 18th centuries, 19th-century French art, 19th- and -20th century American art, African art, photographs and prints. A visit to the museum is a rewarding experience and well worth the two or three hours it will take to complete. Open Tuesday through Saturday from 10 until 5, Friday from 5 until 9, and on Sunday from noon until 5. Admission, $6; children 6-17, $2; free to all on Thursday. Guided tours are available. ☎ 404-733-4200.

World of Coca-Cola, 55 Martin Luther King Jr. Drive at the corner of Central Avenue, is a 45,000-square-foot museum that interprets the history of Coca-Cola in Atlanta and around the world. Inside, you'll find all sorts of interactive displays and exhibits, along with some 1,200 artifacts that date from 1886 through the present. You can see video tapes that explain Coke's development from its invention, visit a soda fountain of the future, and sample Coke products not available in the United States. This is one of Atlanta's not-to-be-missed experiences. Open Monday through Saturday from 10 until 8:30, and on Sunday from noon until 5. Admission, $3.50; children 6-12, $2.50. ☎ 404-676-5151.

Wren's Nest, 1050 Ralph David Abernathy Boulevard, is Atlanta's oldest museum. The turn-of-the-century Wren's Nest was home to Joel Chandler Harris and his family from 1881 until 1908. Harris was 19th-century Georgia's most famous author, journalist, folklore authority, editor of the *Atlanta Constitution,* and author of 30 books. But perhaps he is most famous for preserving the African-American stories of Br'er Rabbit and Br'er Fox. You can tour the museum, which maintains a year-round series of story-telling programs for all ages. The museum shop sells Br'er Rabbit books and tapes. Open Tuesday through Saturday from 10 until 4, and on Sunday from 1 until 4. Admission, $4; children 4-12, $2. ☎ 404-753-7735.

Zoo Atlanta, 800 Cherokee Avenue SE, is home to more than 1,000 animals and birds. Set on 37 acres of parkland, it is famous for its children's zoo, where the kids can meet and interact with all sorts of small, friendly animals, domestic and exotic. The zoo's other exhibits include the Ford African Rain Forest, where the mountain gorillas live; Masai Mara, a small section of East Africa, seemingly lifted right out of the plains and transplanted in the heart of downtown Atlanta, where you can see giraffes, antelope and the endangered black rhino; the Ketambe exhibit, with its rare Sumatran tigers; and Flamingo Plaza, home to more than 50 of the strange pink birds. There's also a reptile house and a troop of monkeys. Refreshments are available, too. Open Monday through Friday from 10 until 4:30, Saturday and Sunday from 10 until 5:30, April through October; open daily the rest of the year from 10 until 4:30. Closed Martin Luther King Jr. Day, and other major holidays. Admission, $7.50; children 3-11, $5.50; seniors over 55, $6.50. ☎ 404-624-5678.

SIGHTSEEING OUT OF TOWN

Kennesaw Civil War Museum, 2829 Cherokee Street, Kennesaw, is a few miles northwest of the city via I-75; just take Exit 118 and follow the signs. The original "Great Locomotive Chase," made famous in several movies, began here in Kennesaw, then known as Big Shanty. The Andrews Raid was a daring but ill-considered Union attempt to disrupt Confederate communications and supply lines. Major James Andrews and a small group of soldiers stole a train pulled by the General locomotive and headed north to do as much damage as possible. The General survived the Civil War, but Andrews and his raiders did not. Most of them were executed. Andrews and his men were among the first recipients of the Medal of Honor. The General is housed in an authentic cotton gin, renovated especially for this famous old locomotive. The museum also houses a large number of Civil War artifacts, weapons and uniforms, and you can view a video interpretation of the raid. Open Monday through Saturday from 9:30 until 5:30, and from noon until 5:30 on Sunday. Admission, $3; children 7-15, $1.50; seniors, $2.50. ☎ 770-427-2117.

Kennesaw Mountain National Battlefield Park is three miles north of Marietta. and is well sign-posted and easily accessible either from US 41 or I-75 at Exit 116, just 20 miles north of Atlanta. There are picnic areas in and around the park, and several hiking trails. The trails start at the visitor center and vary in length from two to 16 miles. They are steep, strenuous, and there is no water or shelter along the way, so be prepared. Bring a camera and plenty to drink.

On May 4th, 1864, General William Tecumseh Sherman set out into the wilds of northwest Georgia with the intention of finding the Confederate Army of Tennessee under the command of General Joseph Eggleston Johnston. The aim was to bring him to battle and destroy him. For almost two months the two armies maneuvered for position. At the beginning of the campaign, Johnston's army numbered close to 70,000 men, and Sherman's almost 100,000. Time and again Sherman and Johnston faced off, and time and again, the wily General Johnston outmaneuvered his Federal opponent. But all the while he was being driven steadily southeast toward Atlanta, the supply center of the Confederacy.

Finally, by June 19, 1864, Sherman's army, now numbering well in excess of 100,000, had forced Johnston to withdraw almost to the outskirts of Atlanta. Johnston's army, now less than 66,000 strong, was occupying a well-prepared and heavily defended position on Kennesaw Mountain less than five miles from Marietta. It was here, he decided, that he would make his stand.

On June 24th, Sherman issued orders for his plan of battle. The main thrust was to be made by General George H. Thomas (The Rock of Chickamauga) and his Army of the Cumberland. He was to assault the enemy center, drive on through, and seize the Western and Atlantic Railroad to the south of Marietta. At the same time, General McPherson, commanding the Army of the Tennessee, would attack the Confederate line south of Kennesaw. Sherman was hoping that Thomas' attack at the Confederate center would cause Johnston to move troops northward to strengthen that position, thus leaving the southern position weak and vulnerable.

The morning of the 27th dawned bright and clear and promised a day of sweltering heat. Skirmishing began around six o'clock in the morning. At eight, the Federal artillery opened fire on the Confederate positions all along the ridge, and McPherson began his feint attack against the Confederate right flank.

The main attack against the mountain began at 8:15, while a secondary attack was made by General Morgan Smith further to the north against the strongly held Confederate positions on Pigeon Hill, a spur of the ridge attached to Little Kennesaw Mountain.

By 10:30 that morning things were not going well for Sherman's divisions. General Morgan Smith's division had all but withdrawn, having done little damage to the Confederate line of battle on the mountain. His attack had cost him more than 850 casualties; the Confederates had suffered less than 200. Meanwhile, 1½ miles away to the south, the main Federal attack on Cheatham Hill was in terrible trouble.

The area Sherman picked for his main thrust against the Confederate line was not a good one. The Confederate positions were a maze of formidable earthworks, dirt embankments and cleverly placed entanglements set out in front of the line of battle, giving little cover but making any advance extremely difficult. Defending these all but impregnable positions were the toughest and most battle-hardened Confederate troops in the entire Army of the Tennessee; two full divisions under the command of General Patrick Cleburne – the general who had inflicted the devastating defeat upon Sherman at Pickett's Mill – and General Benjamin F. Cheatham.

As the Yankee divisions burst from the trees into the valley in front of the lower slopes of Cheatham Hill, it became a Confederate turkey shoot. Thousands of muskets opened up all at once, but the Rebel cannon, more than 25 guns in five batteries, held their fire until, at a distance of less than 50 yards, they opened up a devastating barrage of double-loaded canister that decimated the advancing Federal ranks.

All through the long afternoon the various units continued skirmishing to little or no effect until, by the time darkness had fallen, the battle had dwindled and ended. Sherman had lost more than 3,000 of his men, including two of his best brigade commanders. General Johnston had lost only a third of that number. The battle of Kennesaw Mountain was Sherman's most devastating defeat of the Atlanta campaign.

Touring the Battlefield: You should begin your tour at the visitor center, where there is a video presentation of the battle and the events leading up to it. The center also has a fine museum with authentic uniforms, maps, photographs, artifacts found on and around the battlefield, and a bookstore.

The tour will take the best part of a day, and many miles of driving and walking.

The visitor center and the open fields around it are Stop 1. From there you'll drive to the top of the mountain to Stop 2, and then on to Stops 3, 4 and 5. Along the way there are several hiking trails that lead across the mountain and through the woodland to various significant points of the battlefield.

The visitor center is open from 8 until 5 daily. Kennesaw Mountain National Battlefield, 900 Kennesaw Mountain Drive, Kennesaw, GA 30152. ☎ 770-427-4686.

Six Flags Over Georgia, 12 miles west of downtown Atlanta, off I-20, is a theme park to rival any in the country, even those in and around Orlando, Florida. The 330-acre complex has more than 100 rides, shows and attractions, including NINJA: The Black Belt of Roller Coasters, which will turn you upside-down five times; a triple-loop roller coaster; a whitewater rafting adventure; and a 10-story freefall ride that will leave you breathless. The kids will love the roving Loony Tunes characters and soft play area. Throughout the day you'll enjoy audience-participation shows, Broadway musicals, high-diving exhibits and strolling musical groups. Open daily from 10 until late, Memorial Day through Labor Day; Saturday and Sunday only from mid-March until Memorial Day, and from Labor Day until October 31. Admission, all-inclusive, $28-$57; children 3-9, $19.05; seniors over 54, $14.29. Two-day admission is $32.38, all ages. ☎ 770-739-3400.

Smith Plantation Home, 935 Alpharetta Street in Roswell, was built around 1845 and features 11 of the original outbuildings, including a slave cabin, cookhouse, carriage house, barn, corncrib, and spring house; the 300-year-old white oak tree is the second largest in the state. The main two-story house, home to three generations of the Smith family, contains many original family furnishings. It is one of the best preserved ante-bellum plantation houses in Georgia, and a real example of how a well-to-do, mid-19th-century family lived. Tours Tuesday through Friday from 11 until 2, and on Saturday at 11, noon and 1. Admission, $5; children 6-16, $3. ☎ 770-641-3978.

The Ante-Bellum Plantation, a collection of buildings erected between 1790 and 1845 that portrays the lifestyles of well-to-do, and some not-so-well-to-do, 19th-century Georgians. These include the manor house, cookhouse, gardens, barnyard complex, slave cabins and an overseer's house; all authentically re-create the pre-Civil War days of a major Southern plantation. Open daily, from 10 until 8, June through August; 10 until 5:30 the rest of the year. Admission, $3; children 3-11, $2.

Stone Mountain Park, Highway 78 East, just 16 miles east of Atlanta's downtown district, is a 3,200-acre world of natural beauty and recreation. The signature is, of course, Stone Mountain itself, the world's single largest mass of exposed granite. Stone Mountain has been a popular tourist destination ever since the advent of the railroad in the 1830s made it accessible to all. The park has a number of special attractions and exhibits. You should expect to spend the day and most of the evening, and – if you take the family – a goodly amount of dollars. Admission to the attractions is very reasonable, but it does mount up, and food is always expensive. Of special interest are the following.

Stone Mountain looms over surrounding countryside.

Antique Auto and Music Museum has a number of interesting exhibits, including many vintage and classic autos and accessories, musical instruments and toys. Open daily from 10 until 8:30, June through August; 10 until 5:30 the rest of the year. Admission, $3; children 3-11, $2.

Bells of Stone Mountain: The bell tower rises 13 stories above the park and lakeshore. It's unique in that it uses miniature bell tone rods and amplification to create more than 700 bell sounds. Concerts are given Monday through Saturday at noon and 4, and on Sunday at 1, 3 and 5. Free.

Riverboat Cruises: You can take to the water on the *Scarlett O'Hara* for a 30-minute cruise with magnificent views of the mountain and shoreline. Cruises leave the dock every hour, June through August. Fare, $3; children 3-11, $2.

Scenic Railroad: You can board one of three old-time trains for a five-mile ride around the mountain. The trains are pulled by replicas of locomotives made famous by the Great Locomotive Chase. Train rides run from 10 until 8, June through August; 10 until 5:30 the rest of the year. Admission, $3; children 3-11, $2.

Swiss Skylift offers a cable-car ride to the summit of the mountain and the Plaza of Flags. The views of the great carvings and the surrounding countryside from the top are spectacular; don't miss this one. Rides run daily, weather permitting, from 10 until 8, June through August; 10 until 5:30, the rest of the year. Admission, $3; children 3-11, $2.

The carvings at Stone Mountain.

Stone Mountain Memorial Carvings is dedicated to the memory of three heroes of the Confederacy – Jefferson Davis, Robert E. Lee, and Stonewall Jackson. These carvings are the largest high relief sculpture in the world. The figures are colossal, the area of an entire city block. The one of Lee is as high as a nine-story building. Even so, they are small compared to the massive presence of the mountain.

Wildlife Trails, complete with running streams, allow you to enjoy the animals and plants in a scenic woodland setting. The kids can pet and feed the farm animals. Open daily from 10 until 8, June through August; 10 until 5:30 the rest of the year. Admission, $3; children 3-11, $2.

The park is open daily from 6 am until midnight; opening times for attractions vary. Admission to the park **Beach Complex** is $4; parking, $5. Admission tickets to all attractions are available at the park information center.

SHOPPING

Shopping in Atlanta is not a simple experience, at least as far as deciding where and when. It has more than 130 shopping centers.

The area around the downtown **Five Points** intersection is a modern bazaar, and perhaps one of the premier shopping locations in Atlanta, but the **Peachtree Center** just to the north contains the two largest wholesale markets in the Southeast, as well as a large number of other opportunities. To the west, the **Omni** offers a massive collection of shops, stores, boutiques, restaurants and cafés. Then there's Atlanta's **Underground** (although two stories of it are actually above ground). It offers a unique shopping experience among 12 acres of commercial district that have been in continuous operation since before the Civil War. The **Buckhead district** has a fashionable shopping area with lots of specialty shops, antique stores, art galleries and, of course, Lennox Square and Phipps Plaza Malls. And, if that's not enough, Atlanta is literally ringed with shopping malls: Southlake, Greenbriar, Northlake, Guinnett Place, Outlet Square, Perimeter, North Point, the Galleria, Cumberland, and others.

NIGHTLIFE

As Atlanta is an international city, a cultural melting pot, so its nightlife reflects its diversity. From loud to sophisticated, from rowdy to quiet, you can spend the evening dining and dancing, theater-going or bar-hopping. If you like country music, you'll find a number of bars and night spots to suit, but perhaps the best place to enjoy it is at the **Crystal Chandelier** at 1750 North Roberts Road in Kennesaw. Jazz enthusiast will be right at home in **Dante's Down the Hatch** at 3380 Peachtree Street. Progressive fans will want to dance the night away at Heaven, Hell and Purgatory, three nightclubs that comprise **Masquerade** at 695 North Avenue NE. The Omni is the place to go for big rock concerts.

But there's more, much more; far too much to cover here. For more information and a complete run-down of exactly what's available, contact the Atlanta Convention and Visitors Bureau, 233 Peachtree Street, Atlanta, GA 30303. ☎ 404-521-6600.

ANNUAL EVENTS

In April each year, the **Dogwood Festival** features a big parade, driving tours of Atlanta's residential neighborhoods, a hot-air balloon race, and lots of other special happenings. ☎ 404-892-0538.

The **Peachtree Road Race** is the premier 10K event in the Southeast. Each year, on July 4, more than 50,000 people run through the streets of downtown Atlanta. ☎ 404-521-6600.

In October each year, the Atlanta History Center holds its **Folklife Festival** at the Tullie Smith House. The festival include tours of the house and gardens, as well as demonstrations of such 19th-century crafts as pottery making, yarn spinning, candle dipping, weaving, blacksmithing, and dulcimer music. ☎ 404-814-4000.

In September, the **Arts Festival of Atlanta** is held in Piedmont Park. It features all the usual exhibits of paintings, sculpture, photography and other visual arts, as well as children's workshops,

puppet shows, and dance, music and theater performances.
☎ 404-521-6600.

Allatoona Lake

This vast waterworld, 30 miles northwest of Atlanta off I-75, is on
the Etowah River, a tributary of the Coosa River. It covers more
than 1,100 square miles, and is the Corps of Engineers' oldest
multipurpose project in their South Atlantic Division. Work began
on the site in 1941, but was discontinued at the outbreak of World
War II. The dam itself was completed in 1950. It's one of the most
frequently visited lakes in the nation. Each year, more than 13
million people head out from Atlanta and the surrounding
communities to enjoy time in the outdoors and on the water.

BIRDWATCHING & WILDLIFE

More than 23,000 acres of land adjacent to the lake are forested and
provide homes for a variety of wildlife. Birdwatchers can expect to
see all the usual common birds, along with hawks, owls,
woodpeckers, all sorts of songbirds and, if you're lucky, even the
bald eagle. The forests are also home to the bobcat, fox, wild turkey,
black bear, raccoon, deer, opossum and ground hog. Among the
plants and trees found in the forests around the lake are dogwood,
cherry, redbud, magnolia, gum, sycamore, oak, pine, beech,
hickory and ash.

BOATING & WATERSPORTS

With more than 12,000 acres of water surface available, there's
plenty of room to do your thing, be it fishing, sailing, skiing or
windsurfing. There are 13 swimming beaches in Corps of
Engineers-operated recreation areas and four more at state and
county parks. Eight commercial marinas around the lake provide
for all your boating needs, including rentals. The Corps operates
33 boat ramps, the marinas almost as many more, and the state and
county have them, too.

CAMPING

This is perhaps the best way to enjoy all that Allatoona has to offer. There are 11 campgrounds located at strategic points around the lake. Between them they provide more than 700 campsites, most with water and electric hookups, tables, grills, laundromats and modern bathhouses. And, even if your idea of "roughing it" means a hotel room complete with TV and telephone, you'll find that here, too.

Fees

Camping fees entitle a specified number of people to enjoy the full privileges of the campgrounds and parks, and those visiting campers also pay a modest fee. Visitors to Red Top Mountain State Park are charged, too. Other than that, all other activities in the Corps-operated recreation areas around the lake are free. There are no fees for day-use areas.

Security

Always an important consideration when choosing a campground. Security at all Corps-operated campgrounds, and at Red Top Mountain State Park, is excellent. Gates are locked at night and rangers patrol the grounds around the clock. In an emergency, there's always a number you can call if you need to leave the campground after lock-up.

FISHING

These are gamefish waters where you can hunt striped, white, largemouth, spotted and hybrid bass, along with crappie, sauger, catfish, various bream and sunfish. The lake is almost always busy, but it's still possible to get away from the boating fraternity. The best time to go is in the early morning on weekdays. Access points can be found at all Corps-operated recreation areas and at Red Top Mountain State Park.

HIKING

Many of the Corps-operated recreational areas have designated hiking trails, as does Red Top Mountain State Park, and there are more than 270 miles of shoreline for you to explore. Trails at the recreation areas and parks vary in length from a few hundred yards of pleasant walking to several miles of fairly stiff hiking through the forest. The areas with hiking trails are indicated in the text below.

HOW TO GET THERE

From Atlanta, take I-75 northwest, drive 25 miles and take any of the exits numbered 120 through 125. From each of the exits, feeder roads provide access to the lake. Also, from Atlanta, you can take I-75 northwest to its junction with I-575, where you'll turn north and drive toward Canton; again, a number of feeder roads provide easy access to the eastern section of the lake. From Tennessee, take I-75 southeast for 65 miles to Exits 125 through 120.

The Resource Manager's office is at the north end of the dam and can be reached by taking I-75 to Exit 125 near Cartersville, then GA 20 east to County Road 294N. Turn south there and drive on to the dam. ☎ 770-3820-4700.

WHERE TO STAY

Hotels and motels are located in small communities around the lake.

Acworth

Best Western Frontier Inn, off I-75 at Exit 120, has 120 rooms, a swimming pool, playground, coin-operated laundromat, and a cocktail lounge; there's a restaurant nearby. Pets OK. ☎ 770-974-0116. $.

Quality Inn, 4980 Cowan Road, off I-75 at Exit 120, has 60 rooms, a swimming pool, and there's a small restaurant close by. Pets OK. ☎ 770-974-1922. $.

Ramada Limited, off I-75 near Exit 120, has 40 rooms and there's a restaurant nearby. ☎ 770-975-9000. $.

Travelodge, at 5320 Bartow Road, off I-75 at Exit 120, is typical of the chain: clean, well-managed, and reasonable. All of the 40 rooms are equipped with reclining rockers and a hair dryer. There's a swimming pool, and a restaurant is conveniently close by. ☎ 770-974-5400. $.

Cartersville

Budget Host Inn, 851 Cass/White Road, off I-75 at Exit 127, is just that, a motel for travelers on a budget. It's clean, well-managed, has a swimming pool and a restaurant. Pets are welcome. ☎ 770-386-0350. $.

Days Inn, 5618 Highway 20SE, at Exit 125 on I-75, is typical of the chain: reliable and predictably clean. There's a restaurant next door and a complimentary continental breakfast is provided. ☎ 770-382-1824. $.

Holiday Inn, on I-75 at Exit 126, is good value for money. The rooms are clean, the restaurant service and food is better than most, and there's a lounge, an exercise room and whirlpool. ☎ 770-386-0830. $-$$.

Ramada Limited, 45 Highway 294SE at Exit 125 on I-75, is clean and functional, with a swimming pool and other limited facilities. A complimentary continental breakfast is available, and there's a nice restaurant close by. ☎ 770-382-1515. $-$$.

DINING OUT

Cartersville

There are several nice restaurants in the Cartersville area, though these are not on the level you'll find farther south in Atlanta:

Morrel's, 22 Highway 294 at Exit 120 on I-75, is open from 6 am until 10 pm for breakfast, lunch and dinner. The food is good, and the menu includes prime rib, chicken and barbecue. ☎ 770-382-1222. $.

Winston's, 463 East Main Street in the shopping center, is open between 11 and 10 for lunch and dinner. This is a sort of British pub, with a menu that includes what passes for English "pub grub," fish & chips (French fries), salads and burgers. You can eat inside or outdoors. Beer and other beverages are available in the bar. ☎ 770-387-9479. $.

CORPS RECREATION AREAS

Facilities around the lake – federal, state and county parks and recreation areas, and commercial marinas – are numerous. Each, numbered 1 through 42, is identified on the map and described below.

Allatoona Lake

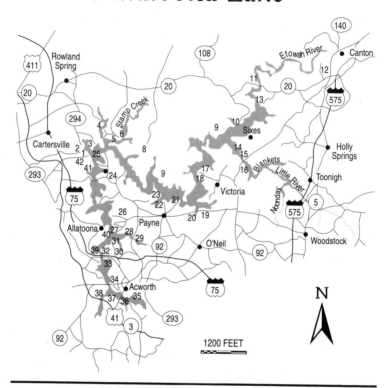

1. Resource Manager's Office and Visitor Center, off I-75 near Exit 125, on County Road 294N, is the best place to begin your visit to Allatoona. The view of the dam from there is unequaled. The visitor center features video displays and exhibits that interpret the history of the area and of the project. You can learn how the power of the great lake is harnessed to create electricity, and see an animated cutaway drawing of the dam. Open daily from 8; closing times vary with the seasons. ☎ 770-382-4700.

38. Allatoona Creek, off US 41 close to the junction with GA 92 (Dallas Road), near Acworth, covers eight acres on the western shore of the lake. Facilities are limited to 30 picnic tables, grills and restrooms.

39. Blockhouse, off GA 293 northwest of Acworth. Facilities include a small number of picnic sites with tables and grills, fresh drinking water, restrooms, fishing pier, and a boat dock and ramps. The area is handicapped-accessible.

16. Cherokee Mills, off Bell's Ferry Road on the eastern shore of the lake, is a boat ramp in one of the more remote areas of the project.

2. Coopers Branch 1 & 2, on the north side of the dam close to the visitor center, has two picnic shelters, 57 picnic sites with tables and grills, a swimming beach, boat ramp with two lanes and a playground for the kids, all set on 29 acres of parkland.

42. Cooper Furnace, also on the north side of the dam close to the visitor center, has two picnic shelters, 20 picnic sites with tables and grills and a playground for the kids.

34. Dallas Road, northwest of Acworth on the eastern shore of the lake, is reached via GA 92 and a network of feeder roads. Facilities include 81 acres, 50 picnic sites with tables and grills, a swimming beach and a one-lane boat ramp.

22. Galts Ferry, north of I-75 via Exit 120, is on the eastern shore of the lake north of Payne. Facilities at the 15-acre site include a picnic shelter, 30 picnic sites with tables and grills, fresh drinking water, restrooms, fishing pier, boat dock, boat ramp with three lanes, and a swimming beach. The area is handicapped-accessible.

19. Kellogg Creek, also north of I-75 via Exit 120, is on the eastern shore of the lake north of Payne. Facilities at the 27-acre site include a picnic shelter, 30 picnic sites with tables and grills, fresh drinking water, restrooms and a swimming beach. There are no boat launching facilities. The area is handicapped-accessible.

11. Knox Bridge, at the north of the eastern branch of the lake near Canton, is accessed via I-575 and GA 20. This is a small recreation area with facilities limited to a one-lane boat ramp.

14. Little River. From I-75, take Bell's Ferry Road exit and go north to the Little River Bridge; the recreation area is to the west on the north side. Again, facilities are limited to a boat ramp with one lane.

33. Old Highway 41, 1 & 2, on the lakeshore off GA 293 northwest of Acworth, is a pair of recreation areas totaling 26 acres. Facilities include two double-lane boat ramps, 52 picnic sites with tables and grills, a boat dock, two swimming beaches and a playground for the kids. Fresh drinking water is available, along with restrooms at both sites. Hiking – just walking, really – is also available on three short lakeside trails. The facilities are handicapped-accessible.

41. Riverside Park, on the south side of the dam, near the powerhouse, has a boat ramp with one lane, two picnic shelters, 28 picnic sites with tables and grills, and a playground for the kids. Fresh drinking water is available, along with restrooms. Hiking is also an option on a short woodland trail. The facilities are handicapped-accessible.

30. Tanyard Creek, northwest of I-75 Exit 120?, is a small recreation area with facilities limited to 20 picnic sites with tables and grills, restrooms, a boat ramp with three lanes, a dock and a small swimming area.

6. Wilderness Camp, no more than a public-access boat ramp, is north of the dam and east of Rowland Springs. From I-75, Exit 25, take GA 20 east and then turn south on the paved road just beyond Rogers Creek.

CORPS CAMPGROUNDS

37. Allatoona Proctor, on the south side of the lake, southwest of Acworth, off US 41, is a 35-acre campground with 44 tent and trailer sites, of which none have water and electric hookups. Other facilities are limited to 60 picnic sites with tables and grills, fresh drinking water, restrooms and a swimming beach. Fees: $10-$15. ☎ 770-382-4700.

28. Clark Creek North, on the north shore of the lake, off I-75, Exit 121, is a small campground with just 24 sites and group camp. Some of the sites do have water and electric hookups, along with picnic tables and grills. Other facilities include a comfort station with hot showers and flush toilets, handicapped-accessible restrooms, a sewage dumping station, laundromat and fresh drinking water. Fees: $10-$14. ☎ 770-382-4700.

29. Clark Creek South, on the south shore of the lake, off I-75, Exit 121, is the larger of the two campgrounds on Clark Creek. Of the 40 sites, 23 have water and electric hookups, picnic tables and grills. Other facilities include a comfort station with hot showers and flush toilets, handicapped-accessible restrooms, public-access picnic sites and a group shelter, a sewage dumping station, laundromat, fresh drinking water, a two-lane boat ramp, a dock and a swimming beach. Open April 1 through September. Fees: $10-$14. ☎ 770-382-4700.

8. Macedonia is on the eastern shore of the western branch of the lake, and is reached via a series of unpaved roads (Old Macedonia Road) from GA 20. This is one of the more remote campgrounds on Allatoona. Facilities here are limited to just 23 campsites – none with hookups – a restroom, fresh drinking water, boat ramp, and a few picnic tables and grills. Open year-round. ☎ 770-382-4700.

4. McKaskey Creek, east of I-75, Exit 124, at the extreme north of the western branch of the lake, via Highway 294N, is a nice, secluded campground with extensive facilities. These include 50 tent and trailer sites (30 have water and electric hookups), picnic tables and grills. Other facilities include a comfort station with hot showers and flush toilets, public-access picnic sites and a group shelter, a sewage dumping station, laundromat, fresh drinking water, a boat ramp with two lanes, a dock, a playground and a swimming beach. There's also a small store where you can buy the essentials. The campground is handicapped-accessible. Open March through November. Fees: $10-$14. ☎ 770-382-4700.

27. McKinney, off I-75 north of Acworth via Glade Road and Kings Camp Road, is a large campground on the eastern shore of the lake at the mouth of Clark Creek. Facilities are extensive and include 150 tent and trailer sites, of which 142 have water and electric hookups, with picnic tables and grills. Other facilities include a comfort station with hot showers and flush toilets, handicapped-accessible restrooms, public-access picnic sites and a group shelter, plus a sewage dumping station, laundromat, fresh drinking water, a boat ramp with one lane, a dock and two swimming beaches. Open March through November. Fees: $10-$14. ☎ 770-382-4700.

32. Old Highway 41 #3 is north of Acworth via Highway 293. Facilities include 50 tent and trailer sites, of which 26 have water and electric hookups, and picnic tables and grills. Other facilities include a comfort station with hot showers and flush toilets, handicapped-accessible restrooms, public-access picnic sites and a group shelter, a sewage dumping station, laundromat, fresh drinking water, a boat ramp with two lanes, a dock and a swimming beach. Open April 1 through September. Fees: $10-$14. ☎ 770-382-4700.

20. Payne is north of Acworth and I-75, Exit 120, via Old Highway 92. Facilities include 57 tent and trailer sites, of which 23 have water and electric hookups, plus picnic tables and grills. Other facilities include a comfort station with hot showers and flush toilets, picnic sites and a group shelter, a sewage dumping station, laundromat, fresh drinking water, a boat ramp with two lanes, a dock and a swimming beach. The campground is handicapped-accessible. Open March through November. Fees: $10-$14. ☎ 770-382-4700.

10. Sweetwater Creek, near Canton on the western shore of the eastern branch of the lake, is reached via Highway 20 and a feeder road that leads south from Sweetwater Corner Store. This is one of the most extensively developed of the Corps-operated campgrounds on Allatoona. There are 149 tent and trailer sites, of which 54 have water and electric hookups, with picnic tables and grills. Other facilities include a group campsite, comfort station with hot showers and flush toilets, public-access picnic sites and a group shelter, a sewage dumping station, laundromat, fresh drinking water, a boat ramp with one lane, a dock, playground for the kids and a swimming beach. There's also a very nice lakeside hiking trail. The campground is handicapped-accessible. Open April 1 through September. Fees: $10-$16. ☎ 770-382-4700.

7. Upper Stamp Creek, east of I-75, Exit 120? at the north end of the western branch of the lake, is reached via Highway 20 and a partially unpaved feeder road. This is a small campground with just 20 sites; none have hookups. Other facilities include toilets, public-access picnic sites, fresh drinking water and a boat ramp. Open year-round. Free. ☎ 770-382-4700.

18. Victoria, west of Woodstock on the eastern shore of the eastern branch of the lake, is reached via Highway 5 south from Woodstock, then west on Highway 92, north on 205 and, finally, west on the feeder road from Victoria. This is one of the more remote, less busy, of the Corps campgrounds. Of the 74 available sites, 64 have water and electric hookups, with picnic tables and grills. Other facilities include a comfort station with hot showers and flush toilets, public-access picnic sites, a sewage dumping station, laundromat, fresh drinking water, a boat ramp with two lanes, a dock and a swimming beach. The campground is handicapped-accessible. Open April 1 through September. Fees: $10-$14. ☎ 770-382-4700.

COMMERCIAL CAMPGROUNDS

Allatoona Campground Beach Marina is a lakeside family campground off I-75 at Exit 122 on Allatoona Road. This is, perhaps, the best developed campground on the lake. Facilities include 129 shaded, paved sites, of which 22 have full hookups, 104 water and electric only, and the rest have no hookups at all. The bathhouse is modern with flush toilets and hot showers; sewage disposal is available to guests; there's also a laundromat, a full-service grocery store that sells the essentials, as well as LP gas by weight or meter; ice is also available. There's a recreation hall, pavilion, swimming pool, boat rentals, lots of court games, a sports field and several hiking trails – lakeside and woodland. A recreation director is on hand to help make your stay as productive and pleasant as possible. Security is good; the campground is gated, with a guard on duty, and locked up at night. Open year-round. Fees start around $16 for two persons per night. ☎ 800-346-7305.

Holiday Marine Harbor & Campground is a lakeside facility with shaded sites on a woodland hillside on the eastern shore of the lake at the mouth of Clark Creek. To find it, from I-75, go east on Glade Road to Tapper Creek Road, turn north, and drive to Groover's Landing Road; the campground is a half-mile farther on. Facilities include 57 sites, of which 39 have water and electric hookups. The bathhouse has flush toilets and hot showers; sewage disposal is offered; there's also a laundromat, a small grocery store for essentials, as well as LP gas by weight or meter; ice is also available. Recreational facilities include a recreation hall, swimming beach, boat rentals, and a boat ramp and dock. Open year-round. Fees start around $15 for two persons per night. ☎ 770-974-2575.

Whispering Pines is a woodland campground close to the lake and can be reached via I-75, Exit 120, and Highway 92. Facilities include 121 sites, of which 82 have full hookups – water, electric, sewage – and 39 offer water and electric only. The bathhouse is kept clean and has flush toilets and hot showers; sewage disposal is available to guests; there's also a laundromat, a small grocery store for the basics, as well as LP gas by weight or meter and ice. There's a recreation hall, swimming pool and several hiking trails – lakeside and woodland. No tents. Open year-round. Fees start around $15 for two persons per night. ☎ 770-974-7380.

RECREATION AREAS & PARKS

35. Acworth Beach, inside the city limits on the north shore of the lake, is the place for a pleasant afternoon in the sun. Facilities include a boat ramp, picnic sites, picnic shelter, fresh drinking water, restrooms and a swimming beach. The park is handicapped-accessible.

9. Allatoona Wildlife Management Area, on the north shore of the lake, is reached via a series of gravel roads from Highway 20. It's a vast wilderness area that takes in many miles of forested shoreline in Bartow and Cherokee counties. There are no facilities here, only the birds, animals and trees. It's a remote area.

23. Bartow Carver Park, on the south shore of the lake, east of Red Top Mountain State Park, can be reached via Exit 123 or Exit

121 off I-75. In either case, just follow the signs for Red Top Mountain State Park; Bartow Carver is at the end of the feeder road. Facilities include a picnic shelter, tables, grills, a boat ramp, playground for the kids, fresh drinking water and restrooms.

3. Bartow County Park is close to the Resource Manager's Office and visitor center at the main dam, off I-75 near Exit 125, on County Road 294N. This is a full-service park. Facilities include 32 campsites, some with water and electric hookups, two picnic shelters, 24 picnic sites, tables, grills, fresh drinking water, restrooms, a boat ramp with two lanes, a swimming beach and a playground. For camping information, contact the Resource Manager's Office, ☎ 770-3820-4700.

12. Canton City Park, west of Canton off GA 5 via Highway 20, has a picnic shelter, tables, grills, fresh drinking water and restrooms. There's also a lakeside walking trail that makes for a very pleasant afternoon out.

13. Cherokee County Park, west of Canton on the eastern shore of the lake, is reached via Highway 20 and a short, paved feeder road. Though it has somewhat limited facilities – just a picnic shelter, four picnic sites and a boat ramp – this 10-acre facility in a fairly remote spot provides for a quiet afternoon beside the lake.

36. Cobb Regional Park, off US 41 and Highway 92, south of Acworth on the southern shore of the lake, has just three picnic shelters and restrooms. Even so, it's a nice, well-kept park and a great place to go walking or shore fishing.

24. Red Top Mountain State Park is two miles east of I-75 via Exit 123. Named for the color of its earth – the region is rich in iron ore and once was an important mining district – this is one of the most extensively developed and popular parks on the lake. The 1,950-acre facility is on a peninsula west of the Corps of Engineers' Visitor Center across the lake. The fine fishing is probably the park's main attraction, but the wildlife and the chance to explore make it an ideal getaway, especially for an extended family outing. And you don't have to rough it. Every type of accommodation is available, from primitive campsites to the very best in hotels to rental cabins. And there's more, much more.

Camping facilities include 125 tent and trailer sites with water and electric hookups, tables, grills, comfort stations with hot showers and flush toilets, a dumping station, and a store where you can buy supplies, as well as souvenirs and hand-made crafts. Fees: $12-$16.

There are 18 rental cottages, complete with all you need to set up housekeeping for a couple of days, or even a couple of weeks. $. For those who like more than a roof overhead, there's a 33-room lodge ($$) that rivals some of the better hotels in the area, even Atlanta. Facilities include a full-service restaurant – and the food is very good – a swimming pool, tennis courts, restrooms, picnic shelters, picnic sites, grills, a playground for the kids, fresh drinking water, boat ramps, a dock and a swimming beach. There's also a marina with two boat ramps and five docks where you can rent a boat or canoe, fishing tackle and purchase boating supplies.

More than seven miles of hiking, walking and nature trails that meander through the forest, up the mountain, and along the lake shore. These make an ideal environment for nature study, birdwatching and wildlife photography. Animals, especially deer, are used to the human presence and can often be seen on the trails and park roads.

Open from 7 am until 10 pm; the park office is open from 8 to 5. For lodge and cabin reservations, contact Red Top Mountain State Park & Lodge, 653 Red Top Mountain Rd. SE, Cartersville, GA 30120. ☎ 770-975-0055.

COMMERCIAL MARINAS

The following is a list of commercial marinas operating on the lake. Most have extensive facilities, including a store, boat ramps and docks, fuel docks, and boat rentals. Fishing tackle is available – for sale or rent – at most facilities, along with camping and boating supplies. Telephone numbers are included and each is numbered for easy location on the map.

5. **Wilderness Camp**	☎ 770-382-9066
15. **Little River Landing**	☎ 770-345-6200
17. **Victoria Landing**	☎ 770-926-7718
21. **Galts Ferry Marina**	☎ 770-974-6422
25. **Park Marina**	☎ 770-974-6063
26. **Glade Marina**	☎ 770-974-6710
31. **Holiday Marina**	☎ 770-974-2574
40. **Allatoona Landing**	☎ 770-974-6089

Athens

The main claim to fame here is the University of Georgia, but it's also an old community, incorporated in 1806. Thus it's one of Georgia's better preserved ante-bellum cities, with old mansions –

some of which are open to visitors – boxwood gardens and pleasant city walks.

Athens is some 60 miles east of Atlanta. Take US 78 from Atlanta and drive east.

WHERE TO STAY

Best Western Colonial Inn, 107 North Milledge, has a restaurant, swimming pool, and provides a complimentary continental breakfast. Pets are welcome. ☎ 706-546-7311. $ (Expect higher rates when there's a university home game).

Holiday Inn, at Broad and Lumpkin streets adjacent to the university, is one of the better examples of the chain. Facilities are extensive and include a luxury level in the Executive Tower, a restaurant – the food and service are excellent – a bar, an indoor swimming pool, an exercise room and a whirlpool. ☎ 706-549-4433. $$, higher when there's a home game at the university.

Ramada Inn, 513 West Broad Street, is typical of the chain, but the service is good, the staff friendly, and facilities provide all you need for a pleasant stay. There's a restaurant – a complimentary continental breakfast is provided – a pool and entertainment Tuesday through Saturday. Pets are welcome. ☎ 706-546-8122. $-$$.

DINING OUT

For something a little different, try the **Varsity** at 1000 West Broad Street. It's open for breakfast, lunch and dinner, and specializes in excellent hamburgers and hot dogs. ☎ 706-548-6325. $.

SIGHTSEEING

You can take a tour of the city's historic homes, including the Taylor-Grady House, 1839; Church-Waddel-Brumby House, 1820; University President's House, 1855; Founder's Memorial Gardens and House, 1857; Ross Crabne House, 1842, and others. Contact the Athens Convention and Visitors Bureau, 220 College Avenue, 7th Floor, 3063. For information, ☎ 706-546-1085.

Georgia Museum of Art, on the university campus, contains several permanent collections, including the Eva Underhill Holbrook Collection, and others. Open daily. Admission, free. ☎ 706-542-3255.

State Botanical Gardens, 2450 South Milledge Avenue, on the university campus, covers some 300 acres and is home to a variety of wildlife and rare plants. Nature trails meander through the gardens. They and the conservatory provide unique opportunities for study and a quiet afternoon out. Admission, free. Open daily. ☎ 706-542-1244.

Collegiate Tennis Hall of Fame, Henry Field Tennis Stadium on the university campus, honors the great college players of the past 100 years. Open during tennis tournaments and home football games. Admission, free. ☎ 706-542-1622.

City Hall Lawn, at College and Hancock Avenues. If you're a Civil War buff, you should check out the unique, double-barreled cannon that sits on the lawn. It was cast at the Athens foundry in 1863 and is thought to be the only one of its type in the world.

The Tree That Owns Itself, at Dearing and Finley streets, is a white oak, the descendent of the original tree that once stood on the spot. What's unique about it? Well, it stands on a plot that's deeded to it, so it owns itself, "believe it or not."

Sandy Creek Park, north of the city on US 441, is an outdoor playground with a swimming beach, tennis courts, basketball courts, playgrounds for the kids, picnic shelters and sites and grills. The fishing is good — crappie, bluegill, sunfish, bream, catfish, etc. — and you can hike or walk the easy trails. Open daily except Wednesday, April through September; Thursday through Sunday the rest of the year. ☎ 706-613-3631.

Sandy Creek Nature Center, off US 41 a half-mile north of the city, is a 200-acre park with live animal exhibits, a 180-year-old cabin, and several nature trails. It's quiet place to spend a few hours walking. Open Monday through Friday, and on Saturday afternoons. Admission, free. ☎ 706-613-3615.

ANNUAL EVENTS

Tour of Historic Homes, last weekend in April. ☎ 706-353-1801.

Marigold Festival, in Winterville the weekend after Father's Day, includes hand-made crafts, antiques and parades. ☎ 706-742-8600.

Crackerland Tennis Tournament, at the Henry Field Tennis Stadium on the university campus, is held at the end of July for juniors, and mid-August for seniors. ☎ 706-542-3354.

Northern Georgia Folk Festival, held at Sandy Creek Park, usually at the end of September. ☎ 706-613-3620.

Augusta

While Atlanta is the premier city in the Piedmont Region, Augusta is the oldest. In fact, it's the second oldest city in the state. Located on the south bank of the Savannah River, it serves the South as an agricultural and manufacturing center.

Often called the Garden City of the South, Augusta has wide, pleasant streets lined with magnolia trees. The city has many fine old mansions. Most were built during the early part of the 19th century and, fortunately, spared by General Sherman. Of special interest is the First Presbyterian Church and its manse, where President Woodrow Wilson lived as a boy. In April each year the world watches as the Masters Invitational Golf Tournament is played at the Augusta National Golf Course.

Named for the Princess of Wales, the mother of King George III, Augusta was founded in 1735 by James Oglethorpe. First, the river city served as an Indian fur-trading post, then as a military outpost for Savannah. Occupation by the British during the American Revolution and the subsequent siege by colonial forces left the countryside around Augusta devastated. But the town was rebuilt and, after war, served as state capital from 1786 to 1795. The immigration of tobacco planters from Virginia during the last quarter of the 18th century brought new industry to the region. The advent of Eli Whitney's cotton gin in 1793 brought even more prosperity. By the turn of the 19th century, Augusta was the second largest inland cotton market in the world. A railroad to Savannah began operating in 1854. Augusta saw more than its fair share of the Civil War. The United States arsenal was quickly taken by the Confederates, and the city became the South's principal supplier of munitions.

Although it was in Sherman's path from Atlanta to Savannah and was the site of the main Confederate powder works, Augusta was spared the Union general's torch. And then came reconstruction. The cotton industry was no more, the countryside lay bare, and the resourses of the area's leading families were seriously depleted. But Augusta had one asset that no war could destroy – its climate. By the 1890s, Augusta had become a major resort area, and many of its citizens opened their homes to paying guests. Augusta's first nine-hole golf course was built during the same period by one of the city's hoteliers. The new game from Scotland proved so popular with his guests that the following year an 18-hole course was built on what was soon to become the Augusta Country Club.

Augusta

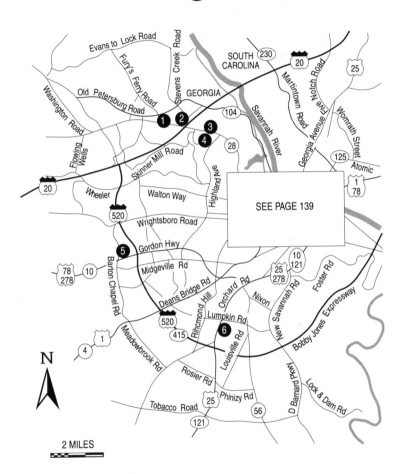

1. National Science Center/Discovery Center
2. Confederate Monument
3. Gertrude Herbert Institute of Art
4. Augusta-Richmond County Convention & Visitors Bureau
5. Ezekiel Harris House
6. Lucy Craft Laney House/Museum

HOW TO GET THERE

By Road

Augusta's main link with the rest of the world is I-20, which connects it with Atlanta to the west and Columbia, South Carolina, to the east. US 25 is the main link north and south.

By Air

Bush Field is Augusta's municipal airport. Served by Delta with regular service to Atlanta, and by USAir Express to Charlotte, NC, the city is easily accessible by air.

By Bus

Greyhound/Trailways. ☎ 404-522-6300, or 1-800-231-2222.

By Rail

Amtrak. ☎ 800-USA-RAIL.

WHEN YOU ARE THERE

The majority of Augusta's attractions are closed on Sunday, Monday and most major holidays.

Entrance fees are, on the whole, very reasonable, averaging $2 for adults and $1 for children.

To make the most of your time in Augusta, you should start at the visitors center, 32 Eighth Street, where you can get detailed maps, brochures and other useful information.

Getting Around

Augusta is laid out like most other Southern cities on the grid system, with its downtown streets running roughly north-south and east-west. The city is ringed by I-520/Bobby Jones Expressway, which is accessed from I-20 at Exit 64. Traffic in the downtown business district can be heavy during rush hours, 7 until 9, and 3:30 until 6, so it's best to avoid the roads during those hours if you can. Other that that, Augusta is easy to negotiate.

All major **car rental** companies are represented at the airport, and metered parking is available on the streets in some areas; other city sections are served by garages, of which there are plenty.

Augusta has a comprehensive **public transportation** service, with routes serving most sections of the city on a regular schedule. **Augusta Public Transit,** ☎ 706-722-0848.

DINING OUT

Augusta is a diverse culinary world. Almost every ethnic cuisine is available; almost every American region is represented; and, as close as it is to the coast, fresh seafood is readily available almost everywhere. The following will start you off.

Calvert's, 475 Highland Avenue, is open for dinner from 5 until 10. Fine, elegant dining is the focus here. Dark paneling, candlelight, fresh seafood, beef and veal, along with a selection of fine wines. It's a good idea to make a reservation, especially on Friday and Saturday. ☎ 706-738-4514. $$.

French Market Grille, in the Surrey Center at 425 Highland Avenue, is arguably one of Augusta's best restaurants. The menu is mostly Cajun or Creole with such specialties as filé gumbo, crawfish étouffée and honey-pecan fried chicken. It can be very busy at times, but well worth a try. Open for lunch and dinner. ☎ 706-737-4865. $$.

T's Restaurant, Highway 56 just south of the Bobby Jones Expressway at Exit 7, is the place to go if you're a seafood lover. The menu includes catfish, fresh shrimp, crab legs and fresh oysters. This is one of Augusta's old, well-established houses. The food is excellent and the service is just as good. Open for dinner. ☎ 706-798-4145. $$.

Villa Europa, Highway 1, just off the Bobby Jones Expressway at Exit 5B, is open for lunch from 11 and dinner from 5. Basically a German-style restaurant serving such specialties as *rahmschnitzel* and *sauerbraten*, but you can also get a good prime rib or even lasagne. Adventurous? Try the *escargots de Bourgogne*. Best on weekends. ☎ 706-798-6211. $$.

WHERE TO STAY

There are plenty of rooms in Augusta, from the top-of-the-line luxury hotels to the mom-'n-pop motel on the corner.

Admiral Inn, 3320 Dean's Bridge Road, ☎ 706-793-9600. A smaller motel with just the basics available. No pets. Restaurant nearby. $.

Courtyard by Marriott Augusta, 1045 Steven's Creek Road at Exit 65 on I-20. ☎ 706-737-3737. Typical of the chain; a nice restaurant open for breakfast, lunch and dinner; heated pool, whirlpool and exercise room. No pets. $-$$.

Hampton Inn, 330 Washington Road northwest of Exit 65 on I-20. Always predictable: clean rooms, economical, pool, whirlpool, exercise room, but no restaurant (there's one within walking distance). No pets. ☎ 706-737-1122. $.

Holiday Inn Express, 1103 15th Street, is economical and predictable. Little in the way of facilities, but most of what you need is available close by. No pets. ☎ 706-714-5560. $.

The Partridge Inn, 2110 Walton Way just off 15th Street, is one of Augusta's historic hotels. Built around 1890, the emphasis is on Southern hospitality. Nice restaurant, buffet breakfast, complimentary beverages, health club privileges, valet parking. Some rooms have kitchens. ☎ 706-737-8888. $-$$.

Perrin Guest House Inn, 208 Lafayette Drive, is a small, two-story, bed and breakfast inn. Expensive, but you do get value for money. ☎ 706-731-0920. $$.

For further information on hotels, motels, camping and other topics, contact the Augusta Convention and Visitors Bureau, 32 Eighth Street, Augusta, GA 30901. ☎ 706-823-6600 or 800-726-0243; fax 706-823-6609.

TOURIST INFORMATION

Augusta-Richmond County Convention and Visitors Bureau, 32 Eighth Street, Augusta, GA 30901. ☎ 706-823-6600 or 800-726-0243; fax 706-823-6609.

SIGHTSEEING

Like Savannah, Augusta is one of Georgia's historic sites with an old-world downtown district, renovated, and returned to its former glory as one of the ante-bellum South's premier cities. The **Olde Towne historic district** is filled with the fine homes of yesteryear. The **Summerfield district**, once a haven for wealthy visitors from the north, is another old and affluent section of the city. You should be sure to visit both.

Brochures and maps for self-guided walking and driving tours of Augusta's historic sites are available at the visitors bureau. The following are just a few of the sights you'll not want to miss.

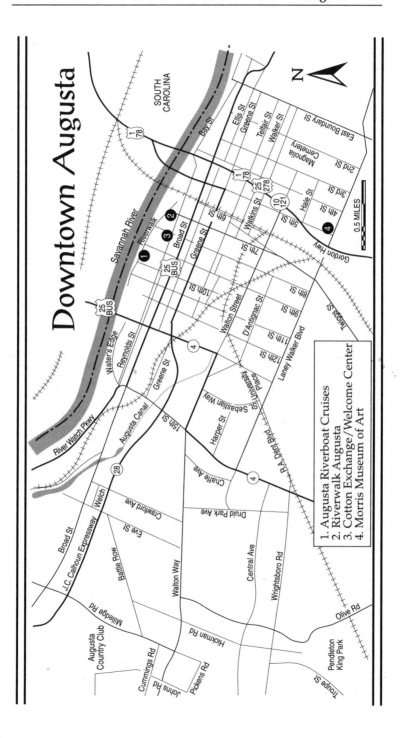

Downtown Augusta

1. Augusta Riverboat Cruises
2. Riverwalk Augusta
3. Cotton Exchange/Welcome Center
4. Morris Museum of Art

Augusta Riverboat Cruises present a unique look at the old city, its surroundings, and the Savannah River. Cruises leave the dock on 10th Street at Riverwalk aboard a replica of a 19th-century stern-wheeler. From February through December, you can take a sightseeing, dinner dance or luncheon cruise. Fares range from $7.50 for an afternoon sightseeing cruise to $36 for the dinner dance, with varying rates in between. Children and seniors receive discounts. ☎ 706-722-5020.

Confederate Monument, on Broad Street between 7th and 8th streets, is a marble obelisk dominated by a statue of a Confederate private soldier, with life-sized figures of Robert E. Lee and Stonewall Jackson.

Confederate Powder Works, 1717 Goodrich Street, is another monument to Augusta's Civil War past and Confederate dead. All that's left of the munitions plant, once the second largest in the world, is its chimney. Standing 176 feet tall, it's a stark reminder of the city's contribution to the Cause.

Gertrude Herbert Institute of Art, 506 Talfair Street, is housed in a three-story Federalist-style house built in 1818 by Nicholas Ware, a Georgia legislator. Even then it was famous for its great cost, more than $40,000, and became known locally as Ware's Folly. Today it contains works by local and nationally known artists. Open Tuesday through Friday from 10 until 5, and on Saturday from 10 until 2. Admission, $2; children 8-12, $1. ☎ 706-724-4174.

This classic building houses the Gertrude Herbert Institute of Art.

Ezekiel Harris House, 1822 Broad Street, was used by visiting tobacco merchants. Built in 1797, the Federalist-style house is furnished with period pieces and displays of artifacts found on the grounds. Open Tuesday through Friday from 1 until 4, and on Saturday from 10 until 1. Admission, $2; children 5-17, $1. ☎ 706-724-0436.

Fort Discovery/National Science Center. Housed in a 128,000-square-foot building on Riverwalk, this high-tech science playground opened in the fall of 1996 as a joint public-private partnership between the US Army and NSC Discovery Inc., a non-profit organization. The facility has a high-tech theater and many interactive exhibits that focus on electronics, computer arts and communications. Open daily from 10 until 5. Admission, $3; children, $1.

Georgia Golf Hall of Fame, scheduled to open in spring, 1998, on Riverwalk, this facility will highlight two of Augusta's claims to fame: golf and gardens. It will contain a museum highlighting the more than 30 members of the Hall of Fame, the Bobby Jones Theater, and high-tech golf displays. An interactive exhibit will put the golf club in your hands and enable you to swing at some of the world's most famous courses to sounds of an enthusiastic gallery – all very exciting.

Lucy Craft Laney Museum of Black History, 1116 Philip Street, is the former home of one of the most influential black educators in America. This lady saw education as the key to the progress of blacks in America. She founded the Haines Normal Institute in 1883 in the lecture room of Christ Presbyterian Church in 1883. The home, now owned by Delta Sigma Theta Sorority, contains many period pieces and is open for tours by appointment. ☎ 706-724-3576.

Meadow Garden, 1320 Independence Drive near the Augusta Canal, is the former home of George Walton, a signer of the Declaration of Independence. It is now a museum opened by the Daughters of the American Revolution. Open Monday through Friday from 10 until 4. Admission, $3; children, $1. ☎ 706-724-4174.

Morris Museum of Art, at One 10th Street, houses one of the finest collections of 18th-century art, portraits, still lifes and contemporary art in the South. Open Tuesday through Saturday from 10 until 5:30, and on Sunday from 12:30 until 5:30. Admission, $2; children 12-18, $1; children under 12, free. ☎ 706-724-7501.

Poet's Monument, on Green Street, honors some of Georgia's most famous scribes: Sidney Lanier, James R. Randall, Paul Hamilton Hayne and Father Ryan.

Riverwalk Augusta, at Eighth and Reynolds streets, with breathtaking views of the Savannah River, spans more than eight city blocks. It has become one of the Georgia's foremost attractions and a popular venue for special events, as well as for picnics, starlit walks and a year-round display of seasonal flowers that turn the walk red, pink, orange, yellow and purple.

The Cotton Exchange, also on Eighth Street, houses Augusta's Welcome Center. Here you can find all the information you need to make your stay in the city as pleasant and productive as possible. ☎ 706-823-6600.

Signer's Monument, on Green Street between 4th and 5th streets, is the final resting place of two of the signers of the Declaration of Independence: George Walton and Lyman Hall.

SHOPPING

Shopping in Augusta can be a unique experience. The downtown district, especially **Broad Street,** has survived the advent of the perimeter mall. There are more than 30 antique stores, a dozen art galleries, and many more specialty shops, stores, restaurants and cafés, all served by pleasant pedestrian walkways. If it's mall shopping you enjoy, try the **Augusta Mall**, at 3450 Wainright Road; **Regency Mall**, at 1700 Gordon Highway; and the **Surrey Center**, at 483 Wylds Road. they offer a couple of hundred shops, stores, restaurants and cafés, all under cover, with plenty of parking.

CAMPING

There are a couple of commercial campgrounds in the closer Augusta area. Neither are very big, but they do offer most of what's needed for a pleasant stay.

Flynn's Inn Camping Village, on Peach Orchard Road, has 56 sites, of which 46 have full hookups; 12 are pull-throughs. Other facilities include a modern bathhouse with flush toilets and hot showers, a laundromat and a sewage dumping facility. Rates start around $14 for two persons. Take Exit 6 off I-520, and drive 3½ miles south on Highway 25 (Peach Orchard Road) ☎ 706-796-8214.

Fox Hollow Camp Grounds, also on Peach Orchard Road, has 31 sites, of which 21 have full hookups. Other facilities include a bathhouse with flush toilets and hot showers, picnic tables and sewage disposal. Rates start around $12 for two persons. Take Exit 6 off I-520, then drive 3½ miles south on Highway 25 (Peach Orchard Road). ☎ 706-592-4563.

John Tanner State Park

John Tanner offers some of the best recreational facilities anywhere in the Georgia. You can enjoy a simple day out in the park, a getaway weekend, or even a couple of weeks of outdoor vacationing. There's great fishing, boating and swimming on two lakes, hiking on backcountry trails, and the largest sandy beach to be found in any of Georgia's state parks. If it's nightlife you're looking for, Atlanta is only half an hour away to the east along I-20.

Major facilities include 78 **tent and trailer sites**, a group lodge, a six-unit motor lodge and a miniature golf course.

Popular activities include hiking the exercise and nature trails, and boating; boat rentals are available by the hour, the half-day, and the full day (private boats are permitted but only powered by electric motors).

Annual special events include an Arts & Crafts Show in the fall, a Triathlon in the summer, and Christmas in Georgia held in mid-December.

Nearby attractions include the Sweetwater Creek State Park in Atlanta, and the Six Flags Over Georgia Theme Park.

The park is open from 7 am to 10 pm and the park office is open from 8 am until 5 pm.

For information and reservations, contact the John Tanner State Park, 354 Tanner's Beach Road, Carrollton, GA 30117. ☎ 404-830-2222.

The park is six miles west of Carrollton off GA 16.

Cartersville

A small community west of Allatoona Lake, Cartersville has a couple of attractions you might like to see.

SIGHTSEEING

Etowah Indian Mounds State Historic Site is five miles southwest of I-75, Exit 124. These flat-topped mounds – the largest is more than 60 feet high and covers more than three acres – were the nucleus of an important religious center and home to several thousand Indians. The mounds were, in fact, the platforms for the temple, the High-Priest's home, and the burial grounds of the Etowah Indians from around 1000 to 1500 AD. Artifacts found at

Etowah Indian carvings.

the site and now on display in the museum help us to understand the lives and culture of the Indians. Exhibits include tools and ceremonial objects made of stone, wood, shell, and copper.

Annual events include an Indian Skills Day in spring, Artifacts Identification Day in April and November, and several astronomy programs.

Open year-round from Tuesday to Saturday, 9 to 5, and on Sunday from 2 to 5. Admission, $2; children 6-18, $1.

Etowah Indian Mounds State Historic Site, 813 Indian Mounds Rd. SW, Cartersville, GA 30120. ☎ 770-387-3747.

William Weinman Mineral Museum, one block from Exit 126, I-75, on US 441, is where you'll learn all about Georgia's geological history and the rocks and minerals found in the local area. Exhibits include a walk-in replica of a limestone cave with a waterfall, fossils, Indian artifacts, displays that interpret the history of mining, gemstone cutting and a slide show. Open Tuesday through Saturday from 10 until 4:30, and on Sunday from 2 until 4:30. Admission, $3; children 6-11, $2; seniors over 54, $2.50. ☎ 770-386-0576.

Clarks Hill/J. Strom Thurmond Lake

Located some 22 miles north of Augusta, the Thurmond Dam and Lake is the first and largest US Army Corps of Engineers project east of the Mississippi. Work began in 1946 and was completed in 1956 on this comprehensive flood control development for the Savannah River. The result, beyond all the flood control benefits to the surrounding countryside and communities, was one of the largest and most diverse outdoor recreation areas in the Southeast. For more than 40 miles the great lake stretches northward up the Savannah River, and for 26 miles up the Little River from Georgia into South Carolina. It covers more than 70,000 acres, with some 1,200 miles of shoreline, making it one of the largest inland bodies of water in the South. The entire project includes more than 150,000 acres of land and water, six state parks (three in Georgia and three in South Carolina), five county parks, 13 Corps campgrounds, five commercial marinas, 10 recreation areas, more than 100 islands, and a diversity of plant and animal life that includes many endangered species, the most notable of which is the red-cockaded woodpecker. The dam itself is more than a mile long and 200 feet high, a concrete causeway flanked by earth embankments.

The region covered by the Thurmond Project is also rich in history. During the early 1800s it was the scene of the nation's first gold rush. Before that it was home to the Shawnee, Cherokee, Creek, Chickasaw and Yuchi Indians. It was the site of several Revolutionary War forts, including Forts James and Charlotte. The French Huguenots first settled here to escape religious persecution at home. All this is documented and interpreted through exhibits at the Thurmond Visitor Center, Route 1, Box 12, Clarks Hill, SC 29821-0010. ☎ 706-722-3770 or 803-333-2476.

HOW TO GET THERE

From Augusta, take Highway 28 and drive north for 21 miles to Clarks Hill and the visitor center. From there you can continue on through South Carolina, taking in the eastern shore of the lake, or you can drive on 221 east to Pollard's Corner, and from there turn north on Highway 47, crossing the Little River, to take in the western shore. From Atlanta, take I-20 to Thomson, GA, and then turn north on Highway 43 to the Little River crossing and on to the western shore. Highway 378 from Washington provides easy access to both shores from Athens, via Highway 78, and from the north via Highway 17. From whichever access point you choose you'll have the option of driving many miles through the more remote stretches of the project, or staying close by at one of the state or county parks.

The visitor center is at the South Carolina end of the dam just off Highway 221. Brochures and other literature are available. Open daily year-round, except Thanksgiving, Christmas and New Year's Day, from 8 until 4:30 from October through March, and from 8 until 8:30 April through September. Contact the Resource Manager, Thurmond Lake, Route 1, Box 12, Clarks Hill, SC 29821-0010. ☎ 803-333-2476 or 706-722-3770.

CAMPING

There are 13 Corps of Engineers campgrounds, two primitive Corps campgrounds, one US Army Campground, six in state parks, two at county parks, and four more at commercial marinas around the lake. Facilities and services range from the primitive to luxurious. Individual campgrounds are covered in detail throughout the following text; check the map for locations.

FISHING

This sport is rivaled in popularity only by boating. Between them, they can turn the surface of the lake into a floating village. But Thurmond really is fishing country. With a vast population of white, striped, hybrid and largemouth bass, the lake could be the bass capital of the two states. Other sport is available in the form of crappie, bluegill and sauger. The lake is easily accessible to all via a system of public-access boat ramps, reached via any one of a number of access roads, or through one of the state or county parks (see the map on page 149).

☞ **Hazards:** Watch for sudden, swift rises in the river level below the dam when water is released for power generation. An air horn will sound one minute prior to release. Be alert for submerged stumps, logs, rocks and other objects in the lake, especially during periods of low water.

HIKING

There are opportunities for hiking, or at least walking, at almost every mile along the entire shoreline. Some state parks, however, and some Corps recreational areas and campgrounds, have designated trails of varying lengths and difficulty. These are covered, along with their individual locations, throughout the following text.

BOATING

Boating is the most popular pastime on Thurmond Lake. With a large number of public-access ramps strategically placed around the lake, you'll have little trouble finding a place to put in. Want a secluded afternoon on the water? You'll have to drive off into the outer reaches to find such a spot, but they are here! (See map on page 149.)

☞ **Hazards:** Watch for sudden, swift rises in the river level below the dam when water is released for power generation. An air horn will sound one minute prior to release. Be alert for submerged stumps, logs, rocks and other objects in the lake, especially during periods of low water.

Commercial Marinas

The following facilities have been numbered for easy location on the map on page 149.

34. Clarks Hill Marina: A full-service marina near Plum Branch at Landon Creek. Facilities include boat ramps, a picnic area, a campground with all the usual facilities (full hookups, a bathhouse with hot showers and flush toilets), rental cabins, sewage disposal, fuel dock, boat rentals, restaurant and a fishing dock. Clarks Hill Marina, PO Box 8A, Plum Branch, SC 29845. ☎ 803-443-5577.

35. Mike's Marina: A full-service marina near Pollard's Corner off GA 104. Facilities include a boat ramp; a campground with all the usual facilities, including full hookups, rental cabins, sewage disposal, fuel dock, a picnic area, restaurant. Mike's Marina, Route 1, Box 172, Appling, GA 30802. ☎ 706-541-1385.

36. Soap Creek Lodge: A full-service marina just east of Lincolnton off US 378. Facilities include a boat ramp, a picnic area, a campground with full hookups, a bathhouse with hot showers and flush toilets, rental cabins, sewage disposal, fuel dock, boat rentals, restaurant and a fishing dock. Soap Creek Lodge, Route 4, Box 323, Lincolnton, GA 30817. ☎ 706-359-3124.

37. Raysville Bridge Marina: A full-service marina on the Little River off Highway 43. Facilities include boat ramps, a picnic area, a campground with full hookups, a bathhouse with hot showers and flush toilets, sewage disposal, fuel dock, boat rentals, restaurant and a fishing dock. Raysville Bridge Marina, Route 6, Box 157, Thomson, GA 30842. ☎ 706-595-5582.

38. Tradewinds Marina & Yacht Club: A marina with limited services at the west end of the Thurmond Dam, near Clarks Hill, off US 221. Facilities include a boat ramp, bathhouse with hot showers and flush toilets, fuel dock and boat rentals. Tradewinds Marina & Yacht Club, Route 2, Box 187, Appling, GA 30802. ☎ 706-541-1380.

CORPS RECREATION AREAS

These areas are dedicated to the casual, day-use visitor. Most have extensive facilities for recreation, including public-access boat ramps and picnic sites. Note: for picnic shelter reservations, ☎ 706-722-3770 or 803-333-2476.

1. Below Dam: As the name suggests, this area is on the Savannah River at the foot of Thurmond Dam. Facilities include a boat ramp, picnic grounds with tables, restrooms, fresh drinking water, a fishing pier and a fish-cleaning station. Off US 221 at Clarks Hill.

2. Visitor Center: On the lake side of Thurmond Dam, off US 221, at the Clarks Hill Visitor Center. Facilities are limited to parking, restrooms and fresh drinking water.

3. Clarks Hill Park: At the east end of Thurmond Dam, off US 221, at Clarks Hill. Facilities include a boat ramp, several picnic shelters with tables, a playground, a swimming beach, restrooms, fresh drinking water and a fish-cleaning station.

4. Parksville: At Catfish Creek, Parksville, in South Carolina on the eastern shore of the lake, off US 221. Facilities include a boat ramp, picnic grounds with tables, several picnic shelters with tables, playground for the kids, a swimming beach, restrooms, fresh drinking water, and a fish-cleaning station.

5. Calhoun Falls Park: At the north end of the lake in South Carolina, off SC 81, near Calhoun Falls. Facilities are limited to parking and a boat ramp.

6. Gill Point: At Newford Creek, north of Lincolnton off GA 79. Facilities include a boat ramp, several picnic shelters with tables, a swimming beach, restrooms, and fresh drinking water.

7. Lake Springs: Just east of Pollard's Corner near the west end of Thurmond Dam, off US 221. Facilities include a boat ramp, several picnic shelters with tables, playground, a swimming beach, restrooms, fresh drinking water, a fishing pier, a short hiking trail and a fish-cleaning station.

8. West Dam: As the name indicates, this area is at the west end of Thurmond Dam on the lake side of US 221. Facilities include several picnic shelters with tables, a playground, a swimming beach, restrooms, fresh drinking water and a fishing pier.

40. Cherokee: On the north side of the Little River off GA 47. Facilities include a boat ramp, restrooms, fresh drinking water, and a fish-cleaning station.

Thurmond Lake

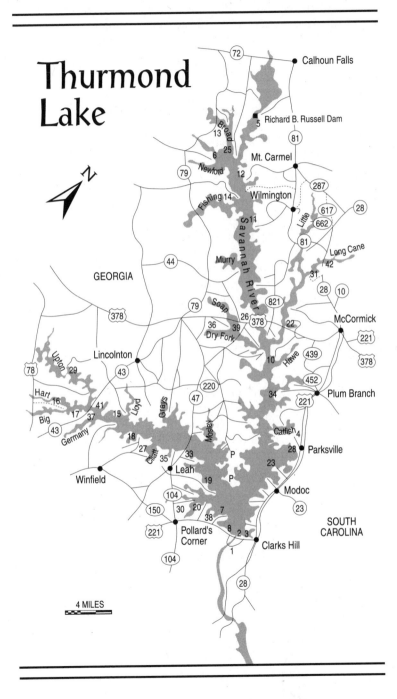

72

Calhoun Falls

Broad
13
25
6

5   Richard B. Russell Dam

81

Newford
79

Mt. Carmel

12

287

Wilmington

Fishing 14

617   28

662

11

Little

81

Savannah River

Long Cane

Murry
44

42

31

GEORGIA

28   10

79

Soap
26
378

821

378

McCormick
221

36
39
Dry Fork

22

378

Hawe   439

10

452

378   Lincolnton
Upton
29

220

34

Plum Branch

43

47

221

78

Hart
16

Lloyd   Grays

Catfish   4

Big   17   37   41   15

Mosley

28   Parksville

43   Germany   18

23

27
35
33

P

Chatt   Leah

Winfield

19

P

23

Modoc

104

30   20

7

23

150

38

8

SOUTH
CAROLINA

221

Pollard's
Corner

2   3

Clarks Hill

104

1

28

4 MILES

41. Amity: On the north side of the Little River off GA 43. Facilities are extensive and include a boat ramp, picnic grounds with tables, several picnic shelters with tables, a playground for the kids, a swimming beach, restrooms, fresh drinking water, a fishing pier, and a fish-cleaning station.

CORPS CAMPGROUNDS

Corps campgrounds are, on the whole, well developed with lots of services and facilities, and well-managed. Fees vary from area to area (see individual campgrounds); attendants are on hand at all Corps campgrounds to register guests and lend assistance. Security is excellent; all Corps-managed campgrounds have gates that are closed and locked at night, and Corps rangers patrol the areas through the year. The letter "P" found at various places on the map indicate a Corps primitive camping area (no fees).

9. Modoc: South of Modoc, SC, off US 221. Facilities include 49 sites, 35 of which have water and electric hookups, 20 are pull-throughs. There is a bathhouse with hot showers and flush toilets, fresh drinking water, sewage disposal, a boat ramp, swimming beach, playground for the kids, picnic areas and a fish-cleaning station. Fees: $8-$10. ☎ 803-333-2272.

10. Hawe Creek: East of McCormick, SC, off US 221 on Hawe Creek. Facilities are somewhat limited but include 28 sites, of which 10 have water and electric hookups. There's also a bathhouse with hot showers and flush toilets, fresh drinking water, sewage disposal, and a boat ramp. Fees: $7-$12. ☎ 803-443-5441.

11. Leroy's Ferry: Southwest of Willington, off SC 81. Facilities are limited to a boat ramp and fresh drinking water; there are no hookups or bathhouse. Fees: $5. There are no telephones at the campground. ☎ 803-333-2467 for information.

12. Mount Caramel: Southwest of Mt. Carmel, SC, off SC 81. Facilities are extensive and include 38 sites, of which 18 have water and electric hookups, 12 are pull-throughs. There is a bathhouse with hot showers and flush toilets, fresh drinking water, sewage disposal, a boat ramp, swimming beach, playground for the kids, picnic areas and a fish-cleaning station. Fees: $7-$12. ☎ 803-391-2711.

13. Broad River: At the north end of the lake on the south bank of the Broad River, off GA 79. Facilities include sites with water and electric hookups, a bathhouse with hot showers and flush toilets, fresh drinking water, sewage disposal, a boat ramp and a fish-cleaning station. Fees: $12-$15. ☎ 706-359-2053.

14. Hester's Ferry: At the north end of the lake on GA 44, off GA 79. Of the 26 campsites, 16 have water and electrical hookups, and 18 are pull-throughs. There's a bathhouse with hot showers and flush toilets, fresh drinking water, sewage disposal, a boat ramp, playground for the kids and a fish-cleaning station. Fees: $7-$10. ☎ 706-359-2746.

15. Clay Hill: On the north shore of the Little River, off GA 43 near Thomson. Facilities include a number of tent and trailer sites with water and electric hookups, a bathhouse with hot showers and flush toilets, fresh drinking water, sewage disposal, a boat ramp and a fish-cleaning station. Fees: $7-$9. There are no telephones at the campground. ☎ 706-722-3770 for information.

16. Big Hart: On a peninsula at the western end of the Little River, off US 78 north of Thomson. This is one of the best developed of the Corps campgrounds. Facilities are extensive and include 31 tent and trailer sites (24 have water and electric hookups), a group campground, a bathhouse with hot showers and flush toilets, fresh drinking water, sewage disposal, a boat ramp, a hiking trail, swimming beach, a playground, picnic areas and a fish-cleaning station. Contact the Resource Center for group camp information, ☎ 706-722-3770. You can call ahead to reserve a site. Fees: $13-$15.

17. Raysville: On the south shore of the Little River, off GA 43, near Thomson. Facilities include 56 tents and trailer sites, all with water and electric hookups, 18 of which are pull-throughs. There's a bathhouse with hot showers and flush toilets, fresh drinking water, sewage disposal, a boat ramp, playground for the kids, and a fish-cleaning station. Fees: $13-$15. ☎ 706-595-6759.

18. Winfield: North of Winfield on the south shore of the Little River. Facilities include tent and trailer sites with water and electric hookups, a bathhouse with hot showers and flush toilets, fresh drinking water, sewage disposal, boat ramp, swimming beach, a playground and a fish-cleaning station. Fees: $13-$15. ☎ 706-541-0147.

19. Ridge Road: East of Leah on a peninsula just north of the Thurmond Dam, off GA 104. Facilities include 52 sites, of which 29 have water and electric hookups and 23 are pull-throughs. There's also a bathhouse with hot showers and flush toilets, fresh drinking water, sewage disposal, boat ramp, swimming beach, playground and a fish-cleaning station. Fees: $10. ☎ 706-541-0282.

20. Petersburg: West of the Thurmond Dam on the south shore of the lake off US 221. Facilities are extensive and include 66 tent and trailer sites, of which 58 have water and electric hookups; 30 are pull-throughs. There's also a bathhouse with hot showers and flush toilets, fresh drinking water, sewage disposal, a boat ramp, swimming beach, playground for the kids, hiking trail and a fish-cleaning station. Fees: $12-$15. ☎ 706-541-9464.

21. Bussey Point: On the north side of the lake southeast of Lincolnton, off GA 47 via a network of access roads. This is a primitive area with a boat ramp, picnic area and hiking trails. No telephone at the site. Contact the Resource Center for information, ☎ 706-722-3770.

STATE PARKS

Facilities at the following state parks in some cases rival those of the Corps-managed areas. In Georgia, the powers that be have gone to great lengths to make their facilities as appealing as possible. In all cases, the parks are set in some of the finest and most spectacular scenery.

Bobby Brown State Park. Named for Lt. Robert T. Brown, who gave his life while serving in the US Navy in World War II, the park is south of Russell Dam at the north end of the Lake, and can be reached either via GA 79 or GA 72. The site is that of the old town of Petersburg, where the Broad and Savannah rivers flow into Clarks Hill Lake. Petersburg, a once-thriving community in the late 1700s, is now a 665-acre park.

Facilities include 61 tent and trailer sites, all with water and electric hookups, sewage disposal, bathhouse with showers and flush toilets, concessions, fresh drinking water, and a store selling a range of supplies. There's also picnic sites, picnic shelters, swimming pool, boat ramp, boat dock, playground, hiking trails, and swimming beach.

Annual events here include the Fall Camper Reunion.

Open daily from 7 am until 10 pm; the park office is open from 8 until 5. Bobby Brown State Park, Route 4, Box 232, Elberton, GA 30635. ☎ 706-213-2046.

26. Elijah Clark State Park. The 447-acre park is on the western shore of Clarks Hill Lake, east of Lincolnton, off US 378. Named for one of Georgia's most famous frontiersman and a leader of pioneers during the Revolutionary War, it features reconstructed cabins, a museum, and a variety of exhibits on everyday life in late 18th-century Georgia. You can tour the cabins and see the grave of Clark and his wife, Hannah.

Facilities include 165 tent and trailer sites, all with water and electric hookups, sewage disposal, bathhouse with showers and flush toilets, concessions, fresh drinking water, and a store for supplies. In addition, you'll find picnic sites, picnic shelters, swimming pool, boat ramp, boat dock, playground, hiking trails and swimming beach.

Annual events include the Pioneer Rendezvous in October, and a Log Cabin Christmas in December.

Open daily from 7 am until 10 pm; the park office is open from 8 until 5. Elijah Clark State Park, Box 293, Route 4, Lincolnton, GA 30817. ☎ 706-359-3458.

27. Mistletoe State Park. On the south shore of the lake at Cliatt Creek, this park takes its name from Mistletoe Junction. In times gone by the local people would meet in the area where the park now stands to gather mistletoe for the holiday season. Today, the 1,900-acre park is more famous as one of the best bass fishing spots in the United States. It's also a great place for hiking, nature study, birdwatching and wildlife photography. Facilities include 107 tent and trailer sites, all with water and electric hookups, 10 rental cottages, four walk-in campsites, a pioneer camp, sewage disposal, bathhouse with showers and flush toilets, concessions, fresh drinking water and a store where you can buy a limited range of supplies. There are also picnic sites, picnic shelters, more than six miles of hiking trails, a swimming pool, three boat ramps, boat dock, playground for the kids and a swimming beach.

Open from 7 am until 10 pm; the park office is open from 8 until 5. Mistletoe State Park, Route 1, Box 335, Appling, GA 30802. ☎ 706-541-0321. The park is off GA 150, 12 miles north of I-20, Exit 60.

22. Baker Creek State Park. On the eastern shore of the lake, just west of McCormick off US 378, Baker's Creek is the best developed of the three South Carolina state parks on Thurmond Lake. The facilities are extensive, as are the opportunities for recreation: miles of hiking trails and lots of wildlife. It's a great place for nature study and photography.

Camping facilities include 100 tent and trailer sites, all with water and electric hookups, tables and grills, walk-in campsites, a pioneer camp, sewage disposal, bathhouse with showers and flush toilets, concessions, fresh drinking water, and a store.

Other facilities: picnic sites and shelters, hiking trails, boat ramps, boat dock, playground and swimming beach.

Open from 7 am until 10 pm; the park office is open from 8 until 5. Bakers Creek State Park, Route 1, Box 12, Clarks Hill, SC 29821. ☎ 803-443-5886.

23. Hamilton Branch State Park. On the eastern shore of the lake, just north of Modoc, off US 221 in South Carolina, this park offers a large campground and lots of opportunity to spend time on the water. It's usually quite busy during the summer months, so if you don't like crowds, this isn't the place for you.

Facilities include 200 tent and trailer sites, all with water and electric hookups, tables and grills, a bathhouse with hot showers and flush toilets, and fresh drinking water. Unfortunately, there are no concessions or store, so you'll need to take all your supplies with you. There are also picnic sites, picnic shelters, and boat ramps.

Open from 7 am until 10 pm; the park office is open from 8 until 5. Hamilton Branch State Park Route 1, Box 12, Clarks Hill, SC 29821. ☎ 803-333-3223.

24. Hickory Knob State Park. On the eastern shore west of McCormick, South Carolina, via US 378, off SC 821, this park has lots to offer. Camping facilities include 75 tent and trailer sites, all with water and electric hookups, tables and grill; sewage disposal; a bathhouse with hot showers and flush toilets; concessions; fresh drinking water; and a store where you can buy a limited range of supplies. There are several miles of hiking trails, boat ramps, boat dock and a playground for the kids.

Open from 7 am until 10 pm; the park office is open from 8 until 5. Hickory Knob State Park, Route 1, Box 12, Clarks Hill, SC 29821. ☎ 803-391-2450.

COUNTY PARKS

28. Parksville Wayside. On the eastern shore of the lake and Catfish Creek, off US 221, a few miles north of Clarks Hill in South Carolina. One of the smaller facilities on the lake.

Facilities are limited to picnic shelters and sites, and fresh drinking water. No telephone.

29. Holiday Park. To reach this park on the north side of the Little River, you'll have to take GA 43 north from Thomson and drive north to the more remote area. This is one of the smaller parks on the lake, with a boat ramp, picnic shelters and sites, a small campground and fresh drinking water. There is no bathhouse or showers. No telephone.

30. Wildwood Park. Twenty-two miles from Augusta via GA 104, just north of Pollard's Corner on the south shore of the lake, Wildwood is something of a surprise. This one rivals its big sister state parks as one of the best parks of the lake. The recreational facilities are extensive; the park is well looked after and kept in pristine condition year-round.

Camping facilities include 62 tent and trailer sites with a maximum capacity of 15 feet, all with water and electric hookups, tables and grills; five are pull-throughs. There is sewage disposal, bathhouse with hot showers and flush toilets, laundromat, concessions, fresh drinking water, and a store where you can buy a limited range of supplies. Other facilities include a recreational pavilion, picnic sites with tables and grills, picnic shelters, several miles of hiking trails, boat ramps, boat dock, a playground and swimming beach. There's also a recreation director on hand.

Open from 7 to 10; the park office is open from 8 to 5.

Wildwood Park, Columbia County Park. ☎ 706-541-0586.

39. Soap Creek. On the west shore of the lake, east of Lincolnton, off US 378, this is a nice, quiet recreation area, small in facilities but big in opportunities for fun in the outdoors. There's a boat ramp, picnic shelters and sites, fresh drinking water and a swimming beach. No telephone.

33. Fort Gordon Recreation Area. North of Pollard's Corner at Leah, off GA 104, this is an off-base recreation area operated by the US Army out of Fort Gordon some 22 miles away to the south. Its facilities – and they are extensive – are open for public use year-round. It has 151 tent and trailer sites, of which 63 have full hookups (water, electric and sewage), 30 water and electric only, and 51 with no hookups; a bathhouse with hot showers and flush toilets; sewage disposal; concessions; fresh drinking water; and a store. There's a recreation hall, a fully-equipped pavilion, picnic sites, picnic shelters, several miles of hiking trails, boat ramps, boat dock, playground for the kids, a swimming beach and lots of court games – badminton, volleyball, etc. You can also rent a sailboat, canoe, pedal boat or motor boat. A recreation director is on hand to help with planning, activities, and to make sure you make the best of your time.

Open from 7 to 10; the park office is open from 8 to 5. ☎ 706-541-0063.

Watson Mill Bridge State Park

Comer is a small community, just 900 people, about 12 miles northwest of Athens off Highway 72. Here you'll find Watson Mill Bridge State Park, one of the most picturesque state parks in Georgia. At 229 feet, the signature piece is the covered bridge built in 1885. Supported by a town lattice truss system and held together by wooden pins, it's the longest covered bridge standing on an original site in Georgia. Even though the fine old bridge is the park's main attraction, there's much more for you to enjoy. It's the ideal spot for an afternoon of picnicking, walking in the forest or along the riverbank, birdwatching, or even an overnight stay in the campground.

River, lake and mill pond **fishing**. There are three picnic shelters, a number of picnic sites with tables and grills, several short but pleasant walking trails; and you can rent a boat or canoe and take to the water. Day and overnight canoe trips are organized and guided by qualified, knowledgeable park staff. Call for details.

Camping: There are 24 tent and trailer sites, of which 21 have water and electric hookups (18 are pull-throughs), a handicapped-accessible bathhouse with hot showers and flush toilets, sewage disposal, a laundromat, picnic tables and grills. Fees: $12 for a site with water and electric.

Annual Events include a Civil War Encampment, Georgia Awareness Weekend in August, and an assortment of outdoor concerts held throughout the summer and at Christmas.

Open daily year-round from 7 am until dark; the office is open from 8 to 5. Reservations: Watson Mill Bridge State Park, Route 1, Box 190, Comer, GA 30629. ☎ 706-783-5349. The park is three miles south of Comer off GA 22.

A.H. Stephens State Historic Park

A.H. Stephens State Historic Park is in the tiny community of Crawfordville, east of Atlanta and just north of I-20 at Exit 55. Named after the Vice President of the Confederacy and one-time Governor of Georgia, this park offers both natural and historic attractions. Liberty Hall was the home Stephens built for himself around 1875. The house and the Confederate museum, which houses one of the most extensive collections of Confederate artifacts and memorabilia to be found anywhere in Georgia, and the beautiful gardens and outdoor facilities make the park a natural choice, not only for the history buff, but for nature lovers, too.

There's a nice **nature trail**, two picnic areas with tables and grills, and a fishing lake. Fishing is good throughout the year. Private boats are allowed (electric motors only); rental boats are available. The museum offers an educational program and an audio-visual show.

A small **campground** has 36 tent or trailer sites, all with water and electric hookups, tables and grills; a bathhouse with hot showers and flush toilets; a dumping station; laundromat; and a small store where you can purchase ice, paper goods, souvenirs, crafts and other goodies. Security is good; the facility is gated and locked up at night. The campground is handicapped-accessible. Fees: $12 per night for two persons.

Annual events include the Stephens' Homecoming in April and the Gaslight Tours in the fall.

Open daily from 7 to 10; office hours are from 8 to 5. Admission, $2. ☎ 706-456-2602.

Take Exit 55 from I-20 and go north on Highway 22 for two miles. Drive east on US 278 for one mile to Crawfordville and follow the Park Service signs.

Elberton

Elberton is a small community west of Richard B. Russell Lake on the Georgia/South Carolina border, the gateway to a vast outdoor playground that includes, not only Russell Lake, but also J. Strom Thurmond Lake and Hartwell Lake. The little city is the largest center for hard-rock mining in the world. There are 45 quarries in the area, along with at least 100 granite manufacturing operations, so it's only natural that this is where you'll find a unique museum dedicated to the industry.

NEARBY ATTRACTIONS

The Elberton Granite Museum is on GA 17, a half-mile west of GA 72. Here you'll find interpretive displays of granite products, antique granite working tools, and you can learn all about the industry – how the stone is taken from the ground, worked, and turned into all sorts of products. Open daily from 2 until 5. Free. ☎ 706-283-2551.

Richard B. Russell State Park, nine miles northeast of Elberton off GA 77 on Ruckersville Road, is situated on a site that was home to the Paleo Indians more than 10,000 years ago. On the shores of the 26,500-acre Russell Lake, it's one of Georgia's newest state recreational areas. The lake itself offers all sorts some of the finest fishing and boating in Georgia. All of the park facilities are wheelchair-accessible.

Facilities include a swimming beach, a boat ramp and dock, three picnic shelters, a number of picnic sites with tables and grills, and a concession stand where you can purchase light refreshments. There's also a pleasant lakeside walking trail, which makes the park a good spot for nature study, birdwatching and wildlife photography.

Open from 7 am until dark; the park office is open from 8 to 5.

Richard B. Russell State Park, Route 2, Box 118, Elberton, GA 30635. ☎ 706-213-2045.

Fort Yargo State Park

Fort Yargo, one mile south of Winder on GA 81, is a unique log fort built in the late 1700s as a protection for the settlers in the area against the local Cherokee and Creek Indians. But more than that, the 1,800-acre park offers some of the best fishing in the Piedmont, and includes the Will-A-Way Recreation Area – a facility designed for use by special populations, with cottages, a 250-capacity group camp, food service facilities, along with picnic and fishing areas.

Boating: Canoes, jon boats and pedal boats are available for rent.

Camping: Facilities include 47 tent and trailer sites with water and electric hookups, a modern bathhouse with hot showers and flush toilets, handicapped-accessible restrooms, picnic tables and grills. Fees: $10.

Fishing: The lake is well-stocked with bass, crappie, bluegill and catfish.

Other facilities include a 260-acre lake with swimming beach, a hiking and nature trail, two tennis courts, 116 picnic sites with tables and grills, five shelters, two family group shelters and a miniature golf course.

Open daily year-round from 7 to 10; the park office is open from 8 to 5.

Fort Yargo State Park, PO Box 764, Winder, GA 30680. ☎ 770-867-9934.

Lake Sidney Lanier

Nestled in the foothills at the southern end of the Blue Ridge Mountains in central Georgia is one of the Piedmont Region's most popular attractions. The 38,000-acre Lake Lanier is the product of the US Corps of Engineers' Buford Dam project. The corps has gone to great lengths to develop the more than 540 miles of shoreline as an outdoor adventureland. So successful were they that Lake

Lanier was chosen to host the 1996 rowing and sprint canoeing competition.

Sidney Clopton Lanier, for whom the lake is named, was born in 1842 in Macon, Georgia. He was a man with an obsession, a poet who spent much of his time in the great outdoors, pen in hand, trying to understand the musical qualities of verse. His writings, among them his famous "Song of the Chattahoochee," reflect his love for the area. He died at age 39 in 1881 of tuberculosis contracted during the Civil War.

Lake Lanier is a vast waterworld that extends more than 30 miles northeast from Cummin, northeast of Atlanta, taking in Gainesville, to the east. With a well-developed network of roads both to the east and west, it's one of most accessible outdoor centers in Georgia.

Recreation is first rate on and around the lake. The Corps of Engineers has developed some 41 day-use recreation areas and nine campgrounds. All are listed in the following text – the campgrounds are described in some detail – and all are numbered for easy location on the map. There are also 11 state and county parks and 10 commercial marinas; these, too, are listed and numbered on the map (see page 163).

Lake Lanier is home to an abundance of wildlife, and one of the main stops on the way south for hundreds of migratory birds. The animal population includes squirrels, rabbits, turtles, raccoons and deer. Though not as heavily forested as its neighbor, Allatoona Lake to the west, Lanier's shoreline is about as beautiful as you could wish for. Flowering dogwoods, majestic hardwoods and pines provide shade and a skyline that's been the subject of artists and photographers for many a year.

Fishing: Although this is one of the busiest lakes in central Georgia, Lanier offers fine fishing throughout the year. And, even though it's accessible at almost every point on its shoreline, it's still possible to find a quiet spot, far away from the crowds, to enjoy a morning's sport. What can you expect to catch? The lake is well-stocked with striped, hybrid, white, largemouth and smallmouth bass, crappie, sunfish, bream, sauger and bluegill. Catfish can be caught everywhere, but the big ones lurk in the dark cool tailwaters below the dam. And, speaking of the water under the dam, it's here you can also catch brook, rainbow and brown trout. Lake Lanier offers anglers all they could wish for.

☞ **A word of warning:** Waters released during power generation cause the levels below the dam to rise suddenly and very quickly. If you decide to try your hand there, and you're in a boat, be on the alert for the warning signal – horns located at strategic points along the river between the dam and the Highway 20 bridge. You can also tune your radio to 1610 on the AM dial for water-release schedules and safety information.

Watersports: Lake Lanier's shoreline offers opportunities for all sorts of fun and action on the water, including waterskiing, sailing, canoeing, windsurfing and swimming. Most of the Corps day-use campgrounds have swimming beaches – unsupervised – as do their campgrounds, and many of the state and county parks.

Picnicking: Well-provided for at almost all of the developed areas around the lake, and in many places you'll discover for yourself. Most of the Corps picnic areas have tables and grills, as do those operated by the state, and some have group shelters that can be reserved by making a phone call.

Camping: Those of you who carry your home around with you will find the lake a haven like no other. The Corps-operated campgrounds are secure – gated and locked at night, patroled by park rangers – and are well looked after, with lots of facilities. Some of the commercial grounds provide more extensive facilities, but none can offer the great parklands, the primitive sites, and the "away-from-it-all" feeling provided by their Corps and state competitors. Fees at Corps and state campgrounds are included in the listings, as are those for commercial campgrounds.

CORPS RECREATION AREAS

Following is a list of all the Corps recreational facilities on the lake. The preceding numbers correspond to those on the map. All but four – Powerhouse, Upper and Lower Overlook, and Buford Dam Park – have at least one boat ramp; most are handicapped-accessible; almost all have restrooms, picnic tables and grills and fresh drinking water; some have picnic shelters and swimming beaches. For more detailed information, call the Resource Manager's Office, Lake Sidney Lanier, Buford, GA 30518. ☎ 770-945-9531.

1. Powerhouse
2. Lower Overlook
3. Upper Overlook
4. Buford Dam Park

50. Bolding Mill Day Use
52. Lumpkin County Park
53. Toto Creek
54. Nix Bridge

6. Shoal Creek Day Use Park	55. Thompson Creek
11. Big Creek	56. War Hill
12. Burton Mill	59. Keith Bridge
13. Van Pugh Day Use Park	60. Long Hollow
18. Old Federal Day Use Park	64. Vann's Tavern
19 Balus Creek	66. Bethel
20. Mountain View	67. Two Mile
30. Belton Ridge	70. Six Mile Creek
31. Lula Park	71. Charleston
36. Little River	75. Young Deer
38. Wahoo Creek	76. Tidwell
39. Thompson Creek	79. Mary Alice
41. Sardis Creek	82. West Bank
42. Simpson Park	83. West Bank Overlook
43. Robinson	84. Lower Pool
45. Duckett Mill Day Use Park	46. Little Hall

The Resource Manager's Office is at Buford Dam, off Buford Dam Road, which can be reached from Atlanta and the southwest via GA 440, Exits 14 or 15 at Cummin. From the south and Gainesville in the east, it can be reached by taking Exit 2 off I-85. The lake itself can be reached by numerous feeder roads off GA 400 or I-85.

CORPS CAMPGROUNDS

The Corps-operated campgrounds here on Lake Lanier are well developed affairs with extensive facilities. They are secure – gated and locked at night – and strategically placed to make the most of the lake and all it has to offer. Campsites cannot be reserved and are available on a first-come basis. Group campsites may be reserved by calling ☎ 770-945-9531.

7. Shoal Creek, at the southern end of the lake, off Buford Dam Road, five miles northwest of Buford, is a fairly large campground with 107 tent and trailer sites, of which 65 have water and electric hookups; 88 are pull-throughs. Other facilities include a bathhouse with hot showers and flush toilets, handicapped-accessible restrooms, tables and grills, fire rings, sewage disposal, a laundromat, three boat ramps and a dock. Open March through October. Fees: $12-$18. ☎ 770-945-9531.

14. Chestnut Ridge is on the western shore of the lake, east of I-985 and US 23, northeast of Buford. There are 70 tent and trailer sites, of which 32 have water and electric hookups; 12 are pull-throughs. Other facilities include a bathhouse with hot showers and flush toilets, handicapped-accessible restrooms, tables and grills, fire rings, sewage disposal, a laundromat, a swimming beach, playground for the kids, a boat ramp and a dock. Open April through September. Fees: $12-$18. ☎ 770-945-9531.

17. Old Federal is on the western shore of the lake, off Jim Crow Road, and east of I-985 and US 23 at Exit 3. Facilities include a number of tent and trailer sites, most with water and electric hookups, a bathhouse with hot showers and flush toilets, handicapped-accessible restrooms, tables and grills, fire rings, sewage disposal, a laundromat, a swimming beach, playground for the kids, a boat ramp and a dock. Open April through September. Fees: $12-$18. ☎ 770-945-9531.

45. Duckett Mill, on the eastern shore of the lake, some six miles west of Dawsonville, is reached by taking Exit 17 off GA 400, then driving northeast on GA 306 for 11 miles, then south on the feeder road that serves the site. Facilities include 111 tent and trailer sites, most with water and electric hookups, a bathhouse with hot showers and flush toilets, handicapped-accessible restrooms, tables and grills, fire rings, sewage disposal, a laundromat, a swimming beach, a playground, a boat ramp and a dock. Open April through September. Fees: $12-$18. ☎ 770-945-9531.

50. Bolding Mill, on the eastern shore of the lake, west of Dawsonville, is reached by taking Exit 17 off GA 400, then driving northeast on GA 306 for 12 miles to the feeder road that serves the site. Turn northwest there and drive on for about five miles. Facilities include 97 tent and trailer sites, most with water and electric hookups, a bathhouse with hot showers and flush toilets, handicapped-accessible restrooms, tables and grills, fire rings, sewage disposal, a laundromat, a swimming beach, playground for the kids, a boat ramp and a dock. Open April through September. Fees: $12-$18. ☎ 770-945-9531.

74. Shady Grove, on the western shore of the lake northeast of Cummin, is reached by taking GA 400 north from the city to Exit 13; from there go northwest on GA 306, southwest on 309, then south on Shady Grove Road. This is one of the Corps' most extensively developed campgrounds. Facilities include 125 tent and trailer sites, of which 45 have water and electric hookups; 35 are pull-throughs. There's a bathhouse with hot showers and flush toilets, handicapped-accessible restrooms, tables and grills, fire rings, sewage disposal, a laundromat, a swimming beach, a playground, a boat ramp and a dock. Open April through September. Fees: $12-$18. ☎ 770-945-9531.

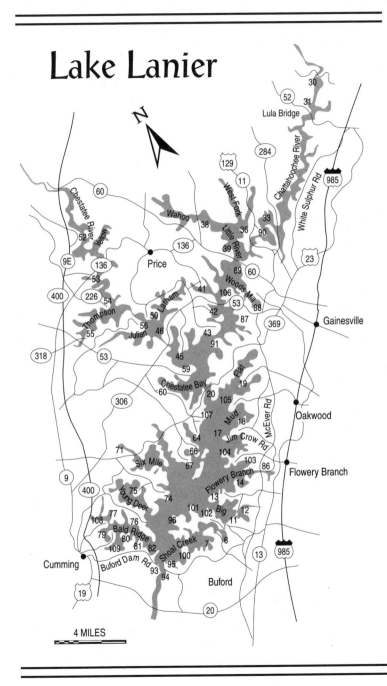

Lake Lanier

4 MILES

77. Bald Ridge is close to Cummin on the western shore of the lake. Take GA 400 and drive northeast for five miles. Facilities include 82 tent and trailer sites, all with water and electric hookups; 11 are pull-throughs. There's a bathhouse with hot showers and flush toilets, handicapped-accessible restrooms, tables and grills, fire rings, sewage disposal, a laundromat, a swimming beach, playground for the kids, a boat ramp and a dock. Open April through September. Fees: $12-$18. ☎ 770-945-9531.

81. Sawnee, east of Cummin, off GA 400 and Buford Dam Road, may be the most accessible of the Corps-operated campgrounds on Lake Lanier. Facilities are extensive and include 56 tent and trailer sites, of which 44 have water and electric hookups. There's a bathhouse with hot showers and flush toilets, handicapped-accessible restrooms, tables and grills, fire rings, sewage disposal, a laundromat, a swimming beach, playground for the kids, a boat ramp and a dock. Open April through September. Fees: $12-$18. ☎ 770-945-9531.

MARINAS

There are 10 commercially operated marinas on and around the lake. All have extensive facilities that include boat launching sites, fuel docks, retail stores selling boating supplies and fishing tackle, and renting boats. Some even have full-service restaurants. They are all listed below, numbered for easy location on the map.

100. Lanier Harbor	☎ 770-945-2884
101. Holiday	☎ 770-945-7201
102. Lazy Days	☎ 770-945-1991
103. Starboard	☎ 770-577-2628
104. Aqualand	☎ 770-967-6811
105. Sunrise	☎ 770-536-8599
106. Gainesville	☎ 770-577-7252
107. Lan Mar	☎ 770-688-2278
108. Bald Ridge	☎ 770-522-9297
109. Habersham	☎ 770-577-6867

STATE, COUNTY & CITY PARKS

The following is a listing, numbered for easy location on the map, of parks and recreation areas with facilities that range from campgrounds to luxury hotels. Lake Lanier Islands, a Corps of Engineers/state of Georgia resort, is covered separately.

33. Clark's Bridge is off GA 284, near the Olympic Rowing site. Facilities include a boat ramp with three lanes, a boat dock, plenty of public parking and a swimming area. ☎ 770-945-9531.

86. Flowery Branch Park, on the eastern shore of the lake, is west of the city of Flowery Branch, off Lights Ferry Road. Facilities include eight picnic sites, a group shelter and a boat dock. ☎ 770-945-9531.

87. Lanier Point is west of the city on the eastern shore of the lake, off GA 53. Facilities include five picnic sites, a group picnic shelter, boat ramp, dock and a playground. ☎ 770-945-9531.

88. Longwood Park sits west of the city, off Jesse Jewell Parkway and Highway 53. Facilities include 50 picnic sites, a group picnic shelter and a playground. ☎ 770-945-9531.

89. Holly Park is east of the city on the western shore of the lake, off GA 60. Facilities at the 27-acre park include 20 picnic sites, two group picnic shelters, a boat ramp and a dock. ☎ 770-945-9531.

90. Laurel Park, is a 133-acre park, west of Gainesville via Limestone Parkway. Facilities include 15 picnic sites, two group picnic shelters, two boat ramps, a dock and an extensive playground for the kids. ☎ 770-945-9531.

91. River Forks, southwest of Gainesville off the Jesse Jewell Parkway, sits on the western shore of the lake. With more than 1.8 million visitors each year, this is one of the busiest of the locally operated parks. Facilities are extensive and include more than 110 acres of lakeside parkland, 80 campsites, 50 picnic sites, three group picnic shelters, tables, grills, a boat ramp, dock, swimming area and a playground. ☎ 770-531-3952.

93. East Bank, on the southern shore of the lake, off Buford Dam Road, covers more than 114 acres and has 22 picnic sites, a boat ramp with four lanes and a dock. ☎ 770-945-9531.

94. Lanier Park, also on the southern shore of the lake, off Buford Dam Road, is a 37-acre facility with 34 picnic sites, a boat ramp and a dock. ☎ 770-945-9531.

95. Gwinnett Park, on the southern shore of the lake, off Buford Dam Road, is a 25-acre park with 42 picnic sites, a group shelter and a boat ramp. ☎ 770-945-9531.

LAKE LANIER ISLANDS RESORT

Situated on a group of islands off the western shore at the southern end of the lake, the Islands is a resort almost without compare. (It is shown as number 96 on the map.). Constructed as a joint project between the US Corps of Engineers and the state of Georgia, it is now one of the most popular outdoor playgrounds in the state. There are two major hotels, two championship golf courses, one of the largest campgrounds in the area, and a plethora of water-related and other outdoor activities with endless supporting facilities.

Lake Lanier Islands is less than 45 minutes from downtown Atlanta. Take I-85 north to I-985 to either Exit 1 or 2, then follow the signs. Or you can take GA 400 to GA 20, Exit 14, and follow the signs.

Where To Stay

Lake Lanier Islands Hilton Resort, 700 Holiday Road, opened in the spring of 1989 and has everything you'll need for an all-inclusive vacation with a difference. The hotel has 224 lake- or forestview rooms, and 11,000 square feet of meeting space. Facilities and services are extensive; they include a heated swimming pool with poolside service, a wading pool, a playground for the kids, a program of supervised children's activities, a snack bar and a world-class restaurant. There are lighted tennis courts, a putting green, driving range and a championship 18-hole golf course (more about that later). For outdoor enjoyment, the hotel has its own beach and a picnic area with tables and grills. There's a water park nearby, and there are boats, bicycles (rentals), lawn games, waterskiing, and so on. There's a large exercise room with weights, bicycles, a sauna and a whirlpool. Trails meander away through the forest and alongside the lake. ☎ 770-945-8787. $$$.

Stouffer PineIsle Resort, 9000 Holiday Road, is a AAA Four Diamond Hotel. There are 250 guest rooms, three restaurants, an indoor/outdoor pool with poolside service and grill, and a program of supervised activities for the kids. The hotel has its own private beach, boat rentals – sailboats, canoes, pontoons, houseboats, etc. – bicycles, and horses (yes, you can take horseback riding lessons, too). The tennis facility has a resident pro and there's a magnificent 18-hole golf course, complete with driving range, putting green and 19th hole. An extensive exercise facility offers weights and machines, as well as instruction. And, as if all that's not enough, you can even get a complimentary shoeshine. ☎ 770-945-8921. $$$.

Dining Out

Aside from the Hilton's fancy restaurant and the three restaurants at the Stouffer, there are a number of other options on the Islands.

The Beachside Café offers the opportunity to make your own hamburgers, hot dogs, grilled chicken sandwich, pizza, fries, etc. $.

The Islands Grill serves great hickory-smoked pork barbecue, all-beef burgers and hot dogs. You can also get a reasonably priced chicken dinner, and an assortment of sandwiches. $.

Wildwaves Refresher is the place to go for a cool afternoon drink or snack.

Boating

You can take your own craft – many people do – or you can rent a boat. You'll find three boat launching areas at strategic locations on the Islands with ramps, plenty of parking, and easy access to the water. You should know, however, that this section of the lake is extremely busy most of the season. If you don't mind making a long haul northward, it's possible to find a quiet area where you can enjoy the lake alone. So, what can you rent? Houseboats to sleep up to 10 people; an Island Skimmer Group Boat to carry as many 20 people, an ideal party boat; group boats to carry as many as 45, fully furnished inside and out with couches, deck chairs, kitchens, restrooms, life jackets, ice chests and ship-to-shore radio, just the boat for a business group; pontoon boats to carry up to eight people; sports boats for cruising or fishing; and ski boats with 90-hp motors that carry up to five. If you want to go sailing, you can not only rent a sailboat – sunfish, day sailors and cruising yachts up to 36 feet – but the Lanier Sailing Academy offers lessons. For boat rental rates and information, call ☎ 770-932-7255; for Lanier Sailing Academy rates and information, ☎ 770-945-8810.

Biking

You can explore almost all of the 1,200 acres on Lake Lanier Islands by bike. For rental information and rates, ☎ 770-932-7233.

Camping

There's probably no other campground in Georgia quite like the one here on Lake Lanier Islands. Facilities include more than 300 sites, of which 74 have full hookups (water, electric and sewer), 198 with water and electric only, and 34 have no hookups; 88 are pull-throughs. The campground is gated, locked at night, and is totally secure. Bathhouses have hot showers and the restrooms have flush toilets and are handicapped-accessible. There's a modern laundromat with plenty of machines so you won't have to wait in line; the camp store carries a range of groceries, paper goods, gifts, ice, gas by meter or weight, and other supplies. There are also 150 picnic sites and 10 group shelters with tables and grills. Open year-round. Fees: from $10. ☎ 770-932-7270.

Fishing

Angling is a big part of the Lake Lanier Islands experience, but only in that it's a good place to launch the boat and park the trailer. This section of the lake is extremely busy most of the year. So, if it's a quiet spot and good sport you're after, you'll have to drive north for quite a distance before you find what you're looking for. When you get there, you'll find there are plenty of good-sized fish in the lake, including hybrid, white, largemouth and smallmouth bass, crappie, bluegill, sunfish, sauger, bream and the inevitable catfish. There is no one good time to go; just head out and hope for the best.

Golf

The Hilton Resort Golf Course is an award-winning design by Joe Lee. It's a par-72, 18-hole championship course that offers quite a bit more than a challenge. There are 75 bunkers out there, all strategically placed to make you think your way around the course. And there are no parallel fairways, so every shot is a challenge. The greens are bent grass and always fast. At the time of writing, green fees were $47.40, including cart. ☎ 770-945-8787.

Stouffer PineIsle Golf Course is also a championship course and hosted the LPGA's Nestlé World Championship from 1985

A golfer tests his skills.

through 1989. It was designed by Gary Player and Ron Kirby & Associates, and is touted as being one of the most scenic courses in Georgia. The course will challenge even the best of players. Eight of the holes are on the water, the fairways are tight and the greens promote target golf.

Fees at the time of writing were from $59, including cart. ☎ 770-945-8922.

Hiking

With more than 1,300 miles of shoreline to explore and some 80,00 acres of forest and parklands. The energetic hiker will enjoy walking and hiking trails, all within easy access of the islands. You can start out almost anywhere and return by the same trail; with so many people around, it's doubtful that you could get lost, but a good local area map and a compass will keep you on the right track.

Horseback Riding

Lake Lanier Islands Stables offers horseback riding along many miles of scenic trail on the lakeshore; pony rides are available for the kids, and riding lessons are offered, too. ☎ 770-932-7233.

Hamburg State Park

Six miles northeast of Warthen, via Hamburg Road off GA 102, this park features an old water-powered grist mill still operating today, much as it did when it was built more than 70 years ago. There's a country store – part of the mill complex – that sells stone-ground cornmeal and an assortment of recipe books to go with it. There's also a museum packed with exhibits, including tools and agricultural implements that were part of the everyday life of a bygone age. But the park is more than an historic site. With its 225-acre lake, it also offers a wonderful outdoor experience, good fishing, walking and picnicking.

You can rent pedal boats, canoes, and fishing boats. There are 30 tent and trailer sites, all with water and electric hookups, a bathhouse with hot showers and flush toilets, handicapped-accessible restrooms, a pioneer campground for those who like to rough it, and supplies are available at the country store. Fees: $10.

The lake is stocked with bass, bluegill, catfish and crappie.

Other facilities include two picnic shelters, picnic sites with tables and grills, and a playground. Educational programs are conducted by the museum staff.

Annual events include Canoe the Ogeechee in March and April, and the Fall Harvest Festival held the third weekend in September.

Open daily year-round from 7 am until 10 pm; the park office is open from 8 to 5. Hamburg State Park, Route 1, Box 233, Mitchell, GA 30820. ☎ 912-552-2393.

Hard Labor Creek State Park

Hard Labor Creek, two miles from Rutledge, off I-20, Exit 49, is on Fairplay Road. Supposedly, it was named either by the slaves who worked the fields nearby, or by local Indians who found the creek difficult to ford; we'll never know for sure. But the 5,800-acre park is now one of Georgia's great outdoor destinations.

Camping: There are 49 tent and trailer sites with water and electric hookups, a modern bathhouse with hot showers and flush toilets, handicapped-accessible restrooms, and a store where you can buy from a limited range of supplies. Fees: $10. For the camper who likes to keep a roof overhead, there are 20 rental cottages fully equipped for housekeeping. Fees: from $50.

Golf: Hard Labor Creek has one of the finest 18-hole courses in Georgia. There's also a full-service pro shop where you can buy or rent equipment, a putting green, driving range and a grill restaurant; rental carts are available, too.

Horseback Riding: This is one of the few parks in Georgia that caters to the equestrian with more than just a few trails. You bring your own horse; sorry, no rentals. But overnight accommodation is available in the form of well-kept and serviced stables, and there are more than 15 miles of bridleways for you and your four-legged friend to explore.

Annual events include the Civilian Conservation Corps Reunion in the Spring, and the Christmas Golf Tournament in December.

Hiking (2½ miles of trails), nature study, birdwatching, wildlife photography and picnicking. Other facilities include two lakes (boat rentals include pedal boats, fishing boats and canoes), two group shelters, a swimming beach, four picnic shelters and a barbecue.

Open daily year-round from 7 am until 10 pm; the park office is open from 8 until 5.

Hard Labor Creek State Park, PO Box 247, Rutledge, GA 30663. ☎ 706-557-3001 or 706-557-3006 (golf course).

Marietta

This community, some 15 miles west of Atlanta, is the result of an 1834 lottery that disposed of Cherokee Indian lands. It has always been a quiet town, a bedroom community for Atlanta. Even during the Civil War it was spared, although a major battle was just beyond the boundaries at Kennesaw Mountain. Today, you can spend time walking the historic district, visit General Sherman's headquarters at Kennesaw House, visit the battlefield itself, or enjoy a picnic in the city park. Beyond that, Marietta has a couple of popular theme parks and an art museum, all of which are worth checking out.

Take I-75 northwest from Atlanta.

WHERE TO STAY

Best Inns of America, 1255 Franklin Road, Marietta, GA 30067. Features large rooms, a pool, free coffee in the lobby and meeting rooms. There's a restaurant close by. No pets. ☎ 770-955-0004. $.

Hampton Inn, 455 Franklin Street, Marietta, GA 30067. Typical of the chain, this is a modern, no frills motel with a swimming pool, wading pool and playground. A free continental breakfast is provided, and free coffee is available in the lobby. No pets. ☎ 404-425-9977. $-$$.

Holiday Inn Northwest, 2255 Delk Road, Marietta, GA 30067, has a pool, restaurant and a bar. Services include health club privileges, data ports and coffee makers in every room. Small pets are permitted. ☎ 770-952-7581. $$.

La Quinta, 2170 Delk Road, I-75 N. Delk Road, Exit 111, features large, comfortable rooms, a pool, and provides free coffee in the lobby. Small pets are permitted. ☎ 770-951-0026. $$.

Marlow House is an historic inn built in 1866. Bed & breakfast. Call for rates. ☎ 770-426-1887.

Sheraton Atlanta Northwest, 1775 Parkway Place, Marietta, GA 30067, is a 10-story hotel with all the services one would expect: restaurant, café, swimming pool, bar. No pets. ☎ 770-428-4400. $$.

Stanley House, an historic bed & breakfast inn, was built in 1895. Call for rates. ☎ 770-426-1881.

DINING OUT

La Strada, 2930 Johnson Ferry Road NE, is open for dinner from 5 until 10. The menu is Italian with specialties that include stuffed shrimp and soft shell crab. ☎ 770-640-7008. $$.

Shilling's on the Square, 19 North Park Square, is open for lunch and dinner from 11 until midnight. Housed in a 100-year-old bar, this restaurant specializes in Black Angus beef and fresh seafood. Soft lights and good music. ☎ 770-428-9520. $$.

SIGHTSEEING & ATTRACTIONS

American Adventures, 250 North Cobb Parkway, is a 10-acre children's amusement park with more than a dozen rides, an arcade, bumper cars, carousel, roller coaster and various organized activities. Open daily from 11 until 8. Ride passes, $4 to $13. Parking, $2. ☎ 770-424-9283.

Whitewater, a water park on North Cobb Parkway, features more than 40 attractions and rides, including a body flume, tidal wave, rapids ride, and Little Squirt's Island, an activity pool just for the kids. Open daily from 10 until dusk, Memorial Day through Labor Day weekend; Saturday and Sunday from 10 until dusk, May 1 through the day before Memorial Day. Admission, $18: children under 48 inches tall, $11; seniors over 62, free. ☎ 770-590-4043.

Kennesaw Museum is six miles north of Marietta off US 41 or I-75 at Exit 118, at 2829 Cherokee Street in Kennesaw. The L&N locomotive, The General, of Andrew's Raiders fame, is permanently housed at the museum. Exhibits include an audio visual presentation of Major James Andrews' famous raid. Open Monday through Saturday from 9:30 until 5:30, and on Sunday from noon until 5:30. Admission, $3; children 7-15, $1.50; seniors 65 and over, $2.50. ☎ 770-427-2117.

Marietta/Cobb Museum of Art, 30 Atlanta Street NE, housed in a Greek Revival post office built in 1909, features a number of permanent collections of 19th- and 20th-century American art. Open Tuesday through Saturday from 11 until 5. Admission, $2; children and young adults 6-21, $1. ☎ 770-428-8142.

Annual Event: The BellSouth Golf Classic, part of the PGA Tour, is held annually in early May at the Atlanta Country Club on Atlanta Country Club Drive in Marietta. ☎ 770-951-8777.

Oconee National Forest

Oconee Lake lies just to the southeast of Atlanta in central Georgia. Though lacking the diversity of recreational facilities found in its larger sister to the north, the Oconee does offer some unique opportunities. There are more than 113,000 acres of virgin forest in two sections, with seven recreational areas that include some 55 campsites and almost as many picnic spots. Nearby Lakes Oconee and Sinclair, the Oconee River, and the Ocmulgee River provide some fine fishing, along with extensive boating and watersports opportunities.

Waterskiing is popular at Oconee Lake.

Oconee Ranger District Headquarters, 349 Forsyth Street, Monticello, GA 31064. ☎ 706-468-2244. Maps are available here.

Fees

A small fee, typically $2 to $5, may be charged for the use of some facilities – camping, in particular. You can check with the Forest Service at the Oconee Ranger District Headquarters. ☎ 706-468-2244.

ACTIVITIES

Public-access **boat ramps** to the lakes and rivers can be found in all sorts of diverse locations, but specifically at the Dyar Pasture, Hillsboro Lake, Redlands, Swords, Lake Sinclair and Oconee River recreation areas.

Three of the Oconee's recreation areas have **campgrounds**. Developed campgrounds can accommodate motor homes and trailers up to 22 feet, but there are no water or electric hookups. Primitive camping is allowed anywhere in the forest, unless posted otherwise. A permit is not needed for a campfire.

As already mentioned, the Oconee offers some of the finest **fishing** in Georgia, specifically at the Dyar Pasture, Lake Sinclair,

Hillsboro Lake, Redlands, Swords and Oconee River recreation areas.

The forest has a number of **hiking trails**; some are long and not too well marked, but most are just as tough as you want to make them. The forest here, like the Chattahoochee, is a vast wilderness where it's easy to get lost. Stay on the trails and prepare properly. Licensed off-road vehicles are permitted on all forest roads unless posted otherwise. Unlicensed ORVs are permitted only on designated trails.

RECREATION AREAS

Dyar Pasture Boat Ramp

On Lake Oconee, this is a wonderful waterfowl conservation area on a headland, surrounded by the great forest, that juts out into the lake. Birdwatching and walking are the focus here.

As Dyar Pasture is one of Lake Oconee's best advertised public-access boat ramps, it's no wonder that the waters can get a little crowded, especially on weekends and public holidays. There are flush toilets here.

Lake Oconee is one of Georgia's premier **fishing** locations, but very busy at times, and the boating crowd can make life difficult. The best times to go are on weekdays and in the early mornings. The lake is stocked with bass, crappie and bluegill.

A pleasant, easy **hiking trail** leads from the parking lot to the lakeshore. From there you can wander the shoreline at will. Very beautiful countryside, with the lake and forest as a spectacular backdrop.

From Greensboro, drive west for eight miles on Highway 278 to Greshamville Road. Turn right and drive one mile to Greshamville. Turn right again onto Copeland Road and drive on for two miles. Cross Greenbriar Creek Bridge and go an eighth of a mile to a dirt road. Turn right there and drive through the pasture to the ramp.

Hillsboro Lake

A woodland recreation area set on the shores of a very small lake, just south of Monticello and Jasper. It offers boating, camping, fishing and picnicking. The campground is very small – just five sites – but there are 23 picnic sites and vault toilets.

From Hillsboro, drive southeast on the paved County Road 11 for three miles.

Redlands Boat Ramp

Set on Lake Oconee, six miles southwest of Greensboro, Redlands has a public-access boat ramp, three picnic sites and flush toilets.

From Greensboro, take Highway 278 and drive west six miles, then go south on Forest Service Road 1255 for one mile.

Lake Sinclair

Located on the shores of this 15,330-acre lake is the best developed of the seven wilderness recreation areas in the Oconee National Forest. It was once the home of Joel Chandler Harris, creator of *Uncle Remus* and *Br'er Rabbit,* and is set among some of the most beautiful countryside in central Georgia. This is outdoor adventure country at its best. The lake is remote, yet accessible; the scenery is often spectacular and, strangely, the lake is not as busy as some.

Boating: Such a large body of water is, of course, very popular with the boating fraternity. Mile after mile, the lake stretches onward, with tributaries that extend in every direction like the fingers of a giant hand. Here, it's an easy task to find that secluded spot and spend a few quiet hours on the water.

Camping: There are 44 wilderness sites capable of taking trailers and RVs as long as 22 feet. Showers, fresh drinking water and flush toilets are also available.

Other Activities: Lake Sinclair is something of an outdoor playground. There's a swimming beach, 12 picnic sites, and lots of room to spread out.. You can walk along the shoreline, waterski, ride your jet-ski and windsurf.

From Eatonton, at the crossroads of Highways 16, 24, 44, 129, and 441, take Highway 129 south for 10 miles to GA 212. Turn left there and go for one mile, then turn left again onto FSR 1062 and follow the signs for two miles to the parking area.

Scull Shoals Historic Area

Near the Oconee River Recreation Area, this is all that remains of the once-prosperous little town of the same name. Just the remnants of a few buildings and factories give evidence that Scull Shoals ever existed. But it was here that Georgia's paper industries had their beginnings. One of the first cotton gins in the state was located here, and so was an early textile factory. There are no facilities, just a hiking trail through the historic site, but it's a quiet, beautiful area, and well worth a visit.

The park can be reached via a one-mile hiking trail that begins at the boat ramp in the Oconee River Recreation Area, or you drive there by taking the Macedonia Church Road to FSR 1234, where you'll turn left and drive on to FSR 1231. Turn left again there.

Swords Boat Ramp

This ramp on Lake Oconee is open to the public. Facilities are a little sparse, but there are a couple of picnic sites and comfort station with flush toilets. It's also a good place to go fishing, swimming and boating.

From Greensboro, take Highway 278 west for 6½ miles to County Road 1135. Turn south and drive four miles to the ramp.

Oconee River

This wilderness recreation area is set among gently rolling hills and woodland to the north of Greensboro. It's a small site, secluded and quiet, with just a few facilities. These include six picnic sites, seven wilderness campsites, vault toilets, cold water showers, a hiking trail and opportunities for boating and fishing surrounded by some of central Georgia's most spectacular backcountry.

From Greensboro, take Highway 15 and drive northwest for 12 miles; the recreation area is adjacent to the highway.

Panola Mountain State Conservation Park

Panola Mountain, 18 miles southeast of Atlanta on GA 155 via I-20 Exit 36, is, in fact, a single 100-acre granite rock very similar in many ways to its northern neighbor, Stone Mountain. Unlike Stone Mountain, however, Panola still wears its mantle of vegetation and is home to a wide variety of wildlife. The mountain is a National Natural Landmark. The Park Service offers an assortment of nature programs, guided hikes and special activities throughout the year.

Facilities include an interpretive center, a picnic area and four shelters, plus an assortment of hiking and nature trails that lend themselves nicely to nature study, birdwatching and wildlife photography.

Hiking: There are more than six miles of trails, including two miles of self-guided nature trails and a 3½-mile nature walk and fitness trail. Guided mountain hikes are conducted by Park Service staff every Saturday and Sunday, and you can attend educational programs about the ecology of the mountain and the forest floor; the interpretive center houses a number of interesting and informative exhibits.

Annual events include Spring Wildflower Walks in April, Fall Wildflower Walks in September, and an Environmental Discovery Program for children aged 5 to 13 June through August.

Open daily from 7 am until 6 (or dark), September 15 to April 14, and from 7 am until 9, April 15 to September 14. The interpretive center is open from 7 am until 5, Tuesday through Friday, and from noon until 5 on Saturday and Sunday.

Panola Mountain State Park, 2600 Highway 155 SW, Stockbridge, GA 30281. ☎ 770-389-7801.

Pickett's Mill State Historic Site

Pickett's Mill is claimed to be one of the best preserved Civil War battlefields in the nation. It was at Pickett's Mill that, on May 27, 1864, a full corps of General Sherman's Union Army suffered a major defeat on its march toward Atlanta.

The visitor center houses a fine museum with authentic clothing and uniforms of the day, weapons, maps, photographs and artifacts found on the battlefield. From time to time, the Park Service offers living history demonstrations in which authentically uniformed personnel act out the everyday lives of the soldiers. It's worth a phone call to find out what's going on, and when.

A tour of the battlefield is an exciting experience, but involves a lot of walking over some fairly rugged terrain. You'll need to be in good shape. Each year, the park holds a Battle of Pickett's Mill Commemoration.

Pickett's Mill State Historic Site is five miles northeast of Dallas just off GA 381. From I-75, take Exit 123 (the Red Top Mountain Exit), turn right and go 500 yards to the junction of Highway 41. Turn left and go eight miles to a stop light at Highway 92. Turn right. Go four more miles to a four-way stop at the junction of highways 92 and 381. Go straight through the stop light onto 381 and then two more miles until you see a Park Service sign on the right and Mt. Tabor Road on the left. Turn left onto Mt. Tabor Road and go about eight-tenths of a mile to the park entrance on your left.

Pickett's Mill State Historic Site, 2640 Mt. Tabor Road, Dallas, GA 30132. ☎ 770-443-7850. The site is open all year, Tuesday through Saturday from 9 until 5, and on Sundays from 2 until 5.

Sweetwater Creek Conservation Park

It's difficult to believe that Sweetwater Creek is only minutes from downtown Atlanta. Almost 2,000 acres of wilderness parkland feature a diversity of natural resources, including more than five miles of trails and meandering streams, the ruins of a Civil War-era textile mill, and George Parks Reservoir.

Facilities include a group shelter and barbecue pit, 11 picnic shelters, a playground and two fishing docks.

Lake and stream fishing is a popular pastime here, with a good supply of bass, crappie, bluegill and catfish. There's a bait & tackle shop, too. **Hikers** enjoy the five-mile nature trail, which also lends itself to birdwatching and wildlife photography. Sweetwater Creek is a great place to spend an afternoon with the kids and a picnic basket, or on the water (small boats with electric motors only). Canoes and fishing boats, are available for rent.

Annual special events include an arts & crafts show (call for dates), year-round naturalist programs and several educational programs conducted by Park Service staff.

Open from 7 am until dark; the park office is open from 8 until 5. Take I-20 west from Atlanta; Exit 12 at Thornton Road; turn left and go a quarter-mile; turn right onto Blairs Bridge Road; then turn left onto Mount Vernon Road. Sweetwater Creek State Conservation Park, PO Box 816, Lithia Springs, GA 30057. ☎ 404-944-1700.

Washington

This neat little community of 4,300, northwest of Augusta at the junction of highways 17 and 78, was incorporated 1773. It's an historic town of ante-bellum mansions, some still owned by descendants of the original settlers, and tree-lined streets. If you're in the area, you should take the time to visit; there are several attractions worth seeing.

SIGHTSEEING

Calloway Plantation, five miles west of the city off US 78, is a working farm with a red Greek Revival house built just after the Civil War in 1869. It is furnished with period pieces. The log kitchen, vintage 1780, offers a look at what life on the farm must have been like more than 200 years ago through exhibits of domestic and agricultural implements. There's also a Federal-style farmhouse, with fields planted just as they would have been during the late Colonial period. Open Tuesday through Saturday from 10 until 5; guided tours are available. Admission, $4; children 6-12, $1. ☎ 706-678-7060.

The **Robert Toombs House State Historic Site** is at 216 East Robert Toombs Avenue. Robert Toombs was a controversial Southerner, a successful planter, then lawyer, state legislator, US congressman and senator. His ambitions to become president of the Confederacy were thwarted, however, with the election of Jefferson Davis. Disappointed, he accepted a commission in the Army of Northern Virginia. His military career was all but a disaster and eventually he resigned to spend the war years at home, here in Washington. When General Sherman sent soldiers to arrest him, Toombs managed to escape and flee the country. He spent the next two years in exile. Upon his return to the United States, he refused to accept a pardon, stating, "I am not loyal to the existing government of the United States and do not wish to be suspected of loyalty."

The Toombs House has been restored to its pre-Civil War condition and is packed full of antiques, exhibits and artifacts of the times. You can view a dramatic film that portrays Toombs in his later life telling his story to a young reporter.

Open year-round Tuesday through Saturday from 9 until 5, and on Sundays from 2 until 5. Admission, $2; children 6-18, $1.

Robert Toombs State Historic Site, PO Box 605, Washington, GA 30673. ☎ 706-678-2226.

Washington Historical Museum, at 308 East Robert Toombs Avenue, was built in 1835 and houses an extensive collection of Confederate relics, including Jefferson Davis' camp chest, battlefield artifacts and uniforms. Open Tuesday through Saturday from 10 until 5, and on Sunday from 2 until 5. Admission, $2; children 6-12, $1. ☎ 706-678-2105.

The Coastal Plain

This area takes in a great stretch of land along Georgia's coast from the Florida border to the South Carolina state line. It's a land of seagrass, dunes and intracoastal waterway with odd pockets of civilization sprinkled around. It's Georgia's most historic area. It was here on these shores that settlers came from England and Europe and the Carolinas to make new homes for themselves in a new land. It is, essentially, the birthplace of Georgia.

The Coastal Plain is certainly not lacking in things to do. It offers deep-sea and inshore fishing for shark, barracuda, whiting, sailfish, marlin; endless miles of sandy beaches; a hundred or so barrier islands; one of Georgia's oldest and most beautiful cities; watersports; and the vast natural area that is the Okefenokee Swamp. But where to begin? How about Savannah, gateway to Georgia's coast and the Golden Isles?

Touring

Savannah

HISTORY

Savannah was founded in 1733 by James Oglethorpe, a British general and noted philanthropist of colonial America, as the headquarters for a buffer colony between Spanish Florida and the English colony in Carolina, and as a haven for English citizens imprisoned for debt.

James, the son of a wealthy baronet, was born on December 22, 1696, in London. He was educated at Eton and Oxford and, in 1716-17, served in the war against the Turks and was praised for his services at the siege of Belgrade. He returned to England and in 1722 was elected to Parliament.

He had a sympathetic attitude toward those less fortunate than himself. He saw the long-established practice of imprisoning English debtors as one of the nation's great injustices, and he also

The Coastal Plain

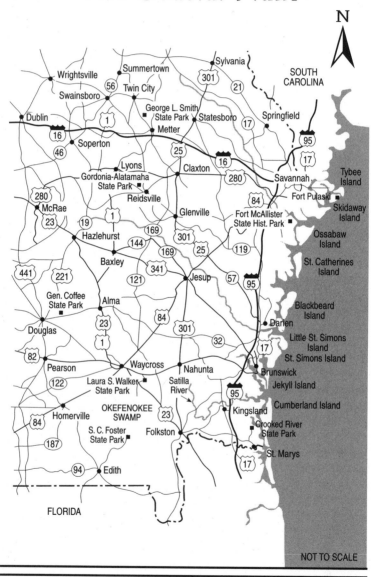

believed that oppressed members of dissenting religious sects deserved a place of refuge. Unable to change the system, he determined to save its victims. And, with that in mind, he suggested a colony in Georgia for them would also serve as a buffer between the English settlers in the Carolinas and the Spaniards in Florida. His heartfelt and persuasive arguments won a charter for the Georgia Colony in 1732.

In 173, Oglethorpe set sail, accompanied by the first party of 120 settlers, and together they founded the city of Savannah. He returned to England the following year, by which time Georgia was already attracting colonists of German Lutherans and Moravians, as well as Scottish Presbyterians.

Oglethorpe returned to Georgia in late 1735, bringing with him the brothers John and Charles Wesley, the founders of the Methodist movement, who conducted preaching missions there and in other colonies.

In 1736 he built Fort Frederica on St. Simons Island as a defense against the Spanish to the south. And, when war broke out between England and Spain in 1739, he led an unsuccessful attack on Spain's St. Augustine settlement and defended his Fort Frederica against the Spanish. Despite his popularity, however, some colonists opposed his rules against drinking and slavery to the point where a subordinate charged him with mismanaging the expeditions to St. Augustine. This led to his being recalled to England in 1743 to stand trial. The court martial vindicated him, but he never returned to Georgia.

In England, Oglethorpe continued to pursue his military career and in 1745 helped put down a Scottish rebellion. James Edward Oglethorpe died at Cranham Hall in Essex, England, on June 30, 1785.

Oglethorpe was missed in Savannah, but the city thrived nonetheless. In 1744, the Port of Savannah was established, turning it into a city of stategic importance. By the outbreak of the American Revolution it was a bustling commercial center with ships coming and going from all points around the globe. War came in 1778 when the city was captured by the British, who held it until the close of hostilities.

From then on until the outbreak of the Civil War, with the growth of the plantation-based economy, tobacco and cotton, the city's port traffic increased steadily; it was a good time to be in Savannah.

Then, in 1861, war came again. During the Civil War, Savannah was an important supply point for the Confederacy. The fall of Fort Pulaski in 1862 closed the port to all sea traffic but a few blockade runners. The city finally fell to General Sherman's troops in December 1864.

Today, Savannah is the oldest and third largest city in Georgia, and is one of the most beautiful cities in the United States. The seat of Chatham County in the southeastern part of the state, it lies only 18 miles from the Atlantic Ocean at the mouth of the Savannah River and remains an important port.

As a center of historical interest, Savannah exceeds all other cities in Georgia and is one of the state's leading tourist attractions. Much of the old city laid out by James Oglethorpe remains. Of the original 24 squares, 20 survive, bordered by handsome townhouses and landscaped with live oaks festooned by Spanish moss, azaleas, fountains and statues. The wide tree-lined streets are crossed at intervals by small parks and squares that bloom with gardenias, camellias and azaleas. Palmettos, magnolias and live oaks give Savannah the name Forest City. Monuments to Confederate and American Revolutionary heroes stand in the parks. The downtown historic district is one of the most extensive and best restored in the country. Fine brick houses with old-world gardens add to the city's charm. Then there are the old churches and the city's historic residential section, a collection of beautiful homes reminiscent of the grand timess before the advent of the Civil War.

Yes, Savannah is truly beautiful, and the best way to see it is on foot. So leave your car at the hotel, put on a pair of comfortable walking shoes, and sally forth; you won't be disappointed.

HOW TO GET THERE

By Air

Savannah International Airport is served by most of the major airlines, including Delta, USAir, and United, with direct service through hubs in Atlanta, Charlotte, Raleigh, Columbia, New York, Dallas, Charleston, Washington, Jacksonville and other major cities. There are 30 flights in and out daily to Atlanta alone. The taxi fare from the airport to the business district (one way) is $18 for one person, plus $5 for each additional person. The limousine fare is $15 one-way, or $25 round-trip.

By Bus

Greyhound/Trailways, ☎ 1-800-231-2222.

By Rail

Amtrak, ☎ 800-USA-RAIL.

By Road

Interstate 95 is the direct connection north and south from New England to Miami, including Georgia. Highway 17, often called the Ocean Highway, offers a more leisurely, picturesque route through the coastal towns and villages north and south from Charleston to Jacksonville. I-16 runs east-west to and from Atlanta via Macon.

WHEN YOU ARE THERE

Most of Savannah's attractions are open daily, although a few do close on Monday, and some open late and close early on Sunday, so you can visit any day that suits you best. You should be aware, however, that to do Savannah properly will take more than a single day, especially if you decide to take in some of the out-of-town attractions.

Getting Around

Getting around in downtown Savannah is a snap; rush hours are never very busy, and there's plenty of parking available. The best strategy is to leave your car at the hotel and catch a shuttle; Savannah is a walking city, and everything can be reached via public transport. The **Chatham Area Transit** (CAT) offers regular, convenient service on electric-powered buses from downtown hotels, inns and the visitors center to the Historic District and other attractions. The fare is a reasonable $1.50 for an all-day pass, or 50¢ per ride.

All major **car rental** companies are represented at the airport.

Climate

The climate is temperate, with a mean temperature of 51° in winter, 66° in spring, 80° in summer, and 66° in the fall. Sunshine is plentiful in all seasons; there are rarely more than two or three days in succession without it. All of which sounds great, but Savannah and the islands can be quite humid in summertime, and subject to frequent afternoon thundershowers. Hurricanes rarely present a problem, but once every 10 years or so you can expect a big blow.

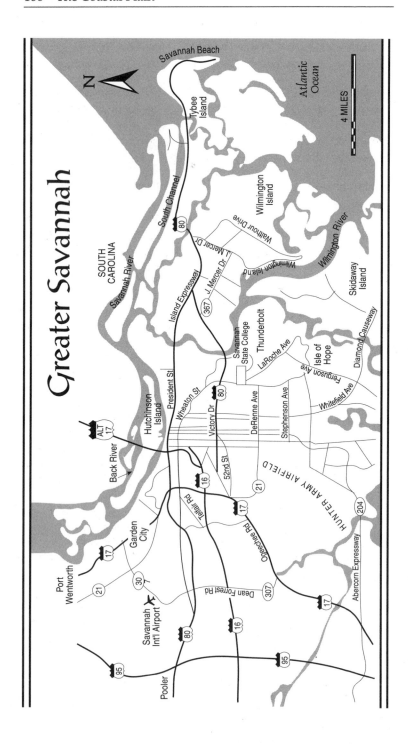

DINING OUT

If you live in the South you already know; if you're here on a visit you're about to find out: Southern cuisine is decidedly different, and especially so in Savannah and the Low Country. Southern cuisine has its roots in the old plantations where, prior to the Civil War, most kitchens were set apart from the main house (the heat from the fire, along with the long hot summer days, would have made life in the living quarters intolerable). This separation between white mistress and black cook led to a specialized labor force that turned the plantation slaves into America's first professional chefs. Their secrets were rarely, if ever, written down; they were simply told and shown to each successive generation. There's nothing quite like a plate of fried catfish and hush puppies, or country ham, eggs and grits.

Savannah also has permanent access to fresh seafood. The shrimp here are always fresh, juicy and delicious, so a meal or two, at least, should be high on your list. Seafood restaurants abound, but Savannah's dining experience is as diverse as it is extensive. You can find just about anything your taste might desire, from Chinese to Mexican, Italian to Greek, and from a New York-style deli to the best of Cajun. Here are one or two good restaurants you might like to try. They are not the only ones, so be sure to explore and find out for yourself.

Garibaldi's Café, 315 West Congress Street, in the Historic District, is open for dinner on weekdays from 6 until 11, and on Friday and Saturday from 5:30 to 11. It's an intimate café with soft lighting set in an old firehouse. The menu includes fresh seafood dishes, veal, beef, chicken and pasta. It can get very busy at times, so you should make a reservation. ☎ 912-232-7118. $$$.

The Pirate's House, 20 East Broad & Bay streets, in the Historic District, is open for lunch from 11:30, and for dinner from 5:30 daily. This is a seafood house, but they also specialize in healthy foods. It's a popular restaurant, often very busy, so a reservation is in order. ☎ 912-233-5757. $$.

River House, 313 East River Street, on the historic waterfront, is open for lunch and dinner from 11 am. The theme is nautical, with a menu dedicated to fresh seafood. Other staples, such as steak and prime rib, are available, too. ☎ 912-234-1900. $$.

WHERE TO STAY

East Bay Inn, 225 East Bay Street, Historic District, is housed in a restored cotton warehouse, circa 1853. The rooms are decorated and furnished in the Georgian style and have 18-foot ceilings. All rooms have coffee-makers, and complimentary beverages are available in the evening. ☎912-238-1225. $$-$$$.

The Forsyth Park Inn, 102 West Hall Street, is an historic bed and breakfast in an elegantly restored Victorian mansion overlooking Forsyth Park. The 10 rooms are all furnished with period pieces. Afternoon tea is served and free beverages are offered in the evening. All rooms have telephones. Pets are not allowed. ☎ 912-233-6800. $$-$$$.

Howard Johnson Lodge, 224 West Boundary, adjacent to the Savannah Visitor Center in the Historic District. No pets are allowed at this motor inn, but it's a great spot to base youself and take in all the sights. There's a nice dining room, a heated indoor pool, and an exercise room. ☎ 912-232-4371. $.

Olde Harbor Inn, 508 East Factors Walk, is another historic bed and breakfast in the Riverfront District. There are several nice restaurants close by. All rooms have coffee-makers and free continental breakfast. Small pets are permitted. ☎ 912-234-4100. $$-$$$

Quality Inn - Heart of Savannah, 300 West Bay Street, Historic District. This hotel is much like any other chain. There is no restaurant on the property, but several may be found nearby. Complimentary continental breakfast is offered in the lobby each morning. ☎ 912-236-6321. $.

Tybee Island

Econo Lodge, 404 Butler Avenue, Tybee Island. ☎ 912-786-4535. Children under 18 stay free. Pool and café. Located on the beach. Credit cards accepted. $.

For further information on hotels, motels, camping and touring, contact the Savannah Area Convention and Visitors Bureau, 222 W. Oglethorpe Avenue, PO Box 1628, Savannah, GA 31402-1628. ☎ 912-944-0456.

TOURIST INFORMATION

Savannah Convention and Visitors Bureau, PO Box 1628, Savannah, GA 31402-1628. ☎ 912-944-0456. Fax 912-944-0648.

SHOPPING

Although at first Savannah might seem to be all cobblestone streets, restored forts and museums, it doesn't take dedicated shoppers long to realize that there's plenty for them, too. The **riverfront** is a world of old cotton warehouses stuffed with galleries, specialty shops, antique stores, boutiques and malls. The streets of the **Historic District** are lined with smaller, old-world shops where you can browse away the hours, always sure that there's something just a little different to be found behind the next tiny shopfront.

Savannah's south side boasts of more than 20 shopping centers, including the huge Oglethorpe and Savannah malls. Farther on, Abercorn (Highway 203) is **Savannah Festival Factory Outlet Center** where you can find all sorts of brand-name bargains.

SIGHTSEEING IN TOWN

To make the most of your time in Savannah you should start out at the visitors center, 301 Martin Luther King Jr. Boulevard, for orientation and a 15-minute video presentation. Next, you might like to visit the Savannah History Museum, next door to the visitors center. There, you can view another film and get a better feel for the old city. A guided trolley or walking tour is also a good idea. Be sure to visit River Street, a nine-block plaza facing the Savannah River, with shops, restaurants, galleries and pubs. Explore the City Market and City Market Arts Center. Take a stroll along the Bull Street corridor and enjoy the old squares. Visit one or two of Savannah's historic inns. If you have the time, a horse and carriage tour is a great way to see the historic district. Finally, no visit to Savannah would be complete without a day trip to Tybee Island and the beaches.

Savannah's **Historic District** contains more than 1,000 historically and architecturally significant buildings, all faithfully restored to their former glory, making it the largest such district in the country. But that's not all; there's much more to see out and about in the greater Savannah area and the islands to the east and south. Thus, planning to see all the sights, even within the city limits, can be a daunting task. A couple of options present themselves. First, you can read through this section – it contains most of the more popular attractions, and then some – and pick out what appeals to you most. Then, using the map, you can plan your route and set out to explore. Your second option is to sign up for one or more of the many organized tours. It's more expensive, but you'll find several tour operators listed at the end of this section. Whatever you decide, it would be best if you put on comfortable walking shoes, lock your keys in the hotel safe, and catch the CAT into the District.

Before you begin, you might like to know what happened to Forrest Gump's bench. If you've seen the movie, you'll remember Forrest sitting on a bench in Chappewa Square in front of the General Oglethorpe Monument. But there is no bench; it was nothing more than a movie prop. Many residents, however, thought a bench should be placed in the square permanently; many more, mostly purists intent on preserving the city's historical authenticity, shuddered at the idea. The solution was reached in June 1995 when the bench found a home in the Savannah History Museum. Now you can see it there, along with the suitcase and box of chocolates, a gift to the city from Paramount Pictures Corporation.

Here's another snippet of interesting information, especially for those who've read John Berendt's best selling novel of Savannah, *Midnight In the Garden of Good and Evil*. The hauntingly beautiful bronze statue on the book's cover, *Bird Girl*, is currently being displayed at the Savannah History Museum.

SPANISH MOSS

One more thing: the Spanish moss you see hanging from all the trees, telephone poles and fences isn't moss at all. It's a flowering plant found all over the southeastern United States and tropical South America, and it's the first indication you'll see that you're entering the deep South. Believe it or not, it's a member of the pineapple family, but it has no roots and can only live in a humid area, absorbing water directly from the air. It blooms from April to July.

☞ **Campers beware:** Don't use Spanish moss to sleep on; it's full of red bugs and chiggers.

Savannah Historic District

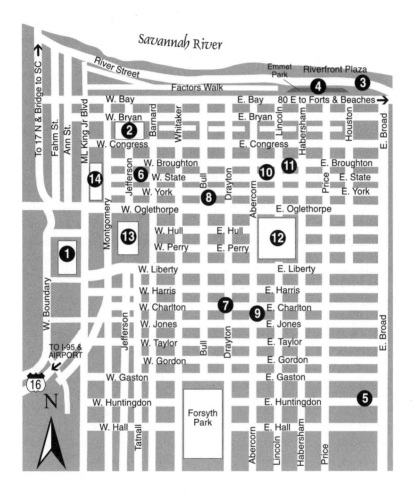

1. Savannah Visitors Center, 1860
2. City Market
3. Ships of the Sea Museum
4. Waving Girl Statue
5. King-Tisdell Cottage
6. Telfair Mansion & Art Museum, 1800s
7. Green-Meldrim House, 1853
8. The Juliette Gordon Low Birthplace, 1820
9. Andrews House, 1849
10. Owens-Thomas House, 1816
11. Davenport House, 1815-1820
12. Colonial Park Cemetery
13. Civic Center
14. County Courthouse

Savannah History Museum: Situated in a restored 19th-century railroad shed behind the visitors center at 303 Martin Luther King Jr. Boulevard, this rather large museum contains a grand hall and two theaters. Here, through multimedia presentations, animated dioramas and static exhibits, the history of Savannah and Eastern Georgia is laid out in an interesting and easy-to-understand manner. One theater focuses on Savannah's history from the earliest times, the other on the battle fought here in 1779 during the American revolution. Other exhibits include a model of the *SS Savannah*, the first steamship to sail across the Atlantic; an 1890 locomotive; an extensive collection of military uniforms; a cotton gin; one of Johnny Mercer's Oscars; and, of course, Forrest Gump's famous bench. Open daily, 8:30 to 5. Admission, $3; children 6-12, $1.75. ☎ 912-238-1779.

Owens-Thomas House: This elegant English villa was designed and built in the Regency style by William Jay in 1817. It was from here in 1825 that the Marquis de Lafayette gave a speech to the citizens of Savannah. Today, the old house offers a treat to the visitor; it's furnished with rare antique pieces of the period, and contains fine collections of rare European and Chinese porcelains, as well as a great many artifacts and pieces of great historical significance. Beyond the main house is the carriage house, connected to it by an exquisite formal, landscaped garden. Guided tours are conducted Tuesday through Saturday from 10 until 5, and on Sunday from 2 to 5; the last tour begins 30 minutes before closing. Closed on all major holidays. Admission, $5; children 6-12, $2. 124 Abercorne Street. ☎ 912-233-9743.

Andrew Low House: Built by Andrew Low, one of Savannah's wealthy merchants, in 1848, this stuccoed brick house is famous for its carved woodwork, crystal chandeliers and fine plaster cornices. It was also the home of Juliette Gordon Low, founder of the Girl Scout movement in the US in 1912. It's always been high on the list of places to visit. General Robert E. Lee and novelist William Makepeace Thackeray are only two of the famous guests to have spent time in the old house, which is packed with period furniture and memorabilia. Open Monday through Wednesday and Friday and Saturday from 10:30 until 4; Sunday from noon until 4. Admission, $5; Girl Scouts, $1. 329 Abacorn Street at Lafayette Square. ☎ 912-233-6854.

City Market: Just east of Franklin Square and Montgomery on West Saint Julian Street, the City Market is a recently restored area with lots of interesting shops and stores, art galleries, studios, restaurants and taverns. It's easy to find, easy to shop, and well worth a little time spent wandering around; who knows what unusual goodies you'll find.

Davenport House: Built during the years 1815-1820 by Isaiah Davenport, this house at 324 East State Street is one of the finest examples of Federal architecture in Savannah. It was condemned in 1950 but saved from demolition by the efforts of the Historic Savannah Foundation. The old building was restored, refurnished with English and American period pieces, and decorated as it might have been during the early 19th century. Today, it's famous for its delicate plasterwork, fine wrought iron and unusual elliptical stairway. Tours are given every 30 minutes. Open daily from 10 until 4. Admission, $4; children 6-18, $3. ☎ 912-236-8097.

Factors Walk: This row of narrow buildings that stretches along the riverfront just north of Bay Street from Martin Luther King to Emmet Park takes its name from the activities of the cotton and other commodities merchants who conducted their business on the street during the 19th century. As you'll see, a network of cobblestone streets and iron and concrete bridges connects the walk and its buildings to the riverfront. The cobblestones were once ballast from visiting ships.

Forsyth Park: Situated at the southern end of the Historic District between Whitaker and Drayton, Forsyth is one of Savannah's most picturesque parks, especially in the spring when the azaleas are in bloom. If you've already done a lot of walking, it's the perfect place to rest and enjoy the tranquility. A lovely old fountain, similar to the one in the Place de la Concorde in Paris, is the park's signature piece. The Confederate Monument is in the extension to the south. Open daily.

Green-Meldrim House: This fine old ante-bellum home at 14 West Macon Street had the rather dubious honor of becoming General Sherman's headquarters during his occupation of Savannah in 1864. It was built in the 1850s and is a fine example of the Gothic Revival architecture so typical of the South prior to the Civil War. Today, it's the Parish House of St. John's Church, but you can still take a tour. Open Tuesday and Thursday through Saturday from 10 until 4; closed holidays and during some church activities. Admission, $3. ☎ 912-233-3845.

Juliette Gordon Low Birthplace: It was here at 142 Bull Street that Juliette Gordon Low, founder of America's Girl Scout movement was born. It's a fine old house, full of period furniture, much of it Low family pieces, and there's a lovely Victorian garden with original outbuildings. The house has been restored and refurnished to its condition of 1886, the year of Juliette's marriage. The house, grounds and buildings are all maintained by the Girl

Scouts as a memorial to their founder. Open Monday and Tuesday and Thursday through Saturday from 10 until 4, and from 12:30 until 4:30 on Sunday. Admission, $5; children 6-18, $4. ☎ 912-233-4501.

King-Tisdale Cottage: This Victorian cottage, built in 1896 and restored almost to its original condition, is Savannah's premier Black Heritage museum. Here, you can sign up for the Negro Heritage Trail Tour, which takes in some 17 significant sites that played important roles in Savannah's Black history. The museum itself is packed full of interesting artifacts, memorabilia and exhibits. The tour departs from the visitors center on Martin Luther King; call for schedules. The museum is open Tuesday through Saturday from noon until 5. Admission, $2.50; trail tour, $10; children under 12, $5. 514 East Huntingdon Street. ☎ 912-234-8000.

River Street Train Museum: If you're a model railroad enthusiast, this is one stop you won't want to miss. Here, housed in an 1856 building at 315 West River Street, you'll find a fine collection of working O-gauge toy trains and rolling stock dating from the 1930s, as well as a large, operating layout with a miniature village, trees and countryside. It's a real treat for kids of all ages. Open Monday through Saturday from 11 until 5:30, and on Sunday from 1 until 6; closed Christmas and Thanksgiving. Admission, $1.50; children, 50¢. ☎ 912-233-6175.

Ships Of The Sea Maritime Museum: Located in an old warehouse built in 1898 on the Savannah riverfront, once the center of Georgia's sea trade around the world, this maritime museum is one of the Historic District's most interesting attractions. Here, you can see collections of early navigational equipment, ships in bottles, model ships, even figureheads. Some of the ships in bottles are exquisitely made, rare and easily worth as much as their life-size counterparts. There's also a shipwright's carpentry shop and a number of exhibits that interpret Savannah's seagoing history. Open daily from 10 until 5; closed St. Patrick's Day, Thanksgiving, Christmas and the New Year. Admission, $3; children 7-12, $1.50. 503 East River Street. ☎ 912-232-1511.

Talfair Mansion & Art Museum: This museum occupies the site of Government House, the one-time residence of Georgia's royal governors. The old house is no more, but the 1818 Regency-style mansion that replaced it was designed and built by English architect William Jay. Its Octagon Room is claimed to be the finest of its type in the United States. The house is extensively furnished with fine antiques and period pieces, many of which once belonged to Governor Edward Telfair. But this is, after all, an art museum, the oldest in the Southeast, and its museum wing is filled with a permanent collection of art dating from the 18th century to the present. The collection includes important American and European paintings, sculptures, prints, silver, fine furniture and decorative arts. Open Tuesday through Saturday from 10 until 5, and on Sunday from 2 until 5; closed most major holidays. Admission, $3; children under 18, free. 121 Barnard Street on Telfair Square. ☎ 912-232-1511.

Trustees Garden Site: Here on East Broad Street you can visit the original site of a 10-acre garden laid out in 1733 and modeled after the Chelsea Gardens in London by the colonists. The peach trees they planted in the garden became the foundation of Georgia's thriving peach industry. From 1762 it was the site of Fort Wayne, which was occupied and strengthened by the British in 1779, and then rebuilt by American engineers in 1812.

TOURS

A number of self-guided and organized educational tours are available at the visitors center, and cassette tapes are provided in several languages for walking or driving tours; tape players are available, too. A list of professional tour operators leaving the Visitors Center daily follows the list of self-guided options below.

Walking Tours (1-2 hours): Four map tours of the Historic District are available, which show the squares and recreation areas.

Driving Tours (1-4 hours): Four map tours are available, including one of Old Savannah and nearby Thunderbolt and Tybee islands. Horse-drawn carriages provide an overview of the Historic District (see list below).

Harbor Tours (1-2 hours): Several options are available (see below).

TOUR OPERATORS

Helen Salter's Savannah Tours, 1113 Winston Avenue, ☎ 912-355-4296. Two-hour guided bus tours of the historic district, museums, historic houses, squares and parks. Call for rates and schedules.

Old Savannah Tours, 516 Lee Boulevard, ☎ 912-354-7913. A full range of guided bus tours of the Historic District, beaches, fort, Low Country and other areas. Specialty tours include Candlelight, Dolphin Watch, and Ghost Tales. Tours leave from the visitors center and many of the downtown hotels and inns. Free all-day on-and-off privileges. Call for schedules and rates.

Old Town Trolley Tours, ☎ 912-233-0083. Trolleys depart every 30 minutes daily from various downtown locations to all the historic attractions and waterfront district. The 90-minute tours feature some 100 points of interest. Adults, $14; children under 12, $6.

Tapestry Tours, ☎ 912-233-7770 or 800-794-7770. Extensive two-hour morning and four-hour walk-on bus tours depart from most downtown hotels and other locations for all the historic points of interest. The two tours can be combined to make a full day's trip. The morning tour departs daily at 10:15; the afternoon tour at 12:15. The fare ranges from $25 to $70, depending upon the option chosen.

Grey Line Tours, ☎ 912-234-8687. This company offers departures every 30 minutes daily from various downtown stops visiting the historic district, old mansions, squares, River Street, the City Market and the Low Country in open-air Red Trolleys or air-conditioned mini-buses. Free on-and-off privileges. Call for rates.

Carriage Tours of Savannah, ☎ 912-236-6756. Tours leave the Historic District daily from a number of locations in the downtown area. Call for rates.

Savannah Riverboat Tours, River Street Riverboat Company, 9 East River Street, Savannah, GA 31412. ☎ 912-232-6404 or 800-786-6404. One-hour narrated sightseeing cruises, $8.50; two-hour evening cruises with entertainment, $9.50; two-hour evening dinner cruises, $30.95 (children under 12, $19.95). Reservations required. Cruises leave daily. Call for schedules.

SIGHTSEEING OUT OF TOWN

From Savannah to Jacksonville, there's so much to see and do you'll never be bored. The 15 Golden Isles and the great swamp just to the west will provide more opportunities than you could handle in a month of Sundays.

Tybee Island. Sand, sea and soft ocean breezes have a charm all their own; combine them with more than a little history and the result is Tybee Island, a little beachfront community just 18 miles from downtown Savannah. Flags of five nations, as well as those of a half-dozen or so pirates, have flown over the island. Tybee is an Indian word for salt.

From her northern shore, Yankees bombarded the supposedly impregnable walls of Fort Pulaski in 1861 and brought the Confederate garrison to defeat after 30 hours.

Thirty-six years after the fall of Fort Pulaski, the Tybee area became the site of other war-related activities; Fort Scraven was established on the northern side of the island. It began as a coastal artillery station and eventually evolved into a training camp for thousands of troops that went off to fight two world wars. Remnants of the wartime installation can be seen all over Fort Scraven. The fort is also home to the Tybee Museum, housed in one of the old coastal batteries built in 1898 – one of the seven batteries that comprised Fort Scraven. It's packed with memorabilia so diverse it defies description, and traces the history of the island from colonial times to 1945. There are exhibits featuring Martello Tower, the Civil War and Fort Scraven; doll collections, gun collections, and a large assortment of military artifacts.

Just across the street from the museum is the Tybee Lighthouse, the oldest active lighthouse in the United States. The climb up the 300 steps to the top is daunting, and you'd better be in good shape, but once there you'll enjoy one of the most dynamic panoramic views in eastern Georgia – a truly awesome experience.

Tybee Island is different from the Golden Isles of St. Simons, Jekyll and Sea Island 60 miles or so to the south. True, it's a year-round haven for several thousand people, many of whom balk at the thought of leaving even in the face of a hurricane, and there have been a few of those. But during the spring and summer, the population swells to almost unimaginable proportions when the summer breezes waft the scent of fresh salt air inland toward the city. They come from Savannah in their thousands for the day, or move the entire family onto the island for an extended stay. Many come just to enjoy the fresh air, which is said to be milder, saltier, and more refreshing than any other.

Tybee Island fronts more than four miles of the Atlantic Ocean and the Savannah River for almost two miles. The beach runs the entire length of the island, with the old coastal defenses and lighthouse located at the north end. There's also a boardwalk, fishing pier, amusements, hotels, motels and several hundred holiday cottages. So, if you like crowds, Tybee is the place for you. If not, you'd better try one of the islands farther to the south.

Fort Pulaski National Monument is just west of Tybee Island on Cockspur Island at the mouth of the Savannah River. It's about 15 miles east of the city and may be reached by way of Highway 80 (the Tybee Highway). The entrance to the fort is located on McQueen's Island at US 80. Cockspur Island is connected by a short road and a bridge across the South Channel of the Savannah River.

The story of Fort Pulaski is interesting. Cockspur Island is a natural defensive position upon which fortifications of one sort or another have been located since Fort George, a palisade log blockhouse, was built in 1761. It was dismantled in 1776 by American patriots who knew the wooden structure could not stand against the guns of a strong British fleet.

In 1794 a new fort was begun on the island. This one was named Fort Greene in honor of the Revolutionary War hero, General Nathaniel Greene. It was very small, constructed of earth and timber with a complement of six guns. Unfortunately, Fort Greene was destroyed by a hurricane some nine years after construction was completed; almost all of the tiny garrison were drowned. It would be more than 26 years before construction of a new fort began on the island.

During the War of 1812 the coastal settlements and cities of the new American nation suffered dreadfully at the hands of the British navy. The coastline for a thousand miles was virtually defenseless. The city of Washington was burned, and settlements along the Mid-Atlantic coast were laid waste. And things might have been even worse were it not for the fact that England was fighting a war with Napoleon and most of her forces were engaged there.

After the Treaty of Ghent in 1814 that ended the war with Britain, President James Madison persuaded Congress to appropriate the necessary funds for a chain of forts to protect the vulnerable American coastline. Cockspur Island was chosen as one of the sites. Work on the new fort, however, did not begin until 1829.

In 1833, the new fort on Cockspur Island was named Fort Pulaski in honor of the Polish hero, Count Casimir Pulaski, who fought in the American Revolution and was killed in the Battle of Savannah on October 9th, 1779. Construction was completed in 1847, but the arming and garrisoning still had not been completed by the time of Lincoln's election as President of the United States in 1860.

The fort's armament was supposed to consist of 145 seacoast guns, but by 1860 only 20 of those guns had been mounted, and the entire garrison consisted of a caretaker and an ordinance sergeant. An interesting footnote to the years of Fort Pulaski's construction is that every engineering officer, with the exception of Major Babcock who died in 1831, employed during the works eventually became a general, either in the Confederate or Union armies.

As to the Civil War years, Fort Pulaski was manned by Confederate forces from the outset. She was thought to be invulnerable, but fell to Union forces on April 10, 1862, after many hours of bombardment by heavy guns on Tybee Island. At the end of the war the fort became a military prison and, for a while, home to many of the Confederate leaders, including Secretary of State Robert Hunter, Secretary of the Treasury George Trenholm, and

Secretary of War James Seddon, as well as several assistant secretaries, and three state governors.

In 1933 the fort was transferred to the jurisdiction of the Department of the Interior, and the National Park Service went to work on its restoration. Today, the fort is open to the public.

Open daily, 8 until 5:15, and from 8 until 6:45 Memorial Day to Labor Day; closed Christmas Day.

Fort Pulaski National Monument, PO Box 30757, Savannah, GA 31410. ☎ 912-786-5787.

Fort Pulaski

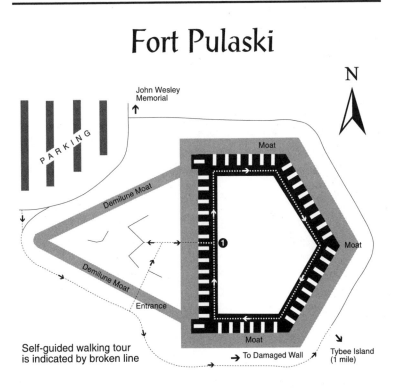

Skidaway Island State Park offers more than 500 acres of salt- and freshwater marshes to make this wild and beautiful park a nature lover's paradise. The Park Service on Skidaway Island offers a complete series of educational programs on the environment, the wild birds that inhabit the area, and the sea life. But visitors to the park will find much more to interest them as they hike the nature trails and explore the park's many historical and archaeological resources.

Major facilities at the park include 88 tent and trailer sites, five picnic shelters, a playground and a swimming pool. The Park Service runs many educational programs, and hiking, nature study, birdwatching, wildlife photography, picnicking and outdoor games are all popular.

Annual events include a Coastal Birds Program in April, Seafood Delights in the fall, and Wild Game Cooking in the winter.

The park is open daily from 7 am until 10 pm pm and the park office hours are from 8 am to 5 pm.

For reservations or more information, contact the Skidaway Island State Park, Savannah, GA 31406. ☎ 912-356-2523 or 356-2524.

The park is located about six miles southeast of Savannah on the Diamond Causeway. Take I-16 to Savannah, then take Exit 34 at I-516. Next, turn right onto Waters Avenue and proceed to Diamond Causeway.

Fort Morris State Historic Park, located on the Medway River, was the site of several attacks by British forces during the Revolutionary War. Twice, the American defenders were able to withstand combined land and sea attacks by the Redcoats. Then, on January 9, 1779, the fort fell to a superior force and remained under British control until they finally evacuated Georgia in 1882. During the occupation several prominent local people were imprisoned at the fort, including George Walton, one of the signers of the Declaration of Independence. When the British moved out, they left the fort and the once-bustling seaport of Sunbury in ruins.

Today, visitors can tour the remains of the earthworks and enjoy the scenic beauty of St. Catherine's Sound. There's also a museum and many exhibits that describe life and times as they must have been in the colonial seaport of Sunbury.

Annual events include a Revolutionary War Battle Reenactment in February; Sunbury –A Town and Its People in April; and Indigo – A Colonial Export in October.

The site is open all year-round Tuesday through Saturday from 9 am until 5 pm and on Sunday from 2 pm until 5:30 pm. The site is closed on Mondays, except for legal holidays, and on Thanksgiving and Christmas Day. There is a small admission fee and group rates are offered with advance notice. Picnic tables and bus parking are available.

For information, contact the Fort Morris State Historic Site, Route 1, Box 236, Midway, GA 31320. ☎ 912-884-5999.

The site is located seven miles east of I-95 Exit 13 on GA 38.

Fort McAllister, in a key position atop a bluff on the south bank of the Ogeechee River, is probably the most complete and best preserved Confederate earthwork fortification in the entire country.

The fort was the southernmost defensive position designed to protect the approaches to the Savannah River some 15 miles to the north, and to defend Confederate blockade runners into Savannah and the approaches to the Ogeechee River. It was also expected to protect the vital Atlantic and Gulf Railroad trestle that lay only a short distance upstream from the fort, and the rice and cotton plantations that lay along the banks of the river.

The massive walls of the fort, still in much the same condition today as when they were built, were designed by Captain John McCrady of the Confederate States Engineers, and were constructed by hand. Work was begun on the site in June, 1861.

Unlike its neighbors to the north, Forts Sumter and Pulaski, McAllister was not an imposing-looking structure. The great brick forts to the north were thought to be impregnable at the beginning of the war. Time and the new, large-caliber rifled guns, however, would prove to be the nemeses of the massive structures. But Fort McAllister would never fall to the great rifles that brought about the demise of its northern neighbors. The spinning projectiles hurtled across distances of more than a mile to shatter the great walls of Fort Pulaski. But the earthen structure of Fort McAllister

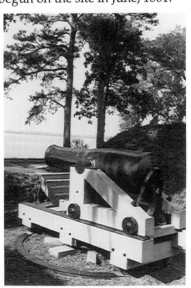

Cannon on display at Fort McAllister.

could absorb the impact of the huge 11-inch guns ranged against it from the ironclad, *USS Montauk*, on the 27th of January, 1863.

The fort, when completed, was equipped with 22 seacoast guns, including several massive eight-inch columbiads and a 32-pounder rifled gun. There was also a 32-pounder hot-shot gun, a dozen or so smaller guns, and a 10-inch seacoast mortar.

By the end of summer, 1864, General Lee was being hard-pressed in Virginia, and Atlanta had fallen to General Sherman; it was only a matter of time before Fort McAllister would have the full attention of the invading Federal forces.

Soon word came that General Sherman was at Savannah, only 15 miles away to the north by sea. With McAllister guarding the southern approaches, Sherman's army, more than 60,000 strong, would be unable to receive supplies from the ships waiting offshore. So, on December 10, 1864, Sherman ordered General Oliver Howard, commander of the right wing of his army, to reduce the fort and open the way for his much-needed food and supplies. Howard, in turn, ordered General William B. Hazen's veteran division of the XV Army Corps to march up the Ogeechee and take the fort.

Hazen's men attacked at 4:15 pm. They stormed over the outer defenses, up the earthen walls, and into the fort. The fighting was, for a short time, desperate and hand-to-hand. The outcome, however, was inevitable; in only 15 minutes Major George Anderson's 200 defenders were overwhelmed. Confederate losses were 16 killed and 54 wounded; Union losses totaled 134, caused mostly by exploding mines in the outer defenses of the fort.

The fall of Fort McAllister marked the end of Sherman's "March to the Sea." With McAllister in Union hands, and supplies flowing into the Federal quartermasters' stores, it soon became obvious that further defense of Savannah was useless and could only end in disaster. So, on December 20, 1864, Confederate Lieutenant General William Hardee gathered together his 10,000 weary soldiers and left the city to General Sherman.

As for Fort McAllister? Tranquility returned to the banks of the Ogeechee and for many years only the raucous seabirds inhabited the once-bustling defenses. Then, in the late 1930s, Henry Ford, the owner of the site, undertook an extensive program of restoration. In 1958 the International Paper Company bought a large tract of the surrounding property, including the fort, from the Ford estate and deeded the site to the state of Georgia. It was then turned into a State Historic Site and placed under the protection of the Georgia Department of Natural Resources, Parks and Historic Sites Division. They, in turn, undertook extensive restoration of the property, returning it to much the same condition as it was during the years 1862-64. A museum was built in 1963 to house the many mementos of the fort's turbulent history, including artifacts recovered from the famous blockade runner, the *Rattlesnake*, now lying in shallow water within sight of the outer walls.

You'll have no difficulty boarding the ship of the imagination and traveling back in time to the days when the fort was bustling with Confederate soldiers. The complex has been so well preserved it could be re-garrisoned and defended again in a very short period. Of course, modern technology would destroy it in a matter of seconds, but you get the idea. The self-guided tour of the fort takes in 15 stops, including the old parade ground, the Hot Shot Gun (a 32-pounder that fired red-hot solid shot), the Hot Furnace, the Center Bombproof, the Left Angle, the eight-inch Columbiad, the Reconstructed Magazine (the storage for shot, shell, and powder), the Rifled Gun Position, the Mortar Battery and the Northwest Angle.

Activities include picnicking, boating on the river, birdwatching, hiking, fishing, audio-visual shows, and educational programs and tours.

Fort McAllister

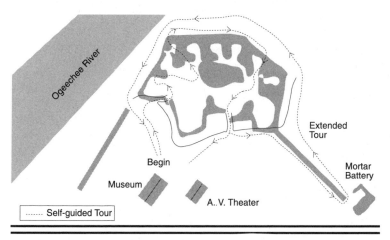

Annual events at the park include a Fourth of July barbecue picnic and craft show, year-round tours of the fort and Labor Day and winter musters.

Facilities include more than 1,700 acres of coastal parkland, 65 tent and trailer sites, hiking trails, boat ramps and a dock, two picnic shelters and one group shelter.

The park is open from 7 am until 10 pm; the park office is open from 8 to 5.

The fort itself is open all year-round, Tuesday through Saturday from 9 until 5, and on Sunday from 2 until 5. Admission, $2; children 6-12, $1. Fort McAllister State Historic Park, Box 394-A, Fort McAllister Road, Richmond Hill, GA 31324. ☎ 912-727-2339.

Drive south from Savannah on I-95 to Exit 15. Fort McAllister is 10 miles east on Georgia Spur 144; follow the signs.

Darien

The quick route to Darien is to take I-95 south from Savannah and drive for 50 miles to Exit 10. Or you can take the picturesque route via the Highway 17 coastal road; the distance is about the same.

In 1721 a small band of scouts from the English colony in South Carolina pushed the boundaries of the King's holdings in the Americas to new limits when they established a small fort on the banks of the Altamaha River. Darien, a small coastal town established near Fort King George in the late 1730s, is another of General James Oglethorpe's creations. It was to be a stronghold to protect the English colony's southern borders at the mouth of the Altamaha River from attack by the Spanish, French and Indians. Populated by Scottish settlers, the little town soon became the center of a thriving plantation economy. By the 1800s timber was being shipped in large quantities from the little river port, and, over the next 200 years, Darien was to become one of the largest timber exporters in the world. The trade continued until the early years of the 20th century, and the ruins of three old sawmills can still be seen.

Today, with one exception, the great plantations are all gone, and the port, once bustling with great ships, is a haven for the local shrimping fleets. But it's still a great little place to visit, a bit out of the way, and quiet. Unfortunately, most of the original city is gone, the victim of a fire that swept through the community in 1863. Still, it's well worth a visit.

SIGHTSEEING

The **Fort King George Historic Site** is a mile east of Highway 17. Established in 1721 by a band of scouts from the colony in South Carolina to prevent expansion into the area by the French and Spanish, it was the first English settlement in Georgia. It was a frontier fort in every sense of the word. An earthwork topped with a stout wooden blockhouse was built on a peninsula on the Altamaha River. For more than 10 years, from 1721 to 1732, Fort King George marked the southernmost limits of the British Empire in North America. The original fort is long gone, but the reconstruction that stands on the site is a faithful representation of the one garrisoned by His Majesty's 41st Independent Company and is open for you to visit. There's also a museum where you can view exhibits that interpret the history of the fort and surrounding area from the earliest times through Indian, Spanish and English occupation. Open Tuesday through Saturday from 9 to 5, and on Sunday from 2 to 5:30; closed Thanksgiving, Christmas and the New Year. Admission, $2. ☎ 912-437-4770.

The Hofwyl-Broadfield Plantation, between Brunswick and Darien on Highway 17, one mile east of I-95 at Exit 9, has its roots deep in the Old South. In 1807, William Brailsford of Charleston established a rice plantation here among the swamps along the Altamaha River. When the rice industry here reached its zenith, the plantation had grown to more than 7,300 acres and employed more than 350 slaves. The Civil War was the beginning of the end for the great plantation. At war's end the slaves were freed and labor to plant rice became short. Rice was last planted at Hofwyl-Broadfield in 1915 when Brailsford's descendants converted the plantation into a dairy. The dairy, too, did not last. It closed in 1943. Eventually, in 1973, the family willed the plantation to the state of Georgia and it was turned into the State Historic Site it is today – a window onto Georgia's turbulent past.

Today, you can wander among the magnolias and the camellias, stroll beneath the oak trees, and visit the fine ante-bellum home. The house is filled with antiques and the bric-a-brac of times gone by. In the museum you'll find a model of a working rice plantation and many exhibits, and you can view a slide show depicting the lives and times of the plantation's slaves and their owners.

Open Tuesday through Saturday 9 to 5, and on Sunday from 2 until 5:30; closed Thanksgiving and Christmas Day. Bus parking is available. Admission, $2. Group rates are available with advance notice. Hofwyl-Broadfield Plantation State Historic Site, Route 10, Box 83, Brunswick, GA 31520. ☎ 912-264-7333.

GOLF

Bacon Park Golf Club: On Shorty Cooper Drive, Savannah, GA 31406. ☎ 912-354-2625. Par 72, 6,740 yards. A nice, challenging course. Green fees, $29; includes half-cart rental.

Black Creek Golf Club: At Bill Futch Road in Ellabell, west of Savannah. ☎ 912-858-4653. Take I-16 to Exit 29, then Highway 280 south for one mile to Bill Futch Road and turn right. A tight, par 72 course of 6,278 yards. Green fees, less than $30.

Mary Calder Golf Club: At Union Camp, Savannah. ☎ 912-238-7100. A short, but challenging experience of 5,799 yards, par 70. Green fees, less than $20.

Sheraton Savannah: At 612 Wilmington Island Road, Savannah, GA 31410. ☎ 912-897-1615. Almost 7,000 yards of picturesque golfing on one of Savannah's major commercial resorts. Par 72. Fees: inexpensive, but subject to change. Call for rates.

Southbridge Golf Club: At 1415 Southbridge Boulevard, Savannah, GA 31405. ☎ 912-651-5455. More than 6,900 yards of tough golfing. Par 72. Green fees, call for rates. Take I-16 east to Dean Forest Road, turn right and drive for two miles; the entrance is on the right.

Brunswick & The Golden Isles

These are Georgia's barrier islands. The Spanish called them Guale, the Golden Isles, so named for the waving marsh grasses that turn a deep bronze color in the fall. Add a wash of setting sunlight and, as far as the eye can see, the marshes turn the color of burnished gold. It's a sight that is never forgotten.

Since the Spanish first set foot ashore in the mid-1500s, the islands have had a significant impact on local and regional development. They have been battlegrounds, playgrounds, and homes; they have provided solitude and inspiration; and they have been both loved and abandoned. The early settlements on the islands are no more than a few ruins; the men and women who built them, adventurers all, are the stuff of legend. Over the last 400 years, the islands off the coast of Georgia have seen it all. The flags and banners of five nations and a half-dozen pirate bands have flown over them. They have suffered and weathered one hurricane after another, protecting the mainland shores from the ravages of the elements. But when the rain is gone and the winds have calmed to cooling ocean breezes, the islands are delightful.

These barrier islands, so named because they form a barrier between the ocean and the mainland, are an integral part of a continuous chain of similar islands and beaches that stretch along the coast from Maine to Florida. Georgia's barrier islands – and there are some 15 large ones, along with untold numbers of tiny rocky outcrops – have become a magnet for adventurers with all sorts of special interests: hikers, divers, shoppers, gamblers, fishermen, naturalists, birdwatchers, shell collectors, turtle watchers, bicyclists, motorists, historians and boaters.

Behind the barrier islands lie Georgia's salt marshes. Here, nutrients from both fresh and salt water mix together to provide an organic material that moves into the ocean and become a major link in the marine food chain. The marshes are also the nurseries for countless marine organisms, including shrimp, oysters and crabs. Not for nothing does this area claim to be the shrimp capital of the world. Without the protection of the barrier islands, these great salt marshes and the tidal creeks that meander through them would not exist, and there would be no place for the birth and development of so many delicate species.

Such an abundance of life in the salt marshes invites other animals to feed, rest or nest. These isles are important to migrating waterfowl, especially those displaced from the rapidly disappearing marshes farther to the north. For the first time ever, the roseate spoonbill, perhaps the most beautiful of wading birds, can be seen on Little St. Simons Island. And there are many more species difficult to find anywhere else. The islands also provide the ideal habitat for a wide variety of plants and animals, including endangered species like the greenfly orchid, American alligator, peregrine falcon, loggerhead sea turtle, and the southern bald eagle.

Anyone who has spent time at the beach is aware of the two major forces that influence the ecology of the barrier islands: wind and tides. The energy released by these two natural elements is awesome and has battered the Atlantic coastline unceasingly since time began. To counter this irresistible force, nature has developed a remarkable defense system: sand. Sand absorbs and dissipates the tremendous energy of the great ocean and its storms. So, next time you're relaxing under your beach umbrella, run some sand through your fingers and wonder at the significance of those tiny grains so important to the life of the islands and the shoreline just to the west.

HOW TO GET THERE

Brunswick and the Isles are served north and south by two main highways. I-95 passes the city some five miles to the west; Highway 17, the scenic route, lies east of I-95 and runs parallel to it and through the city itself. From Albany and Waycross, Highway 82 provides the most direct route.

WHEN YOU ARE THERE

Most of the attractions are open daily, although a few do close on Monday, and some open late and close early on Sunday, so you can visit any day that suits you best.

To make the most of your time here, stop in at the visitors center at the intersection of Highway 17 and the St. Simons Island Causeway in Brunswick for brochures, maps and other information.

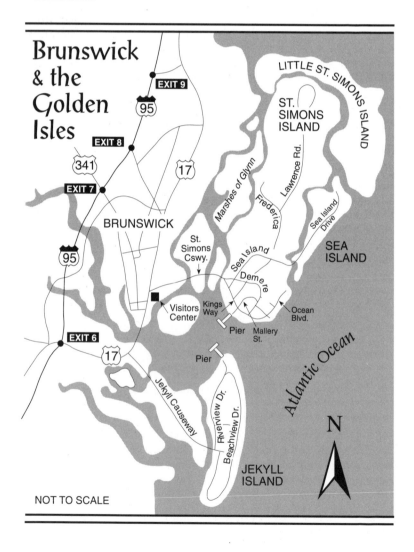

Getting Around

Getting around on the Golden Isles is easy. There are no rush hours as we know them, and even in Brunswick the roads are never very busy. Moreover, there's plenty of parking available. You'll do quite a lot of walking here, but you'll need to ride, too. From island to island, and to get around once you're there, you'll need your car. On St. Simons Island you can take a guided trolley tour; the pickup point is near the lighthouse in the Village.

The weather here is temperate most of the year but, especially at the height of summer, can get very warm. Once on the coast, the heat is tempered somewhat by the constant ocean breeze, and by frequent afternoon showers, not to mention the occasional thunderstorm. This, of course, makes for humidity and, with humidity come the bugs. Though they are confined mostly to the marshes and wooded areas, insects are a consideration. Be sure to take a good repellent with you.

DINING OUT

If Georgia's coast is the shrimp capital of the world, then Brunswick must be its center. If you love seafood, you'll love this area. If you love Low Country cooking, you'll find the best of it right here. After all, it is the home of Brunswick Stew.

You'll find a wide choice of restaurant styles. There are small bistros and cafés, fast food and mom-'n-pop eateries, and there are one or two places where you will dine in surroundings that can only be described as decadent.

☞ **Note**: There are very few fast food eateries on Jekyll Island.

The Cloister on Sea Island has two fabulous restaurants: the Beach Club and the Main Dining Room. The Beach Club is open for breakfast, lunch and dinner and, in the evening, offers a daily seafood buffet with everything from caviar to shrimp, crab, oysters and fresh fish cooked in a variety of ways. The Main Dining Room is also open for breakfast, lunch and dinner but, in the evening, it offers a carefully orchestrated experience in elegant dining. You'll choose your six-course dinner from a set menu, and gentlemen will be required to wear a jacket and tie. On Wednesday and Saturday you'll have to dress for dinner: black tie for gentlemen, evening dress for ladies. Reservations are required. ☎ 912-638-3611. No credit cards. $$$$.

Crabdaddy's Seafood Grill, 1217 Ocean Boulevard, St. Simons Island, is open for dinner from 5:30. The menu is seafood – crab, shrimp, mussels – with steak and chicken, too, cooked in a variety of ways, including mesquite-grilled and blackened. The decor is bare-bones wooden shack, nautical and appealing, and the lighting is dim. It can be busy at times, especially on weekends. ☎ 912-634-1120. $$.

Chelsea, 1226 Ocean Boulevard, St. Simons Island, is open for dinner from 5:30 and offers a continental menu featuring a variety of fresh seafood dishes, chicken, prime rib and pasta. The decor is simple, the dining room clean and comfortable, and the service excellent. Very popular, especially with the locals, so it's best to make a reservation for Friday or Saturday evening. ☎ 912-638-2047. $$.

Blackbeard's, 200 North Beachview Drive, Jekyll Island, is open for lunch and dinner from 11 am. Once again, the emphasis is on fresh seafood, but you can have steak or prime rib, if you like. As the name implies, the theme here is nautical and the view over the ocean is unparalleled. Very popular. ☎ 912-635-3522. $$-$$$.

Denny's, at the Comfort Inn, 711 Beachview Drive, Jekyll Island, is open 24 hours on Friday and Saturday, 6 am to 11 pm, Sunday through Thursday. Breakfast, lunch and dinner. Breakfast is served all day, the prices are reasonable, and you can be sure of what you're getting. Almost always busy. ☎ 912-635-2285. $

TOURIST INFORMATION

Brunswick & The Golden Isles Visitors Bureau, 4 Glynn Avenue, Brunswick, GA 31520. ☎ 912-265-0620. Fax 912-265-0629.

Jekyll Island Authority, 375 Riverview Drive, Jekyll Island, GA 31527. ☎ 912-635-2236. Fax 912-635-4004.

Little St. Simons Island, PO Box 21078, St. Simons Island, GA 31522. Contact Deborah McIntyre, Resident Manager, ☎ 912-638-7472. Fax 912-634-1811.

BRUNSWICK

Sightseeing

Brunswick, the gateway to the Golden Isles, is old-world Southern Georgia. Everywhere, the great limbs of live oaks stretch from one side of the street to the other, festooned with Spanish moss, shading the walkways, and creating the effect of an urban botanical garden that encompasses the entire downtown district. Small and quiet, this is a city with a difference. But it's also an industrial city. Manufacturing – paints, pulp, lumber and machinery – is an important part of its economy, but more so its harbor and processed seafood industry.

Brunswick is a full-service ocean seaport with great ships arriving and leaving regularly. But it's the shrimping industry for which this little city on Georgia's southern coast is famous. The backwash from the marshes, rivers, inlets and estuaries provides all the necessary nutrients for the prized crustaceans to multiply and thrive.

The **Visitors Center**, at the intersection of Highway 17 and the St. Simons Island Causeway, is the first place you should stop. Here, you can not only obtain all the information you'll need to make your visit a special one, but you can also see a replica of one of the Liberty Ships built here during World War II, and the pot in which Brunswick Stew was first made. You can also view a short video that gives a run-down on the sights and sounds of Brunswick and the Golden Isles. Open daily from 9 until 5. ☎ 912-264-5337.

Lover's Oak, at Albany and Prince streets, is a giant oak tree said to be more than 900 years old. The great tree is more than 13 feet around; it's a great photo opportunity.

Old Town Brunswick was laid out according to General James Oglethorpe's standard grid pattern, a city of streets and squares lined with homes noted for their turn-of-the-century architecture and eclectic mix of styles, all nicely restored and kept in pristine condition. This is just the place to go for a stroll under the shade of the ancient live oaks; be sure to take your camera.

The Courthouse, built just after the turn of the century, is an impressive building, made more so by the moss-hung live oaks that surround it.

Mary Miller Doll Museum, 1523 Glynn Avenue, is a stop for all the little girls in the family, even the grown-up ones. Here, you'll find one of the nation's great collections. More than 4,000 tiny people from over 90 countries are on display, along with doll houses, toys, and miniatures, including antiques and works by modern artists. Open daily, except Sunday, from 11 until 5. Admission, $2; children 5-15, $1.50. ☎ 912-267-7569.

The Shrimp Docks, Bay Street, are the place to go to watch the busy unloading of the shrimp boats on most weekdays in the late afternoon. It's fun, interesting, and another great photo opportunity.

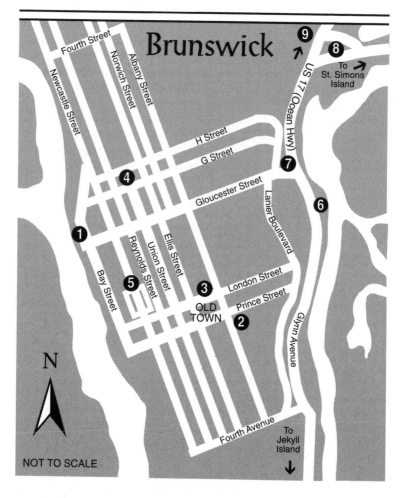

Brunswick Driving Tour

The number in parentheses after each stop
indicates the mileage to the next point of interest.

1. Shrimp Docks (1.1)
2. Lovers' Oak (.4)
3. Old Town National Register District (.7)
4. Courthouse (.1)
5. Main Street Brunswick (1.1)

6. Overlook Park (.2)
7. Lanier Oak (.2)
8. Visitors Center (14.7)
9. Hofwyl-Broadfield Plantation

The Marshes of Glynn separate Brunswick from the Golden Isles: St. Simons Island, Sea Island, Jekyll Island and Little St. Simons Island. The best places to see this vast saltwater biosphere are on, or just off, Ocean Highway (Highway 17). The Marshes of Glynn Overlook Park is perhaps the best vantage point, but it was from under Lanier Oak during the 1870s that Georgia poet, Sidney Lanier, stood and viewed the marshes that inspired him to write *The Marshes of Glynn*, now considered to be his finest work. Another good spot is the visitors center at the intersection of Highway 17 and the St. Simons Island Causeway, or even from the Causeway itself.

Shopping

Glynn Place Mall contains the largest concentration of shops, stores and restaurants in Brunswick. Here, you can shop all the usual national department stores – Sears, Penney, Belk, etc. – as well as a variety of specialty shops and gift stores.

The other great shopping opportunity in Brunswick is the **Outlets Limited Mall.**

Gambling

Casinos are not legal in Georgia, but you can spin the wheel, riffle the cards, crank the slots and toss the dice three miles out to sea aboard the *Emerald Princess*, a 200-foot-long, ocean-going cruise ship. It leaves the dock in Brunswick promptly at 7 in the evening on Thursday, Wednesday, Friday and Saturday, and at 11 am on Wednesday and Saturday, returning at 4 pm to make ready for the evening cruise. On Sunday, the ship leaves the dock at 1 pm, returning at 7 pm. The cost of the cruise, which includes a meal, usually a buffet, ranges from $19.95 to $35 per person. If you've never gambled before, don't worry; the staff offers a brief school just before the casino opens. If you just want to enjoy a few hours at sea and a nice meal, you can do so. The ship's huge observation deck is the place to relax and enjoy a drink. Other on-board entertainment includes scavenger hunts, trivia contests and bingo. In the casino you can play roulette, blackjack, Caribbean poker, craps, draw poker and, of course, the slot machines, where you can risk anything from a quarter on up. The ship is docked at the Brunswick Landing Marina on Newcastle Street. Golden Isles Cruise Lines, Inc., 1 St. Andrews Court, Brunswick, GA 31520. ☎ 912-265-3558 or 800-842-0115 for tickets and reservations.

Walking

As with most historic towns and cities on the Atlantic coast, Brunswick has its own downtown historic district. The **Old Town District** offers the opportunity to stroll around the shaded streets and enjoy the sights, Victorian architecture, ancient live oaks, antique stores and specialty shops. A short distance away are the waterfront and the marshes, where the views are spectacular and unspoiled – views that have inspired poets and artists for more than 250 years. So, park the car, put on a pair of comfortable walking shoes and enjoy.

SEA ISLAND

Just northwest of St. Simons Island, and reached by a causeway, Sea Island is a self-contained five-star resort. Although it is very much an upscale residential community, its main claim to fame is the internationally acclaimed Cloister, one of the world's great hotels.

Where to Stay

The **Cloister** was established in the 1920s by industrialist Howard E. Coffin, the inventor of the Hudson automobile. Since that time, the Sea Island Company has grown to include the Sea Island Golf Club on St. Simons Island, and the Cloister Beach Club, a world-class oceanfront spa. If you're looking for a little gracious living, you'll have to have cash aplenty. A week at the Cloister, including meals, can set you back $5-6,000, and that doesn't include drinks and other extras. It's a once-in-a-lifetime vacation experience, where you'll join the world of the rich and famous, eat the finest food, enjoy a beach that might easily have been transplanted from the French Riviera, swim, splash, relax, wine, dine, and be pampered as you've never been before. This resort has kept the junior members of the family very much in mind. Programs, run by highly qualified staff – all must go to school before being turned loose on the guests – include not only good, wholesome entertainment, but a course in good manners and etiquette. Kids can graduate at the end of the week at a banquet just for them, where they put to good use all that they've learned during the preceding days. The Cloister, Sea Island, GA 31561. ☎ 800-SEA-ISLAND.

LITTLE ST. SIMONS ISLAND

A 20-minute boat ride from St. Simons Island is the nearest thing to paradise you're ever likely to find, at least in Georgia. Virtually untouched for centuries, Little St. Simons Island is a privately owned, 10,000-acre barrier island, a rich and varied natural world of pristine beaches, maritime forests, shimmering marshes, inlets and tidal creeks, seemingly far removed from the rest of the world.

There are no shops here, no houses, no bars, no restaurants, just a small hunting lodge that's been the refuge from the world of business and high finance for the Berolzhiemer family for almost a century. Philip Berolzhiemer, head of the Eagle Pencil Company, bought the island originally for its cedars, but that didn't work out. He fell in love with the island and turned it into a retreat where he could entertain his important contacts. The lodge was built and 12 fallow deer were imported from the Bronx Zoo. Those deer have so multiplied over the years that the size of the herd has to be controlled; annual hunts are conducted during the winter months.

The family still uses the island, usually at Thanksgiving and Christmas. The rest of the year, however, it's open to guests and day visitors. The old lodge still operates as the main guest-house and, together with two guest lodges and one small cottage, it provides accommodation for just 24 overnight guests. There's a large swimming pool, and you're likely to have it all to yourself. There are no telephones in the guest rooms, no televisions, no gift shop, no rental cars, and no roads; there's no transportation available at all, other than a courtesy ride in the back of an old pickup truck, a half-dozen horses and your own two feet. So why should you bother? Here you can spend a few days, or a single day, in complete seclusion, hiking, fishing, canoeing, birding, or simply relaxing.

This is one of the few places left where you can see the America Juan Ponce de Leon saw when he stepped ashore in Florida centuries ago. The island, just nine miles by three, is one of contrast. The

Horses graze in the natural areas.

forests, with their live oaks and cedars, are untouched; no landscaping has been done here, and the small ponds and lakes in the clearings are home to egrets and watering holes for hundreds of fallow deer. The marshes are vast fields of waving seagrass, home to alligators and a hundred other species of marine life. The beaches? Well, to stand at the water's edge in the middle of a stretch of pristine sand that stretches for miles in either direction, with not another human being in sight, is an experience you're not likely to forget.

Hiking

Five trails vary in length from two to almost five miles. Some lead through virgin forest, some through the marshes, and one leads to the beach. All are easy, but you'll need to wear a hat, long sleeves and pants for protection against the sun and insects.

Canoeing

Several trips are recommended. Mitchell Marsh offers a window of opportunity one hour before and one hour after high tide. A one-way trip on Mosquito Creek with the incoming tide is a great ride of about an hour and a half. You can also paddle the marsh creek, leaving from and returning to the dock at the lodge.

Fishing

Surf-casting is best at the north and south end of Main Beach, from mid- to high tide. Good areas for fly fishing are the mouths of Bass Creek and Mosquito Creek. Bass Creek is better at higher tides; Mosquito Creek at lower ones. Creek fishing from a boat is also good.

Birding

Little St. Simons Island is truly a birder's paradise. Shore and marine birds abound, and rare species can often be seen wheeling over the marshes or flitting among the live oaks in the forest.

You'll find all sorts of rare plants and birds here. You can wander the trails, stopping here and there as the mood may take you.

☞ **Note:** This is one of only two barrier islands on the entire east coast where you can see the rare and endangered greenfly orchid.

Shell Collecting

This is one of the few places left in coastal Georgia where you can find sea shells easily, in quantity and all shapes and sizes. Georgia's state shell is the knobbed whelk, and you can find it here. Approximately eight inches long when fully mature, it's a whorled shell with heavy spines and knobs, brownish in color on the outside, pastel orange in the mouth, with a semi-gloss surface. They are found mostly at low tide and within 30 feet of the shoreline. And there are plenty of others; even the usually elusive sand dollar lies liberally scattered across the ocean shallows and beach. Be careful as you wade. Although the shallows stretch outward from the beach for hundreds of feet, rarely more than ankle-deep, they are a favorite haunt of the stingray. Though most are fairly small – not much bigger than the average serving plate – there are lots of them and they can inflict a nasty wound if stepped upon.

The island is reachable only by boat. Casual visitors are discouraged. If you want to visit, or spend a few days on the island, you'll have to call for the shuttle boat, or make arrangements to take your own craft. Parking is available at the marina on the mainland. Little St. Simons Island, PO Box 21078, St. Simons Island, GA 31522. ☎ 912-638-7472. Fax 912-634-1811.

ST. SIMONS ISLAND

This is the most heavily populated and developed of Georgia's Golden Isles. Twelve miles long by three miles wide, the island is linked to the mainland by a four-lane highway and causeway. The small airport has two lighted strips and can handle most corporate jets and small charter aircraft.

Sightseeing

Fort Frederica National Monument. By now you should be familiar with the fact that General James Oglethorpe founded the Georgia colony and Savannah in 1733. He must have been happy with the results of his efforts, for the new town soon began to prosper. But all was not well in Paradise. True, the building of Savannah was proceeding apace, but Oglethorpe knew it was vulnerable to attack from the Spanish, now firmly established in St. Augustine only 130 miles to the south. For more than 100 years they had ruled Florida with an iron hand, and Oglethorpe knew it was only a matter of time before they would visit Savannah, in force. So, with the defense of his new colony uppermost in his mind, he set out down the coast in 1734 looking for places to fortify against the perceived threat from the south. He found a likely site on St. Simons Island, just below the mouth of the Altamaha River. St. Simons in those days bore little resemblance to the idyllic vacation spot it has become today. It was a wilderness island, thick with live oaks draped with moss, but there was good water and fertile upland was available.

Two years later Oglethorpe returned to St. Simons Island with the first settlers, 44 men – mostly craftsmen – and 72 women and children. You have to admire the spirit of the settlers. There were no roads, just a few Indian trails, no shelters, no churches or even supplies of fresh food. Imagine what it must have been like for those women and children.

Oglethorpe and his settlers laid out a military town on a bluff overlooking a sharp bend on the inland passage between the island and the mainland. He named it for his king's only son, Frederick. Ft. Frederica was to become Oglethorpe's favorite town in the new colony.

First, the settlers built the fort, a fairly complicated affair surrounded by a rampart with four bastions that commanded the river in both directions. Next, behind the fort on a large field, Oglethorpe laid out 84 lots, each measuring some 60 feet by 90. Each family received one lot and 50 acres outside the town. The first houses were primitive wooden structures. But these were soon replaced by houses of brick and tabby (a sort of concrete made of powder obtained from burnt oyster shells). The streets were wide and shaded by orange trees. By the mid-1740s the town was like many a little town you might have found, and still can find, in the English countryside.

The fort and town were established and, Oglethorpe's troops well entrenched in the fort. Still, the threat from Spain was an ever-present one and Oglethorpe wasn't about to wait for the enemy. So, with thoughts of conquest in mind, he set out from Fort Frederica in 1740 with a large force – some 900 English veterans and 1,100 Indians – to capture St. Augustine. But it was not to be; by mid-summer Oglethorpe was back in Fort Frederica.

Now it was the Spanish who felt threatened, and they, too, decided to do something about it. They set out for Fort Frederica with a fleet of 50 ships and some 2,000 soldiers in July, 1742. They landed on St. Simons Island and managed to advance to within sight of the fort, but Oglethorpe was waiting for them; the Battle of Bloody Marsh was a decisive victory for the English and, within a week, the Spanish were under full sail once more, heading back to St. Augustine.

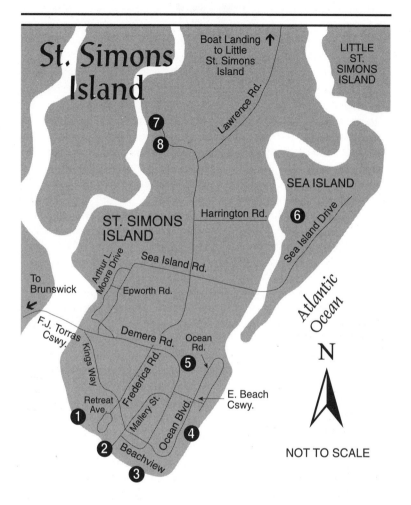

St. Simons Island Driving Tour

The number in parentheses after each stop
indicates the mileage to the next point of interest.

1. Retreat Plantation (.7)
2. Fishing Pier (.2)
3. Museum of Coastal History & St. Simons Lighthouse (1.1)
4. St. Simons Beach (Massengale Park) (1.4)
5. Bloody Marsh Battle Site (National Park Service) (5.2)
6. Sea Island (7)
7. Fort Frederica National Monument (.2)
8. Christ Church, Frederica

When Oglethorpe was recalled to England to stand trail for alleged mismanagement of the St. Augustine campaign, things continued in Frederica just as they had. But with peace between England and Spain, the little community's usefulness became a thing of the past. Oglethorpe's regiment was disbanded in 1749 and, like any small town deprived of its main source of income, Frederica soon dwindled. By 1758 it had been abandoned altogether and fell into ruin, its bricks and masonry carried off to form the foundations of other structures.

Today, all that remains of the fort and the once-bustling little town is the old magazine, and the lately excavated foundations of some houses and shops. It's a neat experience to wander the tiny streets, devoid of buildings though they may be, and try to imagine Frederica as it might have been – to see, through the windows of the imagination, the brightly colored uniforms of the garrison, the gaily dressed ladies and courtly gentlemen going about the business of the day, and the children playing among the trees on a warm summer day. Fort Frederica is a quiet place now, rarely very busy, and just the spot to spend a few moments on the banks of the river, with a picnic lunch, perhaps.

Open daily 8 until 5 from Memorial Day to Labor Day, 9 until 5 the rest of the year. ☎ 912-638-3639.

St. Simons Lighthouse. You'll want to stop in here and visit the Museum of Coastal History. It's filled with all sorts of nautical bits and pieces, artifacts and memorabilia that depict the history of Georgia's coastal communities and the Golden Isles. The first

St. Simons Lighthouse and the Museum of Coastal History.

lighthouse was built in 1810, but was destroyed by Confederate troops in 1862 to prevent its light from guiding Union gunboats onto the island. The one you see now was built in 1872, is 104 feet high, and is the oldest continuously operating lighthouse in the United States. Its Fresnel lens projects a beam of light 500,000 candle-power strong that can be seen more than 18 miles out to sea. Yes, you can climb to the top, but you'll need to be sound of wind and limb. Once there, the panoramic view makes the effort well worthwhile. Open Tuesday through Saturday from 10 until 5, and on Sunday from 1:30 to 5; closed all major holidays. Admission, $3; children 6-11, $1. ☎ 912-638-4666.

St. Simons Beach. Massengale Park and the beaches encompass several miles of public sands and oceanfront off Ocean Boulevard to the north and south of the old US Coast Guard Station. The color of the sand varies from dark gray, due to the backwash of silt from the inlet, to almost white. The waters are, for the most part, calm and safe – great for kids of all ages – and they're fine for windsurfing, jet-skiing and swimming. Lifeguards are on duty in designated spots. You can rent a beach cycle and peddle for miles. There are restroom and picnic facilities. Park hours are 6 am to 10:30 pm.

Bloody Marsh National Battlefield Park. It was here on July 7, 1742, that a largely outnumbered force of British soldiers under the command of General James Oglethorpe defeated Manuel de Montiano's Spanish invasion. De Montiano was governor of Florida. His objective was to destroy Fort Frederica and the town around it, then lay waste to the coast as far north as Port Royal, South Carolina. His fleet of 50 ships successfully ran the gauntlet of British guns at Fort St. Simons and landed troops east of Frederica on the shores of the inlet. Oglethorpe pulled back to Frederica, leaving the way open for the Spanish advance. On July 7 he surprised a force of about 200 Spaniards advancing up the road toward Frederica. These he swiftly routed, and then he waited. Montiano responded by sending reinforcements to support the remains of his retreating advance force; the battle that followed was fierce, bloody and a decisive victory for Oglethorpe. Within a week, Montiano and his army were back aboard ship, making for St. Augustine and safety. The site is east of the Torras Causeway off Demere Road. Open daily 8 until 4 from Memorial Day until Labor Day, and from 9 to 5 the rest of the year. ☎ 912-638-3639.

Shopping

There are no vast department stores here and no giant shopping malls. Everything is on a much smaller scale. That means you'll have to look a little harder to find things, do a little more traveling. Perhaps the best place to begin is at the Village, at the southern end of the island. There, you'll find all sorts of small specialty stores and gift shops, each interesting in their own way and worth the browsing. From there, you can take to the road in almost any direction and find small strip malls and shopping centers, from small, upscale department stores to the larger discount outlets, expensive gift and specialty shops, antique stores and much more.

Golf

The Hampton Club, 100 Tabbystone St. Simons Island, GA 31522. ☎ 912-634-0255. A Joe Lee course, undulating, with large traps that define the fairways and lead to large Bermuda greens. Holes 12 through 15 are set on two small islands in the marshes and are picturesque beyond words. Par 61, 6,465 yards. Very expensive; call for rates.

St. Simons Island Golf Club, 100 Kings Way, St. Simons Island, GA 31522. ☎ 912-638-5130. Another Joe Lee course that, for the first five holes, meanders this way and that through pine and oak forest, then breaks out into some of the most spectacular scenery on the Golden Isles. Par 72, 6,490 yards. Expensive and subject to change; call for rates.

JEKYLL ISLAND

This is the southernmost of the Golden Isles and, like most of Georgia's coastal areas, rich in history and tradition. Its first inhabitants were Guale Indians. How long they had lived on the island before the arrival of Spanish explorers in the mid-16th century, nobody knows – perhaps thousands of years. The Spanish established a mission on the island but, like many others in coastal Georgia, the Mission of Santiago de Ocone fell victim to hostile Indians and pirates. It had long disappeared by the time General James Oglethorpe established Savannah in 1733, the first permanent settlement in Georgia.

Oglethorpe named the island for his friend, Sir Joseph Jekyll, during an expedition in 1734. Another of his friends, William Horton, established a plantation on the island, but it was destroyed by the Spanish when they crossed the island after their defeat by Oglethorpe at the Battle of Bloody Marsh in 1742. But Horton was a tenacious man, and he rebuilt the plantation; the remains of the house still exist.

Horton died in 1749, leaving the island to his son, who showed no interest in it, and ownership passed into other hands; it was purchased by Christopher du Bignon in 1800. The plantation, now producing large quantities of sea-island cotton, thrived under du Bignon and, when he died in 1825, it passed on to his son Henri. It was during his tenure that the slave ship *Wanderer* arrived at Jekyll and unloaded the last cargo of slaves ever to land in the United

States. The plantation was destroyed during the Civil War, never to be rebuilt. Piece by piece the land was sold; one parcel went to John Eugene du Bignon, descendant of Christopher.

Jekyll's modern history really began with John Eugene. The economy of post-Civil War America boomed, and the first great entrepreneurs began to emerge; many of them came south, looking for escape from the cold northern winters, and it was these men that were the target of du Bignon's new enterprise. He determined to obtain ownership of the entire island. By June 16, 1885, he had achieved his goal, at a cost of some $13,000. Negotiations with the members of the prospective Jekyll Island Club, a group of wealthy industrial families, began and were successfully concluded in 1886 with the purchase of the island for the sum of $125,000. The club opened in 1888 and, by 1900, the membership was reputed to represent more than one-sixth of the world's wealth, with such captains of industry as William Rockefeller, Marshall Field, J.P. Morgan, Joseph Pulitzer, Vincent Astor and William K. Vanderbilt on its rolls. The grand hotel and ornate mansions they built on the island – "cottages," they called them – are a testament to that wealth. The unstable politics of the 1930s led ultimately to the club's closing in 1942; the island was purchased by the state of Georgia in 1947.

Since then, efforts have been made to preserve the island as much as possible for public use. The Jekyll Island Authority was established to conserve and develop the island. A causeway was built from the mainland, giving the public direct access to its historic buildings and beaches. The original Jekyll Island Club building, a magnificent structure in the grand style, was reopened and run by the state as a private hotel. It seems, however, that the hotel business was not the forte of the bureaucrats involved. Little effort was made to maintain the old buildings; some even fell into disrepair and disuse. The magnificent wooden paneling inside the Club itself was painted over, the elegant staircase removed in favor of an elevator, great rooms were haphazardly divided, and the grand flavor of the old hotel was lost. The hotel under state management lost money and ultimately was closed again. Then, in 1969, the Authority realized that what they had on Jekyll Island was a piece of American history that, if allowed to further deteriorate, could never be replaced. Restoration work began, first on the McKay-Rockefeller cottage, and then on the other structures in the Historic District. In 1978, the 240-acre Jekyll Island Club Historic District was declared a National Historic Landmark, and the restoration continued. The Jekyll Island Club Hotel reopened under private management determined to return the old club to its

The Jekyll Island Club.

former glory. The panels were stripped of paint and restored, the staircase, now only an image in old photographs, was rebuilt to its former likeness, the dining room extended, and the whole thing restored and redecorated to its turn-of-the-century condition.

Today, the Historic District is the core of Jekyll Island, a state reserve of unparalleled natural beauty where you can stay in relative luxury as a guest at the old Jekyll Island Club, or at any one of the 10 modern hotels on the island.

Still very much the quiet seaside retreat envisioned by the members of the club back in the 1880s, it's a quiet island, with lots of outdoor activities available: golf, hiking, swimming and relaxing in the sunshine far away from the crowds and glitz of the more conventional resorts. You won't find any neon lights on Jekyll.

Sightseeing

Jekyll Island National Historic Landmark District. There are 33 structures and 38 archaeological sites in the Jekyll Island Historic District, making it one of the largest on-going preservation projects in the southeast. Daily guided tours of several turn-of-the-century "cottages" are available and offer a glimpse of life as it must have been for the rich and famous of the Jekyll Island Club era. The old homes contain period furnishings, decorative arts, historical photographs and documents. A behind-the-scenes tour provides an inside look at the craftsmanship involved in the restoration of Moss Cottage, circa 1896. For tour information, ☎ 912-635-2119.

Beaches

Jekyll Island is blessed with more than 10 miles of beaches, sand dunes and sea oats, all of which are accessible by car.

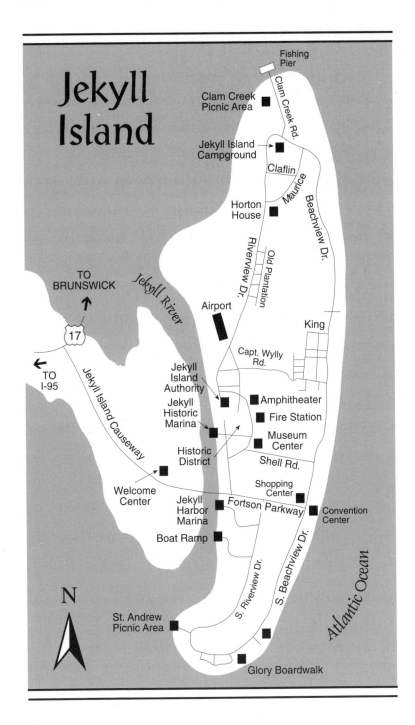

Jekyll Island

Fishing Pier

Clam Creek Picnic Area

Clam Creek Rd.

Jekyll Island Campground

Claflin

Maurice

Beachview Dr.

Horton House

Riverview Dr.

Old Plantation

TO BRUNSWICK

Jekyll River

Airport

King

Capt. Wylly Rd.

17

TO I-95

Jekyll Island Causeway

Jekyll Island Authority

Jekyll Historic Marina

Amphitheater

Fire Station

Museum Center

Historic District

Shell Rd.

Welcome Center

Shopping Center

Jekyll Harbor Marina

Fortson Parkway

Convention Center

Boat Ramp

S. Riverview Dr.

S. Beachview Dr.

Atlantic Ocean

N

St. Andrew Picnic Area

Glory Boardwalk

Here, you can enjoy endless opportunities for shell collecting, beachcombing, driftwood collecting, swimming, fishing, windsurfing or just relaxing. Except at the height of the vacation season, the sands are mostly quiet, with plenty of room to stretch out in comfort. The Authority keeps everything clean and in good order. Public restrooms and showers are located at several beachfront sites and picnic areas.

Fishing

Surf fishing is a popular pastime on Jekyll, as is pier fishing and crabbing. Freshwater fishing is allowed in designated spots, but you'll need a Georgia fishing license if you want to try your hand at that.

Hiking

Jekyll Island is ideally suited for walking and hiking, with more than 10 miles of beaches offering some of the best opportunities, but roads all across the island are quiet and you can walk them without hazard; just walk on the left and watch out for on-coming traffic. For more information, contact the Jekyll Island Welcome Center, 901 Jekyll Island Causway, Jekyll Island, GA 31527. ☎ 800-841-6586 or 912-645-3636.

Turtle Watching

From mid-May to mid-September, Jekyll Island's beaches are visited by nesting loggerhead sea turtles. The female comes ashore at night, making her way slowly up the beach to the dunes where she'll prepare her nest. She does this by wallowing around in a circular motion; then she begins to dig, using her hind flippers. When she reaches a depth of about 14 inches, she stops digging and begins to lay her eggs, anywhere from 80 to 160 of them. When she's finished, she'll cover the nest with sand and return to the ocean. She'll complete the same ritual as many as six times during the nesting season, each time leaving behind a clutch of eggs, of which only 60 to 90% will hatch; the temperature of the sand in the nest will determine the sex of the hatchlings. The tiny, new-born turtles scuttle quickly to the sea to spend the greater part of their lives in deep water, the males never to return; the females return only to nest some 15 to 30 years after birth. You can learn all about these fascinating creatures by joining one of the organized turtle walks conducted by the Jekyll Island Authority. Walks are scheduled

Tuesday, Thursday, Friday and Saturday nights throughout the nesting season. ☎ 912-635-2284 to make a reservation.

Bicycling

There are more than 20 miles of scenic paved bicycle paths on Jekyll Island. They wind through the marshes, beside the beaches, under the massive moss-draped live oaks, and through the Historic District. Rental bikes are available at a number of locations on the island. ☎ 912-635-2648.

Boating

Two marinas serve Jekyll Island. **Jekyll Harbor Marina** has dockage and boat ramps, and offers a number of other services, too. You can go parasailing, charter a fishing boat and captain, join a sightseeing cruise, rent a jet-ski, or enjoy a snack and a drink at **Seajay's Waterfront Café and Pub**. ☎ 912-635-3152. The **Jekyll Wharf**, opposite the Jekyll Island Club in the Historic District, can set you up with a fishing charter, sightseeing cruise, jetboat ride or a sea kayaking trip. Latitude 31, a seafood restaurant overlooking the wharf and dock, is a good place to enjoy an evening meal. ☎ 912-635-3152.

Waterskiing

Always wanted to try it but never able to summon up the nerve? Well, now you don't have to. You can learn quickly and in safety at **Cableway Ski**, 100 South Riverview Drive on Jekyll Island. The unique overhead cable system will tow you quietly around a clean, man-made lake at speeds to suit your experience, or lack of it. You don't need to know one end of the ski from the other. Once you've learned how to do it all, the thrills and spills of waterskiing – double or trick skis, slalom to barefoot skiing – and all the excitement you can handle are available. It's easy, you'll be in good hands and it's safer than being towed behind a boat. There's also a snack bar and ski shop. Open daily 9 until 8. Instruction Monday, Tuesday, Thursday and Friday from 9:30 until 11:30, $15 per person per session. Skiing prices: one hour, $9.99; three hours, $16.19; all day, $22.85. Prices include use of skis and life jacket. ☎ 912-635-3080.

Picnicking

The **South Dunes Picnic Area**, of South Beachview Drive, has covered picnic shelters, a screened-in serving shelter, and lots of individual sites close to the beach under a canopy of live oaks. The **Clam Creek Picnic Area**, off Riverview Drive and Clam Creek Road at the north end of the island, is close to the fishing pier and Driftwood Beach, and has plenty of room at individual sites. Perhaps the best spot is the **St. Andrews Picnic Area,** off South Riverview Drive, close to the Summer Waves Water Park, at the south end of the island. Here you seine (cast-net) for shrimp and small fish, and watch the dolphins at play. For more picnic information, ☎ 912-635-3400.

Shopping

If your idea of adventure is a week spent browsing the stores and shops in search of something special, you won't like Jekyll Island. True, there are a few shops on the island, but you could do them all in less than an hour. There's a small shopping center, a strip mall really, with one or two specialty shops, a limited grocery store, and a drug store. And there are a couple of shops in the Historic District – several gift shops, a sweet shop, and a used book store where you can buy rare collectibles and first editions.

Golf

Jekyll Island claims to be Georgia's largest public golf resort, with 63 holes on four courses; three with 18 holes and one with nine holes. **The Oleander** was laid out by Dick Wilson and measures 6,679 yards; **Indian Mound** was designed by Joe Lee and measures 6,596 yards; **Pine Lakes**, also designed by Dick Wilson, is 6,802 yards. **Oceanside** is a long nine holes, originally laid out for the members of the Jekyll Island Club in 1898. It was remodeled in the 1920s by Walter Travis and measures some 3,298 yards. The clubhouse has a full-service pro shop where you can rent equipment and carts, have a lesson, or tune up your swing on the driving range. **Morgan's Grill** is a full-service restaurant and lounge with a panoramic view of the courses. ☎ 912-635-2368 or 635-3464 for tee times.

Tennis

The Jekyll Island Tennis Center, just off Captain Wylly Road in the center of the island, was selected by *Tennis Magazine* as one of the 25 best municipal tennis centers in the country. There are 13 clay courts tucked away among the live oaks and pines, seven of them lighted for play at night. There's also a full-service pro shop where a USPTA professional offers private or group lessons, and games can be arranged for players without a partner. The facility organizes junior summer tennis camps and numerous other programs. Open daily; lessons and matches available from 9 until noon, and from 2 until 6. ☎ 912-635-3154.

Summer Waves Water Park

This water park in the grand style is the only real concession to the popular concept of a resort on the island. It is one of the best of its type, and a real bargain. The 11-acre park is a vast, watery fairyland of pools and rides, a playground for kids and grown-ups alike. The Pirate's Passage is a five-story, totally enclosed tube ride that, the first time at least, takes you on a high-speed ride into the unknown; Force Three is a ride with inner tubes and body flumes; the Frantic Atlantic is a vast wave pool where the water rises and falls; then there's the Hurricane and Tornado body slides, and the Slow Motion Endless River, where you can relax in an inner tube and drift with the current for hours. For the younger set, the Kiddie Pool provides endless hours of carefully supervised fun in the water, where many of the rides available to the adults are reproduced in miniature for the kids. There's even a McDonald's (the only one on the island) inside the park, along with a gift shop where you can buy the inevitable tee-shirt complete with funny logo. Open daily, 10 until 6, later on Saturday. Admission, $11.95; under 48 inches, $9.95. ☎ 912-635-2074 or 800-841-6586.

Camping

Jekyll Island is a state park. It incorporates one of the best campgrounds in Georgia. Of the 220 sites, 98 have full-service facilities (water, electricity and sewer), 64 have water and electricity only, and 58 are primitive sites suitable for tents only; all sites are equipped with picnic tables. There's a camp store where you can stock up on food, ice, bait, propane and other supplies. There are two bathhouses with hot showers and restrooms. Cable TV and firewood are available, too, and you can rent a bike at the camp store. Rates: tent sites, $11 per day; water and electric hookups, $14 per day; full-service hookups, $16 per day; cable TV, $2 per day. Visa, Mastercard and Discover cards are accepted. Payment is due on registration. One vehicle or tent permitted per site. Tents only on tent sites. Driver's license required on checking in. Checkout time is 12 noon; $2 per hour late charge for checking out after 12 noon. The campground is located at the north end of the island on Riverview Drive. ☎ 912-635-3021.

CUMBERLAND ISLAND

Located just to the south of Jekyll Island, Cumberland is the largest of Georgia's barrier islands. Its former owners, conservationists and the National Park Service have all gone to great lengths to ensure that it will remain in the unspoiled pristine condition in which you'll find it today. Only the ruins of Dungeness Mansion and the homes of the Carnegie Estate betray the hand of man on the island. Here, you can hike the Dungeness Trail, get a glimpse of the island's history, enjoy scenes of breathtaking natural beauty, walk deserted beaches beyond the massive sand dunes, and, if you're lucky, spot some of the wild horses that inhabit the island. As there are no concessions here, and no facilities other than restrooms and drinking water, take along a picnic lunch; there are plenty of places to stop and enjoy it. Wear appropriate clothing for the weather and the season; bug spray is a good idea, as is sunscreen. Open 8 to 4:30 daily. Ferry service from St. Marys is provided twice daily, and you can expect to be on the island for at least six hours. ☎ 912-882-4336.

WATER ADVENTURES

As you might imagine, the opportunities around the Golden Isles for watersports are virtually boundless. Unfortunately, because of the backwash from the many river inlets and estuaries, the waters inshore can be a little on the murky side at best, and downright muddy at worst. Offshore, however, things change dramatically.

Snorkeling

Take your pick. You can put on the fins and mask and cruise the surface of the waters just about anywhere, but the waters off the eastern shores of the islands are often clearer and, therefore, better suited to snorkeling. The popular beaches on Jekyll perhaps provide the best opportunities.

Diving

Two sites are popular with dive operators in this region of the Atlantic coast. There are more, of course, and shipwrecks litter the ocean floor from one end of coastal Georgia to the other, but finding them is another task entirely, and well beyond the scope of this book.

Both popular sites are well out to sea, and require a boat and some fairly specialized local knowledge.

Gray's Reef National Marine Sanctuary, also known as the Sapelo Live Bottom, was awarded National Marine Sanctuary status by President Jimmy Carter in 1989. The site is located some 20 miles east of Sapelo Island and constitutes the largest near-shore live bottom off the Georgia coast; it's also the most accessible. Covering a 17-square-mile area, the underwater terrain ranges from low relief hardpan to rocky ledges rising up to eight feet from the ocean floor; live bottom occurs here and there across the entire area. Certain activities are prohibited on the reef, including trapping and collecting. The live bottom is delicate; don't touch.

Reef G is the largest of Georgia's artificial reefs. It's some 26 miles east of Little Cumberland Island and consists of 3,000 tires located 100 to 250 yards to the north, northeast, south and west of the marker buoy. There are also several shipwrecks on the site, including a 441-foot Liberty Ship; the *Nettleton*, a 33-foot utility boat; the 100-foot tugboat *Tampa;* and another tugboat, the 108-foot *Recife*. The wrecks *Nettleton* and *Recife* are some distance from the buoy in deeper water, but are often identifiable by the schools of baitfish that surround them.

DIVE OPERATORS

Island Dive Center, at 101 Marina Drive, St. Simons Island, GA 31522, is a full-service operator offering daily schedules of two- and three-tank dives to Gray's Reef and Reef G. Rental equipment is available, including tanks, regulators, weight belts and weights, wetsuits and computers. Several courses of lessons are available for beginners through advanced divers. ☎ 912-638-6590 or 800-940-3483.

Hammerhead Dive Center, at 1200 Glynn Avenue, Suite 3, Brunswick, GA 31520, is also a full-service operator. Trips, not only to sites off the coast of Georgia, but also to the Bahamas, Jamaica, Puerto Rico, Mexico and the Florida Keys. Classes are conducted every three weeks in February, March, April, May and June. Call for rates, schedules and equipment details. ☎ 912-262-1778.

Deep-sea Charter Fishing

The Golden Isles are blessed with competent charter captains who stand ready to accommodate you for a day out in search of the big gamefish: tarpon, shark, sailfish, marlin and many more. There's little difference between one captain or another; all have their on and off days, and all boats must comply with US Coast Guard safety regulations. A half-day out beyond the reef, either four or six hours, will cost you between $250 and $350. For a full nine hours, you can expect to pay at least $450. If you want a chance at the big one, you'll need to book for a full day so that you'll have time to reach good waters up to 20 miles off-shore. The costs are not too bad if split by a small group, say up to six anglers. The following list of charter captains will get you started, but it is not a recommendation.

DEEP-SEA CHARTERS

Captain Vernon Reynolds: 30 years experience in local waters; offshore fishing for tarpon, shark, king mackerel, Spanish mackerel, cobia, amberjack and barracuda; inshore fishing for trout, flounder and bass. Half-day and full-day fishing and sightseeing trips available. Captain Reynolds also offers dolphin watch tours; coastal birding excursions to see great blue herons, white egrets, wood storks, ospreys and many others; sand dollar wading tours along the Pelican Split sand bar in St. Andrews Sound; marsh nature tours; sunset cruises; moonlight cruises. Captain Vernon Reynolds, 3202 East 3rd Street, Brunswick, GA 31520. ☎ 912-265-0392.

Captains Jim and Rudolph Beggs will take you aboard the *Osprey* for a day or a half-day fishing for tarpon, shark, reds and trout. They will also take you birding or sightseeing. Both captains have more than 40 years experience of these waters, and both are naturalists with degrees from the University of Georgia. Jim or Rudolph Beggs, 510 Longview Road, St. Simons Island, GA 31522. ☎ 912-638-2874.

Captain Greg Smith will take you on a half- or full-day trip fishing for tarpon or shark aboard the *Ducky II*. Call ☎ 912-634-0312 for rates and information.

Cap Fendig has more than 20 years experience in these waters. He offers offshore fishing trips for black sea bass, cobia, king mackerel, tarpon and shark. He also offers inshore trips to the sand bars and tidal creeks for trout, flounder, whiting, red fish and bass. Half-day and full-day trips are available. ☎ 912-638-5678.

Captain Rob and the *Full Tilt* offer a full range of trips from a short four hours to a full 12-hour day to the deep waters more than 20 miles offshore. Captain Rob, 344 Fancy Bluff Road, Brunswick, GA 31520. ☎ 912-261-1426.

Fishing The Coastal Waters

In the coastal waters, inshore and offshore, around the Golden Isles, you can expect to enjoy plenty of good sport. You can hit the surf, marsh creeks, salt river inlets and streams almost anywhere along the coast and on the barrier islands and have a good day out. All the popular species are available in abundant numbers. You can expect to catch Atlantic croaker, red drum, black drum, whiting, flounder, sheepshead, spotted sea trout,and striped bass.

Shark Fishing

The following article is reproduced by kind permission of Captain Vernon Reynolds of Brunswick.

CUMBERLAND SHARK ACTION

The slack tide had given way to gentle movement of the flood. The water's surface was as slick as the proverbial sheet of glass. Gulls and pelicans circled pods of baitfish, screeching and diving for their morning meal. Sand bars rose from the water's surface, glistening white in the morning sun. Numerous shrimp boats slowly criss-crossed St. Andrews Sound between Jekyll and Cumberland islands as dolphins followed the boats, feeding on the bycatch of baitfish shoveled over the side.

Our boat hardly made a sound as it drifted with the tide. Two stout boat rods stood in rod holders, trailing fresh baitfish. Suddenly, the port reel clicker began to sound with the slow, methodical click that generally means a larger fish. Fishing partner Don Jordan retrieved the rod from the holder and waited as the fish eased away. Twenty seconds later, the clicking stopped and we both knew the fish was swallowing the bait.

Captain Reynolds.

Next came the steady, strong movement of a large fish continuing to search for its prey, not realizing it had just inhaled the business end of a shark rig. The morning calm took an unexpected course change as Don dropped the reel drag into lock and heaved back on the rod. The rod bowed and the reel wailed as the fish immediately stripped off 75 yards of line. A 10-foot circle of white froth formed far beneath the boat as the fish thrashed the surface. Moments later, a 100-plus-pound blacktip sailed 10 feet into the air.

The big shark sounded upon re-entry, peeling off another 50 yards of line. The ensuing 30-minute battle, a give-and-take affair, provided several more jumps and backbreaking strain. It all ended with the unharmed release of the blacktip.

The waters of Cumberland Island, in south Georgia's Golden Isles, have long been reputed to be the largest shark breeding grounds along the east coast. Blacktips, spinners, hammerheads, bulls and tigers are the better-known sharks that cruise these seas.

As water temperature rises in the spring, sharks come here to birth pups. This spring migration begins the prime fishing season, which continues through October. Warm waters protected by a natural chain of sand bars, and the abundance of available baitfish provide the ideal habitat for these great gamefish.

The blacktips and spinners are two of the most abundant and most sought-after sharks along Georgia's coastline. The main reason for their popularity is the formidable fight provided, each being a strong and fast swimmer with unusual jumping ability. Blacktips and spinners are closely related and difficult to differentiate, even for experienced fishermen. Only subtle differences between fin placement and teeth shape exist. The two can be distinguished by their different aerial capers. The blacktip resembles a Polaris missile leaving the water with a vertical leap and the head well above the tail. Re-entry is a fall incorporating violent head-shaking.

The spinner, as its name implies, has a more horizontal jump, with the body spinning at almost unbelievable speed. Hooking either is a heart-stopping event that no angler ever forgets. The Georgia state record blacktip weighs in at 131 pounds. There is no category for the spinner.

The state record for the hammerhead shark is 770 pounds, taken near the "80-Foot Hole" on the south end of Cumberland Island. The hammerhead may be the best-known of the Georgia sharks, mainly due to easy identification provided by the unique shape of its head. Hammerheads, although not known for their jumping ability, do surface.

The bull shark is most easily identified by a very short, extremely rounded snout and rotund body-to-length ratio. The bull is a very strong fish that will bulldog his way deep when hooked. The state record is 455 pounds.

The tiger shark is distinguished by conspicuous dark brown tiger-striped sides, although these markings pale with maturity. The tiger is possibly the largest shark visiting Georgia waters. The state record tiger weighed 794 pounds and was taken near "STS" buoy in the St. Simons Island shipping channel. Tigers are noted for their habit of eating almost anything. Some articles removed from specimens' stomachs include boat cushions, driftwood, lumps of coal and a coil of copper wire. The tiger is a strong fighter, providing the fisherman with long runs when hooked.

Fishing techniques vary slightly, with drift fishing being the most productive. Obtaining bait is a simple matter of taking poagie with a cast net or catching bottom baitfish with shrimp on hook and line. Croaker, spots, whiting and most other bottom fish make ideal shark bait. Cut bait from larger fish works well, also. Bait can be presented live or dead with the same results. Sharks are scavengers and it makes little difference to them. It is sometimes helpful to cut bait near the tail, providing a blood trail for the sharks to follow.

One advantage to drift fishing is it enables the angler to cover more water. Sharks are forever on the move and can cover considerable distances while feeding. An even more important advantage is that of mobility, allowing the fisherman to take advantage of chum lines created by shrimp boat bycatches. This bycatch is said to be five to 10 pounds for every pound of shrimp taken and is mainly comprised of unusable baitfish.

Once the shrimp and salable fish are separated from the rest of the catch, the remaining baitfish are returned to the sea stunned or dead. This creates a large chum line that attracts sharks from miles away. While drift fishing, the captain can position the boat directly behind a shrimp boat and drift in this chum lime. The results can be spectacular.

☞   **A word of caution:** When drifting in these waters, keep a close eye on the depth sounder; sand bars are numerous and the inattentive boater can easily find himself in a shallow spot. It is also a good idea to give the shrimp boats right of way; otherwise, you may receive a stern talking to from one of the captains.

The alternative to drifting is to anchor. This can be effective around deep holes and sandbars. The method is the same, except for the addition of a sinker to take the bait deep.

Tackle consists of medium-heavy to heavy-action rods coupled with reels capable of holding 300 to 400 yards of 40-pound test line. This gear is inadequate for 200-plus-pound fish, but provides excellent fun with the many 50- to 100-pound sharks that travel these waters.

Terminal gear includes six feet of 90- to 120-pound nylon-coated wire as a leader, connected to the line with a size 5/0 swivel. I prefer somewhat smaller cadmium-plated hooks, 8/0 and 12/0, connected to the leader via a snell knot.

Sharks can also be taken from the shore. Most will be of the smaller variety, 20 pounds or less, but on light tackle they can be exciting to catch. The Clam Creek area on the north end of Jekyll Island and the St. Andrews picnic area on the south end are two good locations.

Since sharks became table fare, their numbers have declined dramatically. Due to their lengthy maturation period and small number of offspring produced annually, restocking could take decades. The federal and state governments have placed creel limits on sharks. I prefer, and ask readers, to keep only one shark for the table and release others unharmed. Simply cut the leader and leave the hook in place; it will dissolve or dislodge in a matter of days.

To book a shark-fishing trip in the Cumberland-Jekyll-St. Simons Island area, call Captain Reynolds at ☎ 912-265-0392.

Crooked River State Park

This park is one of Georgia's most popular outdoor adventure centers. Situated on the banks of the river from which it takes its name, the park offers a range of activities and facilities that includes swimming, hiking, camping, fishing, hiking and miniature golf. There are more than seven miles of canoe trails to explore, as well as a 400-acre lake. The freshwater fishing is good all year round, though private boats are limited to 10 HP. Of special interest are the ruins of the old McIntosh Sugar Works. The mill was built around 1825 and was used during the Civil War years to produce starch. Crooked River is an exciting and unique outdoor experience.

Camping facilities at the park include 21 tent and trailer sites, a winterized group shelter, four picnic shelters, and canoe and fishing boat rentals.

Annual events include a Saltwater Fishing Clinic in February, Wildflower Day in March, and an Arts & Crafts Show in September.

Crooked River State Park, 3092 Spur 40, St. Mary's, GA 31558. ☎ 912-882-5256.

The park is 10 miles north of St. Mary's on Georgia Spur 40, or east of Kingsland, 12 miles off US 17, and eight miles off I-95. Open from 7 am until dark; the park office is open from 8 to 5.

Douglas

Named for Stephen A. Douglas, one of Abraham Lincoln's fiercest political opponents, this little city is one of Coastal Georgia's most progressive communities. Its beautiful farmland and fruit orchards can be seen along the backroads. It's a land of lush scenery. Its historic downtown district is one of brick sidewalks, period lamp posts, park benches, and unique shops and restaurants. Douglas is a major tobacco market and boasts one of the largest hog markets in Georgia.

CRAFT HUNTING

The **Southeast Georgia Fair** is held in October and features not only crafts, but rodeos and local foods. ☎ 912-384-1873.

SIGHTSEEING

General Coffee State Park. The land for the park, which is named for General John Coffee, a famous local planter, US Congressman, and Indian fighter, was donated to the state by a group of Coffee County citizens in 1970. The park sits on both sides of the Seventeen-Mile River, which winds its way through the 1,500 acres of parkland, creating four small lakes along. It is a mecca for wildlife enthusiasts, home to a wide variety of birds, snakes, turtles, mammals and wildflowers, including several endangered species, among them the indigo snake and the gopher turtle. One of Georgia's unique and unforgettable outdoor experiences.

There's a small, riverside **campground** with just 25 tent and trailer sites, a comfort station and bathhouse. Campers have free access to the rest of the park's facilities.

There's a four-acre lake, winterized group shelter, swimming pool and bathhouse, six picnic shelters, several nature trails, and a log cabin donated to the park by the Douglas Exchange Club after it was used in the city's 1976 Bicentennial Celebration. There's hiking, fishing, nature study, birdwatching, wildlife photography and picnicking, plus Fishing Rodeo and a Pioneer Skills event in June, and an Archery Demonstration in August.

The park, six miles east of Douglas on GA 32, is open from 7 am until 10 pm; the park office from 8 to 5.

General Coffee State Park, Route 2, Box 83, Nicholls, GA 31554. ☎ 912-384-7082.

Little Ocmulgee State Park

In Eastman, Little Ocmulgee is one of Georgia's best state park resorts. In 1935 the local landowners along the Little Ocmulgee River began donating the land to the state of Georgia and, with the help of the Civilian Conservation Corps and the National Parks Service, a dam was built, roads were installed, and facilities were added until, in 1940, the park was opened to the public. Today the park is a full-service state resort offering all sorts of special and unique amenities, including a magnificent, 18-hole public golf course.

Camping: A large riverside campground, well-developed, with 58 tent and trailer sites, a pioneer campground, group camp, comfort station with flush toilets and hot showers, and a dumping station. For the camper who prefers a roof overhead, there's a 30-room lodge with a restaurant and swimming pool, and 10 rental cottages. Campers and guests at the lodge and cottages have free access to all other park facilities, except the golf course.

There are 1,400 acres of scenic parkland, a 260-acre lake and two tennis courts. The **fishing** is good (rental boats are available); you can go boating and waterskiing (private boats are permitted). The **hiking** trails (a foot trail and a boardwalk) offer unique opportunities for nature study, birdwatching and wildlife photography. There's even miniature golf.

An Arts & Crafts Festival is held over the first weekend in April; the Civilian Conservation Corps reunion is held the first Saturday in April; and a Christmas Decorations Workshop is held on the first Saturday in December.

The park, two miles north of McRae via US 319 and 441, is open from 7 am until 10 pm; the park office is open from 8 to 5.

Little Ocmulgee State Park and Lodge, PO Box 149, McRae, GA 31055. ☎ 912-868-7474 or 912-868-6651 (golf course).

George L. Smith State Park

This is one of Georgia's favorite recreational parks. The surrounding natural beauty, combined with Watson Mill, the dam, the mill pond with its cypress trees, the covered bridge, the wildlife and the fine fishing, make this 1,350-acre park a treat to be enjoyed.

There are 21 tent and trailer sites, a 400-acre lake, a winterized group shelter, fishing boat and canoe rentals, and four picnic shelters. There's year-round fresh water **fishing** for bass, crappie, bluegill and catfish; **boating** (private boats are permitted but are limited to motors of 10 HP or less); canoeing (there are more than seven miles of canoe trails to explore); nature study and birdwatching; wildlife photography; and picnicking. Annual events include a Fishing Tournament in May, and an Arts & Crafts Festival in October.

The park, four miles southeast of Twin City off GA 23, is open from 7 am until 10 pm; the office is open from 8 to 5.

George L. Smith State Park, PO Box 57, Twin City, GA 30471. ☎ 912-763-2579.

Gordonia-Alatamaha State Park

This is a place that, for more than 20 million years, time forgot. Then, about a million years ago, the area emerged from the oceans, the climate tempered, and life spread into this new coastal region from the mainland. Today, it's become something of an outdoor resort.

Camping facilities include 23 tent and trailer sites. There's also a nine-hole golf course, a tennis court, a swimming pool, four picnic shelters, a winterized group shelter and a miniature golf course.

Popular activities include nature study, birdwatching, wildlife photography, picnicking, golfing, exploring, hiking and lake fishing; no private boats are permitted.

Annual special events include Wildflower Day in April, and the Fourth of July Fireworks.

Gordonia-Alatamaha State Park, PO Box 1047, Reidsville, GA 30453. ☎ 912-557-6444 and 912-557-6445 (golf course).

The park, in Reidsville off US 280, is open from 7 am until 10 pm; the office is open from 8 to 5.

Magnolia Springs State Park

During the Civil War this beautiful Southern recreation area was the site of Camp Lawton, a Confederate prisoner-of-war camp. Today, little is left of the prison, just a few rotting timbers that do little to conjure up the images of Camp Lawton and its turbulent past. The natural spring from which the park takes its name pumps into the lake some nine million gallons of sparkling water every day. The 948-acre park with its abundance of wildlife offers the visitor plenty to see and do throughout the year.

Camping facilities include 26 tent and trailer sites, a swimming pool, three group shelters, eight picnic shelters, an 85-capacity group camp, five cottages, a boat dock and three playgrounds.

Activities include hiking along the two well-laid-out nature trails, nature study, birdwatching, wildlife photography, picnicking, fishing and boating. Private boats are permitted and rental fishing boats and canoes are available. There's a fishing tournament in May, Canoe the Ogeechee in October, and a clogging and square dancing weekend in November.

Magnolia Springs State Park, Route 5, Box 488, Millen, GA 30442. ☎ 912-982-1660.

The park, five miles north of Millen on US Highway 25, is open from 7 am until 10 pm; office hours are 8 to 5.

St. Mary's

This picturesque little town is less than an hour south of Brunswick. It's an old town, with lots of early homes and historic structures; it's also the departure point for the ferry to Cumberland Island, and the home of the vast King's Bay Naval Submarine Base, with the US Navy's fleet of nuclear-powered submarines. For more information, call the Campden County-King's Bay Chamber of Commerce at ☎ 912-729-5840.

Okefenokee Swamp

Waycross is the gateway to the Okefenokee Swamp, around which much of its economy revolves.

The Okefenokee is a vast, primitive world of water and cypress swamp that covers an area of more than 600 square miles in southeast Georgia, a watershed fed almost entirely by rainfall, the origin of two of Georgia's great rivers, the Suwannee and the St. Mary's. It's not really a swamp at all, for the word swamp means a low-lying area of stagnant water. The Okefenokee is more than 100 feet above sea level, and its waters are constantly on the move, flowing through the thousands of channels that meander this way and that over the great wetland. Its waters are dark and mysterious, the color of old tea that gives the impression of dirt and contamination; in fact, the opposite is true. The waters of the Okefenokee are pure and quite drinkable. The discoloration comes from tannic acid, the by-product of decaying vegetation in the water, and there's plenty of that. The bed is a layer of peat at least five feet thick, more in places. The dark color of the water provides photographers with many unique opportunities. It gives the surface a mirror-like quality, and when the waters are still and silent, as they are in the interior, the images produced on film are so clear and sharp, it's often difficult to determine which way is up.

The Okefenokee is a strange land of diverse habitats: hammocks, islands, lakes and prairies. Yes, prairies, great open expanses covered with aquatic plants and surrounded by dense stands of cypress. But, even as the Okefenokee is not really a swamp, so these vast open areas are not really prairies in the true sense of the word. They are actually areas of water, one to two feet deep, covered with water lilies, swamp iris, never-wets and numerous other aquatic plants and grasses. Some of them are truly huge. The Grand Prairie is some five miles long and more than three miles wide; the Chase Prairie is a little larger, but they are not the only ones. There are thought to be at least 60,000 acres of them within the swamp, all quiet, all populated by an abundance of wildlife, and all beautiful in a unique way.

The lakes are famous for the good fishing they provide, and for the wildlife that makes a home around them: the sandhill crane, osprey, anhinga, great egret, great blue heron, white ibis and yellow-crowned night heron are just a few of the delights waiting for birdwatchers.

There are some 70 islands in the Okefenokee; most of them are large enough to have names. Many have been inhabited by settlers for more than 150 years. Before that, there were only Indians and wildlife. The Indians are long gone now, chased away by soldiers during the early part of the 19th century, but the wildlife remains very much intact.

The Okefenokee is home to the American alligator. Once hunted almost to extinction for its skin, it is now protected and there are lots of them living here in the swamp. The female lays 30 to 60 eggs at a time. When they hatch, the baby alligators are a little less than six inches long. They grow about a foot a year for the first six years or so. Those that make it through those early years into adulthood can reach 12 to 15 feet and weigh 700 pounds or more. The alligator looks deceptively slow, even clumsy; he's not. He feeds on small animals, birds, fish, turtles, snakes and just about anything he can catch or sink his teeth into, even baby alligators.

An alligator basks in the swamplands at Okefenokee.

The Okefenokee is also home to a variety of other animals, including the white-tail deer, the otter and the black bear. There are also, along with 27 species of snakes, including the venomous water moccasin. It can strike, empty its venom sacs, and return to its coiled position in about a half-second; keep a sharp lookout for them.

There are several entrances to the Okefenokee Swamp, a couple of state parks, and several points of special historical interest. The easiest route into the swamp is via the city of Waycross, just to the north of the swamp on Highway 82, going east and west, and Highway 84 from the northeast and southwest. From there, you'll take Highway 23 and the 121 Spur to the eastern entrance at the Suwannee Canal Recreation Area. Alternatively, for a quick visit, you can head for the Okefenokee Swamp Park just eight miles south of Waycross on Highways 1 and 23. From the southwest, you can enter the swamp at the Stephen C. Foster State Park via Highways 441 and 177.

SIGHTSEEING

Obediah's Okefenokee: A unique outdoor attraction offering self-guided nature walks, including a 1,100-foot boardwalk, through the Okefenokee Swamp. Of special interest is an 1840s swampland homestead containing interpretive exhibits and displays.

Open daily from 10 until 5. Admission, $4.50; children 6-17, $3. From Waycross, take Highway 83 east to the Gillmore Street Exit, then drive south for 8½ miles to 500 Obediah Trail. ☎ 912-287-0090.

Okefenokee Swamp Park: Cowhouse Island has been the headquarters for this 1,600-acre wilderness park since 1945. Operated by a private non-profit organization created for the purpose of making the great swamp accessible to the public. Aside from providing easy access to the Okefenokee, the park has its own museum with all sorts of interpretive exhibits; the Swamp Creation Center interprets the evolution of the swamp through dioramas, animated exhibits, aquariums and charts; the Living Swamp Ecological Center provides insight to the wildlife; there's an exhibition of carnivorous plants native to the swamp; insects; a serpentarium; bear observatory; and films that interpret the ecosystem of the swamp. Out in the park, a 90-foot observation tower provides a panoramic view. Price of admission includes a two-mile boat ride. A guided, two-hour, 10-mile boat trip departs daily at 10, 1 and 3. Open daily from 9 until 6:30, June through August, 9 until 5 the rest of the year. Admission, $10; children 5-11, $7. The fare for the two-hour boat ride is $6 and reservations are required. ☎ 912-283-0583.

Laura S. Walker State Park: The 300-acre park nine miles southeast of Waycross on Route 177, is named for one of Georgia's most famous citizens. A naturalist, teacher, writer and civic leader, Laura Walker was a lover of nature and the outdoors, especially the trees. She was also a dedicated worker for the preservation of Georgia's natural beauty. The park is located close to the Okefenokee Swamp and is famous for its wildlife: birds, animals and wildflowers.

There are 44 tent and trailer sites, a bathhouse, a group camp, picnic tables and grills, a 120-acre lake and pool, nine picnic shelters, four group shelters, a nature trail, a dock and a boat ramp.

The **fishing** here is good: lots of bass, bluegill, crappie, and catfish (private boats are permitted). You can bring your own **boat**, or you can rent one at the park office. If you like to waterski, that's available, too.

Hiking is popular at Laura Walker. The nature trail offers a nice easy stroll and opportunities for nature study, birdwatching and wildlife photography. Picnicking is also popular, and the picnic area is big enough for family reunions and group outings. Open daily from 7 am until 10 pm; the park office hours are 8 to 5. Laura S. Walker State Park, 5653 Laura Walker Road, Waycross, GA 31501. ☎ 912-287-4900.

Stephen C. Foster State Park: The park, situated on Jones Island, is the western entrance to the wild and wonderful world of the great Okefenokee Swamp. Named after the famous songwriter, this is the mysterious, quiet side of the Okefenokee, where the number of visitors is but a fraction of those at the other entrances. This is your introduction to an alien land set deep in the heart of southern Georgia. The lush vegetation of the cypress swamp and its waterways are inhabited by a population of more than 200 species of birds, 40 species of mammals, at least 50 different reptiles and some 60 different species of amphibians. Stephen C. Foster is a lonely place, approached by a long, often-deserted road that seems to go on forever. At night, when the hot, Southern sun has disappeared below the treetops, this vast, subtropical world comes to life with sounds of the swamp. The guest cabins, set back from the road under a canopy of trees, look primitive and uninviting. In fact, they are quite comfortable, with screened-in porches where you can sit and listen to the sounds of the swamp at night.

Here, you can enjoy the Okefenokee from the comfort of an elevated boardwalk, or get really close to nature by taking a guided boat tour through the maze of silent waterways. Stephen C. Foster is a world all its own – one you really should take time out to visit.

There are 66 tent and trailer sites, nine cottages and a bathhouse with hot showers and restrooms. You'll need nerves of steel to spend a night here, but it's an unforgettable camping experience. There are also three picnic shelters and an interpretive center.

This is not really hiking country. However, the half-mile Trembling Earth Nature Trail offers an easy walk through the swamp and a close-up look at the birds and other wildlife.

You can take a guided boat tour, or rent one (canoes, motorboats, and jon boats are available at the visitors center), then go off on your own. Nature study, birdwatching, wildlife photography and exploring the more than 25 miles of public-use waterways are all popular.

Annual events include Man in the Swamp in November, Okefenokee Birding, and a variety of interpretive programs all year.

Open daily from 7 am until 7, September 15 to February 28, and from 7 to 5, March 1 to September 14. Office hours are from 8 until 5.00. Stephen C. Foster State Park, Route 1, Box 131, Fargo, GA 31631. ☎ 912-637-5274.

Visitors paddle through some of Okefenokee's waterways.

Satilla River

East of Waycross and northwest of the Okefenokee Swamp, the Satilla River is recognized as the last of Georgia's wild and scenic rivers. It offers a number of unique, outdoor opportunities found nowhere else in Coastal Georgia. The map provides the locations of campgrounds, boat ramps and fish camps.

Canoeing: The Satilla offers canoeists 149 miles of scenic paddling, with snow-white sand bars, ideal for camping, picnicking and swimming, around almost every bend. Each bridge along the way has at least one boat ramp, and you can pick up supplies in Waycross, Atkinson and Woodbine.

Fishing: Anglers, too, will find the Satilla an exciting experience. Good fishing is available year-round, and the river is well-stocked with bass, bream, catfish, red bellies and crappie.

Nature Watching: Wildlife enthusiasts will find all sorts of species make their homes along its banks: snow-white cranes, white-tail deer, ducks of every shape and size, blue herons, raccoons, squirrels, gopher tortoises and wild turkeys.

Southeast Georgia Regional Development Center, 3395 Harris Road, Waycross, GA 31503. ☎ 912-285-6097.

Satilla River

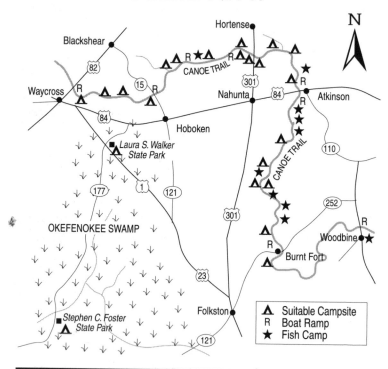

The Plains Region

The land west of the Flint River to the Chattahoochee River on the Alabama border is Georgia's section of the East Gulf Coastal Plain, part of a vast upland section of the southeastern United States that slopes southward to the Gulf of Mexico. It's a flat limestone plain, deeply cut by narrow valleys where the Flint and Chattahoochee rivers flow south and join on the Florida border to form the Apalachicola River. This is a largely uninteresting section of the state, sparsely populated and old-world. But, in places, it offers outdoor adventurers opportunities not to be missed.

How To Get There

This section of the state is served north and south by I-75, and US Highways 19 and 27; east and west by US Highways 82 and 84, and a series of lesser Georgia highways.

Climate

This region is steamy during the summer, often uncomfortably hot in July and August, and temperate during the winter. When it rains, it seems as if the skies have opened, but for the outdoor adventurer, the long summers and short winters, rainy times and all, are a boon indeed.

Where To Stay

Most hotels in this section of Georgia are found at the exits off I-75, although Albany seems to have more than its fair share. Other than that, decent accommodations are hard to find. You'll find some of what's available listed by section below.

The Plains Region

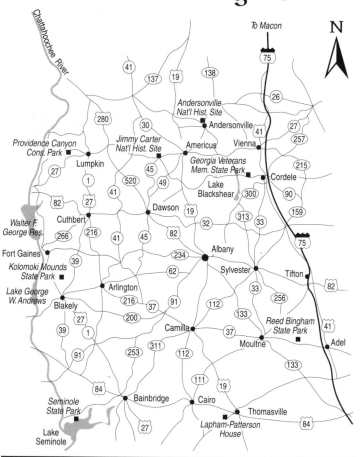

To Macon

75

Chattahoochee River

41
137   19   138
26
280
30   Andersonville Nat'l Hist. Site
Andersonville   41   27
Providence Canyon Cons. Park   Jimmy Carter Nat'l Hist. Site   Americus   Vienna   257
27   Lumpkin   45   Georgia Veterans Mem. State Park   215
1   520   49   Lake Blackshear   300   Cordele
82   27   41   90
Walter F. George Res.   Cuthbert   Dawson   19   32   313   33   159
266   216   41   45   82   75
Fort Gaines   234   Albany
Kolomoki Mounds State Park   39   62   Sylvester   Tifton
Lake George W. Andrews   Arlington   33   256   82
Blakely   216   37   91   112   133
27   200   133   Reed Bingham State Park   41
39   1   Camilla   37   Moultrie   Adel
91   253   311   112
111   19
84   Bainbridge   Cairo   Thomasville
Seminole State Park   27   Lapham-Patterson House   84
Lake Seminole

Dining Out

Again, most of the decent restaurants are confined to Albany, but
there are a few nice places scattered about the region; you'll find
them listed throughout the following text.

INFORMATION

Albany Convention & Visitors Bureau, 225 West Broad Avenue, Albany, GA 31701. ☎ 912-434-8700 or 800-475-8700.

Touring

Reed Bingham State Park

Stop in Adel for lunch, then head west on GA 37 to Reed. This 1,600-acre recreation area is one of the most popular centers for outdoor activities in Southwest Georgia. It's a land of forest, woodland, meadow and lake where you can get far away from the hustle and bustle of city life to spend a few hours fishing, hiking or picnicking.

Camping: Facilities include 85 tent and trailer sites with water and electric hookups, a bathhouse with hot showers and flush toilets, and handicapped-accessible restrooms.

Fishing & Boating: The 375-acre lake, well-stocked with bass, crappie, bream, bluegill and catfish, offers fine sport, as well as canoeing and waterskiing. Four boat ramps and three fishing docks are an added bonus.

Hiking: The park has almost four miles of well-marked hiking and nature trails, all pleasant walks through the countryside, that offer lots of opportunities for nature study and birdwatching.

Other facilities include a swimming beach, seven picnic shelters, four group shelters, and numerous individual picnic sites with tables and grills.

Annual events include a Fourth of July music and fireworks celebration, Old-fashioned Games on Memorial Day and Labor Day, and Buzzard Day the first Saturday in December.

Open daily from 7 am until 10 pm; the park office is open from 8 to 5.

Reed Bingham State Park, Route 2, Box 394B-1, Adel, GA 31620. ☎ 912-896-3551.

Albany

Situated on the Flint River, Albany is the major city in this section. It's not a large city, compared to those farther to the north and east, but it's a very pleasant spot, often overlooked by travelers heading south for warmer climes. Once cotton country, Albany is now one of the centers of the pecan industry. As you head into the city along GA 300 and US 82, you'll see old plantations with avenues of old-growth pecan trees lined up in pristine order. There's not much to see in Albany, but it's a nice place to spend the night and do a little shopping. If you can visit the third weekend in May, the Chehaw Indian Festival is a spectacle worth seeing. More than 10 tribes participate, with Indian dancing, crafts, hide tanning, and arrow-making demonstrations. For more information, ☎ 912-434-8700.

WHERE TO STAY

Comfort Suites Merry Acres, 1400 Dawson Road, is a bit on the expensive side for its location, but you do get great value for your money. All rooms have coffee-makers, and guests have access to the facilities at the Quality Inn Merry Acres. ☎ 912-888-3939. $$.

Holiday Inn Albany, 2701 Dawson Road, is an older example of the chain, but nicely renovated and remodeled to bring it up to standard. There's a good restaurant, a pleasant, landscaped courtyard where you can sit among the greenery and enjoy early morning coffee, and there's a cocktail lounge. ☎ 912-883-8100. $-$$.

Quality Inn Merry Acres, 1500 Dawson Road, is a nice place to stay, although the rates do seem a little on the high side for a rural community. There's a nice restaurant, pool, playground, and an exercise room. ☎ 912-435-7721. $$.

DINING OUT

Villa Gargano, in the Albany Mall at 2601 Dawson Road, is open for lunch and dinner. The restaurant is family-owned, the cuisine is Italian, and it's good. ☎ 912-436-7265.

Andersonville National Historic Site

There is, perhaps, no more infamous name in Georgia history than Andersonville, the one-time Confederate prisoner-of-war camp. Contrary to what most people believe, Andersonville saw service only during the latter 18 months of the Civil War, but during those months thousands of captured Union soldiers died of dreadful diseases, neglect or mistreatment. So bad were the conditions within the 26-acre compound, even the guards were reluctant to enter, and, at the end of the war, the camp commandant, Captain

Henry Wirz, was hanged for war crimes. The prison, 10 miles northeast of Americus on GA 49, is now a national monument, dedicated to those who were interred there, and the more than 16,000 veterans and their dependents buried on the site.

The monument at Andersonville stands as a tribute to all those who died.

The visitors center and museum have a number of interesting exhibits and artifacts that interpret the history of Andersonville, and you can take a self-guided walking tour or, on weekends during the summer, a guided tour of the site. Open daily from 8 until 5; the museum is open from 8:30 to 5. Admission, free. ☎ 912-924-0343.

The site is off Highway 49, 10 miles north of Americus.

Bainbridge

On the banks of the Flint River, southwest of Albany at the junction of US Highways 84 and 27, Bainbridge is the gateway to the great outdoor adventureland that is Lake Seminole. It's also an historic little town. Although its population is still less than 11,000, it has the distinction of being Georgia's first inland port. Andrew Jackson built a fort here to defend the town during the Indian Wars of 1817-1821. Today, Bainbridge is a town where great water oaks and live oaks grow, and it's a fine place to use as a base for a vacation in the great outdoors.

From Albany, take US 19 south to Camilla, then GA 97 south into the city; the scenic route is to take GA 97 to its junction with GA 311, and then south along the Flint. From Thomasville, take US 84 west.

WHERE TO STAY

The Charterhouse Inn, at the junction of US 27 and 84 on the bypass, is perhaps your best choice. There's a restaurant open for breakfast, lunch and dinner, a swimming pool and a bar. ☎ 912-246-8550. $.

Holiday Inn Express, 751 Shotwell Street, is predictable and a safe bet. There's a restaurant nearby, a heated pool, whirlpool and a free continental breakfast. ☎ 912-246-0015. $.

DINING OUT

There are a number of country restaurants and cafés in and around the city.

Johnny's Seafood, on US 27 one mile south of the US 84 Bypass, is open for lunch and dinner from 11 until 9. The menu features a buffet lunch and all sorts of fresh seafood dishes – the Gulf Coast is only a short distance away to the south.

Lake Seminole

Yet another of the great projects undertaken by the US Corps of Engineers. Lake Seminole has, for more years than can be remembered, been one of the bass fishing centers of the Southeast. However, although it's billed as "wet & wild," Seminole is more than just a fishing center. Whatever your outdoor pleasure – hiking, swimming, hunting, watersports, camping, birdwatching or nature photography – you'll find it here, at the outer limits of southwest Georgia.

The terrain close to the lake varies from flat to gently rolling downs, except for a hilly region known as the Apalachicola Bluff that originates in southwest Georgia and extends along the Flint River from above the dam for about 25 miles into Florida. The bluffs are cut by ravines and small valleys, containing a variety of plants that have attracted botanists from all over the United States. The remainder of the area is underlaid by limestone and is dominated by sloughs, sinks and pine forest, a habitat for a variety of wildlife and plants. This is country for nature lovers, birdwatchers and photographers.

Boating: As one might imagine, this lake is very popular with the boating crowd. On any given day, winter or summer, the lake is dotted with crafts of all shapes and sizes. Public-access boat ramps are available at all Corps recreation areas, and at Seminole State Park (check the map for locations).

Anglers take to the calm waters of Lake Seminole.

Fishing: Lake Seminole is deep in the subtropical lowlands of the tri-state region of Georgia, Alabama and Florida. Extensive stump and grass beds provide cover where anglers can hunt trophy-sized largemouth, hybrid, white and striped bass, along with goodly numbers of catfish, bream and crappie. Huge catfish can be caught in the waters of the tailrace below the dam. The lake is always crowded with boat people, but finding a quiet spot is never a problem. Public-access boat ramps are located at all Corps-operated recreation areas, and at Seminole State Park. Be sure to check local fishing regulations for license requirements.

CORPS RECREATION AREAS & CAMPGROUNDS

The Corps also maintains a number of recreation areas with facilities for picnicking, swimming and watersports. These, too, are listed and numbered in the following text.

1. Woodruff Dam: West Overlook, at the southern end of the lake off US 90, is a good place to begin your visit. From Bainbridge, take GA 97 south to US 90 west and follow the signs. The view over the lake and dam is spectacular.

3. Sneads Park, at the southern end of the lake off US 90, is a public-access area with boat ramps, picnic areas, fresh drinking water, handicapped-accessible restrooms, a playground for the kids and a swimming beach. ☎ 912-662-2001.

Camping facilities include a small number of tent and trailer sites with water and electric hookups, a bathhouse with hot showers and flush toilets, handicapped-accessible restrooms, fresh drinking water and a picnic area. Fees: $8-$12. ☎ 912-662-2001.

8. Neal's Landing is also on the western shore of the lake off Highway 271. It, too, is best reached by taking US 84 west from Bainbridge to its junction with Highway 285. Drive on west to Highway 91 and cross the Chattahoochee, then take 271 south.

Camping facilities include a small campground with 10 tent and trailer sites, water and electric hookups, a bathhouse with hot showers and flush toilets, handicapped-accessible restrooms, fresh drinking water, a picnic area and a sewage disposal unit. Fees: $8-$12. ☎ 912-662-2001.

9. Desser Access Area, on the eastern shore of the lake, west of Desser, via Highway 253 from Bainbridge, is a lake-access site with a boat ramp, dock, parking, restrooms and fresh drinking water.

10. Fairchild's Park, on the eastern shore off Highway 253, is another lake-access area with facilities limited to a two-lane boat ramp, parking, restrooms and a group camp.

12. Cummings Landing, on the north shore at the southern end of the lake, is off Highway 39. Facilities include a boat ramp, parking, fresh drinking water, and a small campground with just 15 tent and trailer sites, a comfort station and access to the rest of the facilities. Fees: $8. ☎ 912-662-2001.

13. Rays Lake Access Area, on a small area of the lake north of the main waters at the southern end of the lake, is off Highway 253 west of Bainbridge. Facilities include a public-access boat ramp, restrooms, fresh drinking water and plenty of parking.

17. Cypress Pond Access Area, on the north shore at the southern end of the lake via Highways 253 and 374, has a public-access boat ramp with a parking area and dock, a picnic area, restrooms and fresh drinking water.

19. Reynoldsville Park, on the western shore of Spring Creek on the eastern side of the lake, is reached by taking Highway 253 west from Bainbridge. Facilities here are limited to a picnic area, boat ramp and dock, parking, restrooms and fresh drinking water.

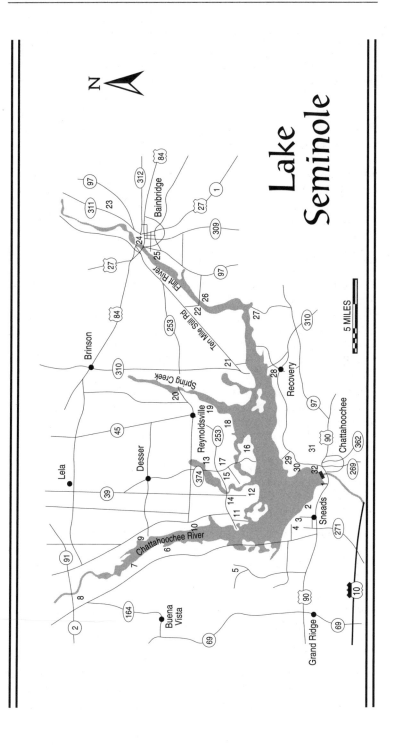

N

Lake
Seminole

5 MILES

22. Hale's Landing Access Area is on the shores of the Flint River, north of the lake and south of Bainbridge via Ten Mile Still Road. Facilities here include a small campground with 10 tent and trailer sites, restrooms, fresh drinking water and a parking area. Fees: $8. ☎ 912-662-2814.

27. Faceville Landing Access Area is on the southern shore at the south end of the lake, off Highway 97. Facilities include a small campground with six tent and trailer sites, six picnic sites, a group picnic site, boat ramp, dock and parking. There's also a restroom and fresh drinking water.

29. River Junction Access Area, on the southern shore of the lake off Highway 310, is a nice park with a small campground, restrooms, fresh drinking water, a boat dock and ramp, and plenty of parking. Camping facilities include 16 tent and trailer sites with water and electric hookups, a comfort station, restrooms and fresh drinking water. Fees: $8. ☎ 912-662-2001.

30. Chattahoochee Park, also at the southern end of the lake on the south shore off Highway US 90, has a playground for the kids, 30 picnic sites, three group picnic areas, a comfort station with flush toilets, fresh drinking water, a swimming beach, bathhouse, boat ramp with three lanes, a dock, and plenty of parking.

31. Woodruff Dam: East Bank Public Use Area, at the southern end of the lake off US 90, is a good place to begin your visit to Lake Seminole. From Bainbridge, take GA 97 south to US 90 and then drive west and follow the signs. Facilities include restrooms, fresh drinking water, and plenty of parking.

32. Woodruff Dam: Fishing Deck and Powerhouse, at the southern end of the lake off US 90, is a great place to hunt those giant catfish. Facilities include a comfort station with toilets and fresh drinking water.

CITY & STATE PARKS

5. Apalachee Game Management Area (state of Florida), a vast wilderness area on the western shore of the lake off Highway 271, is primarily a hunting preserve, but there is a small campground with 10 sites and a public-access boat ramp. ☎ 912-662-2001.

24. Bainbridge Municipal Park, in Bainbridge, is one of the nice areas where you can turn the kids loose in the playground and settle down to enjoy a picnic on a sunny afternoon, seemingly far away from the hustle and bustle of city life. Facilities include picnic sites, restrooms, fresh drinking water, a boat ramp and a parking lot.

25. Bainbridge Bypass Park is on the southern edge of the city, off the bypass. There's a playground for the kids, two public-access boat ramps, three docks, a swimming area, six picnic areas, seven group picnic sites, restrooms and fresh drinking water.

23. Big Slough Park Access Area is a Decatur County Park on the Flint River, north of Bainbridge, off Highway 331. Facilities are limited to a boat ramp and dock.

7. Buena Vista Access Area and Campground, is a Jackson County Park on the western shore of the lake off Highway 271, and is best reached by taking US 84 west from Bainbridge to its junction with Highway 285; from there, drive on west to Highway 91 and cross the Chattahoochee, then take 271 south. This is primarily a campground, but there is a public-access boat ramp with parking available.

20. Decatur Lake No. 2 Access Area, also on Spring Creek, north of Reynoldsville Park, off Highway 253 from Bainbridge, is a county park, and no more than a lake-access area with a boat ramp and dock.

15. Harvel Pond Access Area is a part of Seminole State Park on the north shore at the southern end of the lake via Highway 253.

26. Horseshoe Bend Park is another Decatur County Park on the Flint River, south of Bainbridge, off Highway 97. Facilities are limited to a public-access boat ramp.

16. Sealy Point Access Area is a Seminole County Park. Public-access boat ramp.

21. Ten Mile Still Landing, at the southern end of the lake on the shores of the Flint River, is reached by taking Ten Mile Still Road south from Bainbridge. It has a boat ramp, dock and a parking area.

4. Three Rivers State Park (in Florida) is at the southern end of the lake off US 90 and Highway 271. The tri-state location of Three Rivers, the hardwood and pine forests, the hilly terrain, Lake Seminole, the Flint, Apalachicola and Chattahoochee rivers, all contribute to a setting of unparalleled natural beauty for one of Florida's premier recreation areas, and it's easily accessible from Bainbridge, Georgia. It is also home to a variety of wildlife, thus making it a magnet for nature lovers. White-tailed deer and gray foxes roam the woodlands, while squirrels and birds inhabit the treetops. If ever there was a place to get away from it all, this is it. The fishing, both on the lake and on the rivers, is excellent: largemouth and smallmouth bass, catfish, bluegill, speckled perch and bream are only a few of the species anglers can expect to find here. From waterskiing to canoeing, from hiking to picnicking, there's something for just about everyone. There's a swimming area, several nature trails, a boat ramp and a picnic area. Open

8-sunset daily. ☎ 904-482-9006. Handicapped-accessible. Admission $3.25 per vehicle.

14. Seminole State Park is 16 miles south of Donalsonville via GA 39, or 23 miles west of Bainbridge on GA 253.

Compared to many of Georgia's great parks, Seminole is quite small, only 340 acres, but what it lacks in size it more that makes up for with its great natural beauty, abundant wildlife, wildflowers, woodland and recreational facilities. It is the best developed park on the lake.

Camping facilities include 50 tent and trailer sites with water and electric hookups, 10 rental cottages, a bathhouse with hot showers and flush toilets, handicapped-accessible restrooms, fresh drinking water, a dumping station and a laundromat. Fees: $10 for campsites; cottages, $40 to $59.

There is a swimming beach, two fishing docks, three boat ramps with six lanes, a nature trail, miniature golf course, a playground for the kids, 200 picnic sites with tables and grills, plus six family and group shelters. Park staff conduct a program of summer nature programs.

Open from 7 am until 10 pm; the park office is open from 8 until 5. Admission, $2 per vehicle.

Seminole State Park, Route 2, Donalsonville, GA 31745. ☎ 912-861-3137.

MARINAS

The following is a list of commercial marinas operating on the lake. Most have extensive facilities, including a store, boat ramps and docks, fuel docks, and boat rentals of one sort or another. Fishing tackle is available – for sale or rent – at most facilities, along with camping and boating supplies. Each is numbered for easy location on the map.

2. Sneads Landing & Seminole Lodge
6. Paramore Landing
11. Butler's Ferry Landing
18. Spring Creek Landing
28. Hutchinson's Ferry Landing and Wingate's Lodge

COMMERCIAL CAMPGROUNDS

28. Jack Wingate's Bass Island Campground, south of Bainbridge via Highways 97 and 310, is a well-developed facility, dedicated to anglers as well as campers, on the southern shore of the lake adjacent to Hutchinson's Ferry.

There are 84 tent and trailer sites, of which 24 have full hookups, 58 have water and electric only, and 48 are pull-throughs. There's a modern bathhouse, kept scrupulously clean, with hot showers and flush toilets, a laundromat, sewage disposal, and a store where you can purchase groceries, ice and RV supplies, rent or buy fishing tackle, and refill your propane tanks by weight or meter. Recreational facilities include a hall, pavilion, swimming area, boat ramp and dock, a sports field and a fishing pier. Fishing guides are also available. Open year-round. Fees start at around $15. ☎ 912-246-0658.

Live Oaks Campground is just south of the Bainbridge city limits. It's a fairly small campground, but quite pleasant and within easy reach of the lake.

There are 26 sites, of which 13 have full hookups, nine water and electric only and four have no hookups. The bathhouse has hot showers and flush toilets, and there's a store where you can stock up on groceries and other supplies. Open year-round. Fees start at around $15 per night for two persons. ☎ 912-246-2231.

Kolomoki Mounds State Historic Park

Six miles north of Blakely off US 27, Kolomoki is not only an important archaeological site, it's a popular recreational area. The seven mounds from which the park takes its name were built by the Swift Creek and Weeden Island Indians during a period that encompassed most of the 12th and 13th centuries. They include Georgia's oldest temple mound, two burial mounds and four ceremonial mounds. The museum and interpretive center has a number of interesting and informative exhibits where you can learn more about the Indians and their culture.

Camping facilities include 35 tent and trailer sites with water and electric hookups, a group camp, a bathhouse with hot showers and flush toilets, handicapped-accessible restrooms, picnic tables and grills. Fees: $10 per night.

There are more than 1,300 acres of parkland, with several miles of **hiking and nature trails** that meander through the woods and meadows, and provide unique opportunities for birdwatching, nature study and wildlife photography. There are also two lakes; a boat dock and ramp (private boats are permitted and rental boats are available); two swimming pools; a miniature golf course; a large number of picnic sites with tables and grills; and seven picnic shelters.

Annual events include a Biathlon in July, and Indian Artifacts Day in October. Open from 7 am until 10 pm; the park office is open from 8 am until 5. Kolomoki Mounds State Historic Park, Route 1, Box 114, Blakely, GA 31723. ☎ 912-723-5296.

Georgia Veterans Memorial State Park

Nine miles west of Cordele on US 280, this is more than 1,300 acres of gardens, groves and woodland located on the shores of Lake Blackshear. Established as a permanent memorial to all US veterans who served, fought, and died for freedom, it's a quiet place to spend a few hours, or even a few days, relaxing in the serenity of one of Georgia's most beautiful and sacred places. If it's outdoor activities that you're looking for, there's plenty here for you to see and do: golf, swimming, boating, waterskiing, camping, fishing, hiking, nature study, birdwatching, wildlife photography, picnicking and lots more.

Camping facilities are 83 tent and trailer sites with water and electric hookups (73 are pull-throughs), 10 rental cottages, a bathhouse with hot showers and flush toilets, handicapped-accessible restrooms, a laundromat, sewage disposal, picnic tables and grills. Fees: $10; cottages from $45.

This is a large, flat park with lots of opportunity for walking, especially along the shores of Lake Blackshear. The going is easy, just a stroll in the park.

Fishing on the lake is considered good, but it can be a little crowded at times. Best go mid-week, early in the morning. Bass, crappie, bream and lots of catfish.

The 18-hole **golf course** here is picturesque, challenging and quiet. There's a pro shop, an elevated lounge/restaurant with a view over the course, a putting green, and equipment is available for rent. There's also a swimming pool and beach, a model aircraft flying field, picnic tables, a winterized group shelter, a boat ramp and a dock.

In Cordele the **Watermelon Festival** is held early to mid-July and includes such attractions as a watermelon eating contest, seed spitting, and the Miss Heart of Georgia Contest. At the park there is a Memorial Celebration, Veterans Day Ceremonies, a Catfish Festival in May, and Christmas on the Flint in December.

Open year-round from 7 am until 10 pm; the park office hours are from 8 until 5.

Georgia Veterans Memorial State Park, 2459-A US Highway 280W, Cordele, GA 31015. ☎ 912-276-2371 or 276-2377.

Fort Gaines

Fort Gaines Frontier Village, 100 Bluff Street, overlooking the Chattahoochee River, is an open-air museum with exhibits that interpret early pioneer living in southwest Georgia. Log cabins, cane mills, grist mills, a smokehouse, and Civil War relics and memorabilia, along with a replica of the original 1814 frontier fort, make the village an interesting stop on the way to Walter F. George Lake and its three-mile-long dam. Free. ☎ 912-768-2934.

Lakes Walter F. George & George W. Andrews

The small community of Georgetown on the shores of Lake Walter F. George is a very pleasant, friendly little town. It's rural, dedicated mostly to farming, but it's also the fast track from Western Georgia into Alabama, and one of the main access point to the great lake. From Albany, take US 82; from Columbus, take US 27 south to its junction with GA 27, then drive southwest into the city.

While George W. Andrews is little more than a significant widening of the Chattahoochee River south of Fort Gaines, Lake Walter F. George to the north is a huge waterworld of more than 45,000 acres, and is considered to be one of the bass fishing capitals of the Southeast. Anglers from around the nation arrive here in droves to test their skills and hunt the "big one."

Walter F. George, sometimes called Lake Eufaula, extends some 85 miles along the Chattahoochee River, incorporating along the way some 640 miles of shoreline; it's one of the top outdoor playgrounds for both Georgia and Alabama.

George W. Andrews is directly south of Walter F. George Lock and Dam and, like its larger sister to the north, abounds with excellent fishing and outdoor recreational opportunities.

Both lakes are the result of the River and Harbor Act of 1946, and both fall under the jurisdiction of the US Corps of Engineers, who also control most of the recreational facilities on the two lakes. These include, along with several state and county parks, a number of recreation areas and campgrounds. The campgrounds are, as always, well developed with modern amenities, and secure. The state parks are among the best in Georgia, and they, too, are extensively developed with plenty to see and do, offering campgrounds, lodges, rental cottages, playgrounds, picnic areas, boat ramps and docks. Add a half-dozen commercial marinas and fishing villages, some commercial campgrounds, and you have the makings of a tremendous inland resort where adventure is the name of the game. All of these facilities are listed below and numbered for easy location on the map, but first let's take a look at what's available.

Boating: While boating is available on both lakes, Walter F. George, the larger of the two, is the most popular. A navigable channel 100 feet by nine feet is maintained as far north as Columbus. There are boat ramps at most Corps areas, state parks, marinas and other strategic locations.

Fishing: These lakes are an angler's paradise, famous for the gamefish therein. These include trophy-sized largemouth bass, white bass, hybrids, crappie, bream and channel catfish. Georgia and Alabama have a reciprocal agreement with regard to fishing licenses: Each state's license is accepted on either side of Walter F. George. You should be aware, however, that regulations as to daily limits and size restrictions differ. Most of the lake's submerged vegetation has long disappeared, but the Corps has gone to great lengths to maintain the underwater habitat. Fish attractors, cedars, old tire structures, and other such contraptions have been strategically placed around the lake to create new fish concentration areas. These attractors are marked with permanent pilings and signs. Bank fishing is excellent in many locations, and anglers without boats are well catered for. Many recreation areas and parks have fishing decks, and floating decks located below the two dams also offer excellent opportunities. The tailwaters below Walter F. George also offer good fishing, especially for catfish. Be aware, though, that such waters also pose special dangers: Waters rise rapidly and almost without warning during periods of power generation.

A quiet moment on the lake at dawn.

Nature & Wildlife: Stands of hardwood, large areas of forest and woodland, and great expanses of open water provide habitats for all sorts of wildlife and birds. If you're a nature lover or birdwatcher, you'll find this section of southwestern Georgia much to your liking, for it's home to bobcats, deer, eagles, hawks, waterfowl and a wide variety of songbirds.

RECREATION & CAMPING AREAS

The following areas offer campsites. The numbers shown relate to those indicated on the map.

1. River Bend Park, off GA 26 near its junction with US 27, is the northernmost of the Corps-operated parks. The 187-acre park is quite remote, but well equipped. Facilities include 14 picnic sites with tables and grills, a group picnic area, a boat ramp with two lanes, and a boat dock where you can fish, too.

2. Bluff Creek Park Campground, on the west bank, off SR 165 north of Cottonton, Alabama, is one of the Corps-operated campgrounds. The 71-acre park has 88 tent and trailer sites, all with water and electric hookups. Six are pull-throughs. Other facilities include a bathhouse with hot showers and flush toilets, handicapped-accessible restrooms, a laundromat, sewage disposal, picnic tables and grills, fire rings and a pavilion. Open year-round. Fees: $14 per night; visitor fee, $2. ☎ 205-855-2746.

Lakes Walter F. George & George W. Andrews

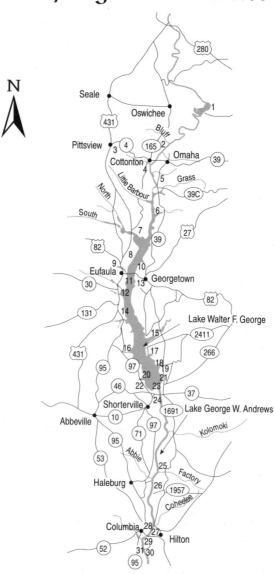

3. Briar Creek Park, in Alabama east of Pittsview off SR 4, is no more than a public-access area for Lake Walter F. George. Facilities are limited to a boat ramp with a single lane and a parking area.

4. Hatchechubbee Creek Park, on the west shore in Alabama off SR 165 just south of Cottonton, is a Corps recreation area with 23 picnic sites, tables and grills, a group picnic area, a boat ramp and a dock.

5. Florence Landing & Marina, on the east shore at the northern end of Walter F. George, south of Omaha, is on GA 39, near Lumpkin. This is a mecca for those who love watersports. The area is rich in early American history and the Kirby Interpretive Center offers visitors a peek into local history from Paleolithic times through the early pioneer days to the present. The lakeside park is extensively developed – a little out of the way, but one of those places you won't regret going out of your way for.

Facilities include 44 tent and trailer sites with water and electric hookups, 10 rental cottages, a bathhouse with hot showers and flush toilets, handicapped-accessible restrooms, a laundromat, sewage disposal, tables and grills. Supplies are available at the marina stores. Fees: campsites $10; cottages from $49. There's a full-service marina with 66 boat slips, two tennis courts, a swimming pool, a lighted fishing pier, a miniature golf course, a clubhouse, and an interpretive center. There's also a public-access boat ramp and six docks.

Annual events include a Crappie Fishing Tournament in March, an Easter Egg Hunt, Astronomy Evening in August, Native American Day in September, and Haunted Halloween.

Open from 7 am until 10 pm; the park office is open from 8 am to 5. Florence Marina State Park, Route 1, Box 36, Omaha, GA 31821. ☎ 912-838-6870.

6. Rood Creek Park, on the east shore of Walter F. George, south of Omaha on GA 39, is another of the Corps-operated campgrounds/recreation areas. The 142-acre park has 33 tent and trailer sites, flush toilets, fresh drinking water, tables, grills and a boat ramp.

7. Lakepoint Resort State Park, seven miles north of Eufaula off Highway 431, is one of Alabama's great state parks. The focus is, of course, on the water and all that goes along with it. It's a picturesque resort, with something special for almost everyone. The scenic outdoor setting and the modern facilities offer a variety of fun-filled activities, along with a year-round schedule of recreational and educational programs provided by the park's naturalist staff. These include environmental slide shows, guest speakers, birdwatching and nature walks. Family and group vacationers can enjoy tours and activities tailored to their ages and interests, and a special summer camp provides "an introduction to the world of conservation," where specialists from the Alabama Department of Conservation share their expertise in the fields of wildlife, marine biology, fisheries management and natural resource conservation.

Facilities include 253 woodland campsites, of which 88 have full hookups, 165 water and electric only. There are bathhouses with hot showers and flush toilets, handicapped-accessible restrooms, sewage disposal, tables, grills, a laundromat and grocery store. There are also 29 rustic, lakeside and woodland cottages fully equipped for housekeeping. Fees: campsites from $10; call for cottage rental rates.

There's a fine 18-hole golf course with a pro shop, putting green, refreshments, and equipment rental. There are 115 picnic areas with tables and grills, three group picnic areas, two playgrounds for the kids, three boat ramps with a total of six lanes, a dock and two swimming areas.

Lakepoint Inn is a deluxe resort, with 101 guest rooms, most with balconies overlooking the lake, and six luxury suites, a superb restaurant with spectacular views of the lake, a swimming pool and lighted tennis courts. Call ☎ 800-544-5253 for rates.

You can go hiking or horseback riding along almost five miles of woodland trails that lend themselves to all sorts of other activities, especially bird and wildlife watching. If you like to go sightseeing, there are several nearby historic ante-bellum homes where you'll be greeted by young ladies decked out in period costumes of the pre-Civil War South.

Annual events include Watchable Wildlife in January, a Eufaula Pilgrimage in April, and the 4-H National Wildlife Habitat Judging in August.

Open from 7 am until 10 pm; the park office is open from 8 am until 5. Lakepoint State Park, Route 2, Box 94, Eufaula, AL 36027-9202. ☎ 205-687-6676.

8. Old Creek Town Park, just north of Eufaula in Alabama on the west shore, is a town park with 63 picnic sites, a group picnic area, tables, grills, fresh drinking water, restrooms, a swimming beach, boat ramp, dock and a playground.

9. Chewalla Creek Marina, in Eufaula, has boat ramps, restrooms, and other facilities available to the public.

10. River Bluff Park, just north of Georgetown on the east shore off GA 39, is a public-access area with a boat ramp and a dock.

11. Barbour Creek Landing, south of Eufaula in Alabama off US 431, is on the west shore of the lake. Facilities are limited to eight picnic sites, a boat ramp and a dock.

12. Cheneyhatchee Creek Park, south of Eufaula in Alabama, off US 431, is also a public-access area in Alabama on the west shore of the lake. There are eight picnic sites, a boat ramp, and a dock.

13. Cool Branch Park, south of Georgetown off GA 39 on the east shore, is a 154-acre Corps recreation area. There are 22 picnic sites, primitive campsites, restrooms, showers, fresh drinking water, a boat ramp and a dock.

14. White Oak Creek Park Campground, south of Eufaula in Alabama, off US 431, is a fully developed Corps campground and public recreation area. Facilities include 130 tent and trailer sites with water and electric hookups, a bathhouse with hot showers and flush toilets, handicapped-accessible restrooms, 36 picnic sites, two boat ramps with four lanes, a dock, a laundromat, sewage disposal, three playgrounds, tables and grills. Fees from $10. ☎ 912-768-2516.

15. Patuala Creek Park, south of Georgetown, off GA 39 on the east shore, is a Corps recreation area. Its 289 acres have eight picnic sites, two group sites, fresh water, restrooms, a boat ramp and a dock.

16. Thomas Mill Creek Park, south of Eufaula in Alabama off SR 97, is a public-access area with a boat ramp and dock.

17. Sandy Branch Park, north of Fort Gaines off GA 2411, is a small recreation area with six picnic sites, a boat ramp, and a dock.

18. Cotton Hill Park, north of Fort Gaines, off GA 39.

19. George T. Bagley State Park, three miles north of Fort Gaines off GA 39, at the southern end of 48,000-acre Lake Walter E. George, is a 300-acre wild and scenic area of open water and big skies, where you can really get away from it all. If you're looking for comfort along with your outdoor experience, you'll find that here, too; there's a modern lodge with all the comforts you'd expect at a major resort hotel.

Private boats are permitted with no restrictions. The boat ramp has two lanes, and there are two docks, and plenty of parking.

There are five rental cottages, each costing $45 per night, and a store at the marina where you can stock up supplies.

There are 41 picnic sites with tables and grill, a group picnic shelter (handicapped-accessible), a swimming beach and a marina with a full-service dock and boat ramp.

The modern 30-room lodge, complete with a restaurant and gift shop, offers all the amenities of a large hotel and yet is able to maintain an atmosphere of isolation, serenity, and even adventure.

Anglers can expect fine sport here, perhaps the best to found anywhere in Georgia. All the members of the bass family are represented in the cool deep waters of the lake; giant catfish can be caught below the tailraces of the dams, crappie, bream and more are present in good quantities. Fort Gaines is one of the major access points to Walter F. George Lake, so you'll probably have to drive the boat a fair distance north to find a quiet spot, but find it you will and, once there, you're assured of a great day out.

There are several easy trails here, and the lakeshore is a pleasant place for a stroll. Bring your camera along; this is also a great place for birdwatching.

Annual events include a Crappie Fishing Tournament held in April, and a Halloween Hayride.

Open year-round from 7 am until 10 pm; the park office hours are from 8 to 5.

George T. Bagby State Park & Lodge, Route 1, Box 201, Fort Gaines, GA 31751. ☎ 912-768-2571.

20. Hardridge Creek Park, northwest of Fort Gaines in Alabama, off SR 97, is a fully developed Corps campground/public recreation area. Facilities include 77 tent and trailer sites with water and electric hookups, a bathhouse with hot showers and flush toilets, handicapped-accessible restrooms, 48 picnic sites, a boat ramp with two lanes, a dock, a laundromat, sewage disposal, tables and grills, and a swimming area. Fees: from $10. ☎ 912-768-2516.

21. East Bank Park and Resource Manager's Office, north of Fort Gaines, off GA 39. ☎ 912-768-2516.

22. Highland Park, northwest of Fort Gaines in Alabama, off SR 97, is a 238-acre Corps recreation area with 25 picnic sites, tables, grills, restrooms, a boat ramp, dock, swimming area and a playground.

23. Walter F. George Dam Area, in Fort Gaines, is a small recreation area with public restrooms, drinking water and fishing deck.

24. Franklin Landing, in Fort Gaines, is a public-access area with a boat ramp and fresh drinking water.

25. Abbie Creek Park is north of Columbia on the east bank of George W. Andrews Lake, off GA 1691. It's a small recreation area with five primitive campsites, six picnic sites, fresh drinking water, a boat ramp and a dock. Fees: none.

26. Odom Creek Park, north of Columbia on the east bank of George W. Andrews, off GA 1691, is a small county park with four picnic sites, a boat ramp, dock and fresh drinking water.

27. Coheelee Creek Park, east of Columbia on the Georgia side of the lake, is a Corps recreation area with seven primitive campsites, 19 picnic sites, tables, grills, a boat ramp, dock, fresh drinking water and pit toilets. Fees: none.

28. Columbia Boat Ramp, in Columbia, Alabama, is a public-access boat ramp.

29. Omussee Creek Park, south of Columbia on the east bank of Lake George W. Andrews, is a recreation area operated and maintained by the state of Alabama. Facilities include 32 picnic sites, tables, grills, a picnic shelter, restrooms, fresh drinking water and two boat ramps.

30. George W. Andrews Lock & Dam, south of Columbia in the east bank of Lake George W. Andrews, has public restrooms, fresh drinking water, and a splendid view of the project.

31. West Bank Dam Site Area, south of Columbia on the west bank of Lake George W. Andrews in Alabama, off SR 95, is a 110-acre Corps recreation area. Facilities are limited to a couple of picnic sites, restrooms, drinking water and fishing dock.

Jackson

A small town north of Macon, six miles east of I-75, is where you'll find a couple of Georgia's best developed state parks. Both are handy to the interstate, and well worth time out for a visit. The views are spectacular, and both parks are well-suited to wildlife and landscape photography.

SIGHTSEEING

High Falls State Park, two miles east of I-75 and Exit 65 on High Falls Road, was once the site of a thriving little industrial town, but no more. It became a ghost town toward the end of the 19th century when it was bypassed by the railroad. Today, the park is a wild and scenic place that attracts visitors from around the state. The 650-acre lake offers fine fishing, hiking trails and isolated areas of great natural beauty.

Camping facilities include 142 tent and trailer sites with water and electric hookups – 25 are pull-throughs – a bathhouse with hot showers and flush toilets, handicapped-accessible restrooms, a laundromat, sewage disposal, picnic tables and grills. Fees: $10.

Fishing here is quite good. The lake is stocked with bass, crappie, bream and catfish. It doesn't seem to be overly busy, especially on weekdays.

There are several **hiking** trails here. One leads along the lakeshore and river bank for several miles and on through the woods. The going is a little strenuous in places, especially around the falls, but it's nothing most people couldn't handle. Other activities include canoeing and picnicking.

Annual events include a Forsythia Festival and Crappie Tournament in March, the Fall Family Camp-out Weekend, and the Christmas Tree Trimming Program.

Open daily 7 am until 10 pm; the park office hours are from 8 until 5. High Falls State Park, Route 5, Box 202-A, Jackson, GA 30233. ☎ 912-994-5080.

Indian Springs State Park: Located south of Jackson on GA 42, is thought to be the oldest state park in the United States. Its claim to fame is its sulfur spring, a one-time gathering and healing place for the Creek Indians. The Creeks signed away their rights to the land in 1821 and the government disposed of all but 10 acres of what was then called the Indian Springs Reserve. Residents of Butts County, however, purchased some 513 acres adjoining the reserve and donated it to the state. Today, the 523-acre park includes the original mineral spring, a 105-acre lake and a museum.

Facilities for **camping** include 90 tent and trailer sites with water and electric hookups – some are pull-throughs – 10 holiday cottages, a bathhouse with hot showers and flush toilets, handicapped-accessible restrooms, a laundromat, sewage disposal, picnic tables and grills. Fees: campsites, $10; cottages from $45.

There are seven picnic shelters, the museum, a miniature golf course, and the lake (private boats with small motors are permitted; rental boats are available).

There are several miles of nature trails; the going is quite easy, and the trails are well suited for nature study, birdwatching and wildlife photography.

Annual events include a week-long astronomy program in August, a Southeastern Indian Celebration in September, and a Christmas Decorations Workshop in December.

Open daily from 7 am until 10 pm; the park office hours are from 8 until 5. Indian Springs State Park, Route 1, Box 439, Flovilla, GA 30216. ☎ 706-775-7241

Juliette

If you've seen the movie, *Fried Green Tomatoes*, you've seen Juliette. This once-thriving little industrial mill town was virtually abandoned when it was discovered by the movie people. Today, you can walk down Main Street and see it just as it was in the movie, but it's all a facade; the buildings are little more than sets, fronts only. Still, it's interesting, and well worth a visit, if only to sample fried green tomatoes at the **Whistle Stop Café** in the railroad depot.

NEARBY SIGHTSEEING

Jarrell Plantation State Historic Site, southeast of Juliette, and 18 miles from I-75, Exit 60, is a Southern plantation founded in the early 1840s by John Fitz Jarrell. The original house, along with some 20 other buildings, still stands. The buildings, the original tools and machinery, and the many family heirlooms and antiques offer a peek into Georgia's past. You can tour the old home, the three-story barn, the smokehouses, the cane furnace, the steam-powered grist mill, the saw mill, the shingle mill, the blacksmith shop and the syrup mill.

Annual events include 100 Years of Jarrell Clothing, Sheep Shearing, Spinning and Weaving, a Fourth of July Celebration, Labor Day on the Farm, Cane Grinding and Syrup Making, and Christmas Candlelight Tours.

Open year-round, Tuesday through Saturday, from 9 until 5, and on Sunday from 2 until 5.

Jarrell Plantation State Historic Site, Route 2, Box 220, Juliette, GA 31046. ☎ 912-986-5172.

Lumpkin

Named for Wilson Lumpkin, and the center of one of Georgia's premier agricultural areas, this little country town has more than 20 antebellum homes and is truly representative of the Old South. The homes can be seen on a driving tour that follows the route of a one-time stagecoach trail.

SIGHTSEEING

Providence Canyon State Conservation Park, seven miles west of Lumpkin on GA 39, is unique in that, although formed by the action of water, there is no great river flowing along its bottom. Instead, the canyon was formed by the action of rainfall during the last few hundred years. Folklore has it that the great canyon began to form when the run-off from one of Georgia's pioneer settler's plowed fields washed out a tiny gully. The next rainfall washed away a little more, and subsequent downpours continued the erosion, thus creating a natural phenomenon that continues to grow even now. It's been said that a single heavy storm can increase the depth of the canyon by several inches.

Providence Canyon is a wild and beautiful place where the canyon walls provide a splendid backdrop of natural colors for trees and the wildflowers that grow in abundance throughout the area. Be sure to bring your camera.

The afternoon sun bounces off the canyon walls.

Facilities include two picnic shelters, a family group shelter, handicapped-accessible restrooms, a pioneer campsite and an interpretive center.

There are more than 10 miles of hiking and backcountry trails here. Those that follow a steep route from the park office down the canyon walls to the bottom are the most attractive, not to mention challenging. These trails present easy going on the way down, although you do have to watch where you put your feet, and it's a long hard climb on the way back. You'll need to be in good physical condition.

Annual events include Spring and Fall Wildflower Days, and the Kudzu Takeover Day in August.

Open daily from 7 am until 6, September 15 through April 14, and 7 until 9 the rest of the year. The park office is open from 8 until 5.

Providence Canyon State Park, Route 1, Box 158, Lumpkin, GA 31815. ☎ 912-838-6202.

Jimmy Carter National Historic Site

No visit to this part of Georgia would be complete without a visit to Plains, the birthplace and home of President Jimmy Carter.

The Jimmy Carter National Historic Site encompasses almost all of the tiny community called Plains. You can take a self-guided driving tour that begins at the railroad depot and takes in the former president's birthplace, boyhood homes, his school, the Carter peanut warehouse, family homes, and even brother Billy's service station. ☎ 912-824-3413.

Thomasville

One of the oldest inland communities in Georgia, the Thomasville of today was created by the influx of snowbirds during the 1880s when it became a famous vacation spot and the location of some of the country's best hotels. Today, it's very much a quiet rural community, a stop on the way south to Florida, where you can enjoy a few hours sightseeing, or a lunch of the best Southern cuisine.

SIGHTSEEING

Lapham-Patterson House State Historic Site, in the heart of Thomasville at 626 North Dawson Street, is one of the most extraordinary examples of a Victorian resort house in the nation. Built in 1885 as the winter home of Chicago shoe merchant, C.W. Lapham, the old house is famous for its magnificent architecture, which includes fish-scale shingles, oriental porch decorations, pine floors, a cantilevered balcony, and a fine example of a double-flue chimney and walk-through stairway.

Annual events include a Victorian Christmas, a quilt show, a Rose Festival in April and various Victorian culture programs.

The house is open year-round, Tuesday through Saturday, from 9 am until 5, and on Sundays from 2 until 5. Admission, $3; children 6-12, $1.

Lapham-Patterson House State Historic Site, 626 N. Dawson Street, Thomasville, GA 31792. ☎ 912-225-4004.

Warm Springs

This is another one-time Indian healing places. The warm, soothing waters of the spring lured Indians and later visitors from around the nation, including Franklin D. Roosevelt.

SIGHTSEEING

Franklin D. Roosevelt State Park, on Pine Mountain, just off I-85, west of Warm Springs on GA 190, was a large part of the four-term president's life. It was here that Roosevelt sought treatment for the polio that struck him down in 1921. Since then, the 10,000-acre park has become one of Georgia's top outdoor attractions. The facilities are extensive, and activities include everything from fishing to boating to hiking. This is a family park, with lots of facilities for a day out and a picnic with kids. In short, there's something here for just about everyone.

Facilities include 140 tent and trailer sites with water and electric hookups, a bathhouse with hot showers and flush toilets, handicapped-accessible restrooms, 21 holiday cabins, a laundromat, sewage disposal, tables and grills. Fees: $10; cabins, from $49.

There are two lakes (the fishing is good), a swimming pool, lots of picnic sites, a family or group shelter and a nature lodge.

If you like to hike, you can spend several days here, walking the more than 23 miles of woodland and lakeside trails. The going is almost always easy and, if you just want a short stroll in the sunshine, you can do that, too.

Annual events include Orientation Meetings, a 46-mile Ultra Run, a series of environmental and educational activities, and the Civilian Conservation Corps Reunion held in September.

Open daily year-round from 7 am until 10 pm; the park office hours are from 8 until 5, Saturday through Thursday, and from 8 until 8 on Fridays.

F.D. Roosevelt State Park, 2870 GA 190, Pine Mountain, GA 31822. ☎ 706-663-4858.

Index